KU-029-328

MODERNISM AND THE THEATRE
OF THE BAROQUE

Edinburgh Critical Studies in Modernism, Drama and Performance

Series Editor:
Olga Taxidou

Editorial Board:
Penny Farfan (University of Calgary); Robert Leach (formerly of Edinburgh and Birmingham Universities); Ben Levitas (Goldsmiths, University of London); John London (Goldsmiths, University of London); Laura Marcus (University of Oxford); Marjorie Perloff (University of Stanford); Kirsten Shepherd-Barr (University of Oxford); Alexandra Smith (University of Edinburgh)

Edinburgh Critical Studies in Modernism, Drama and Performance addresses the somewhat neglected areas of drama and performance within Modernist Studies, and is in many ways conceived of in response to a number of intellectual and institutional shifts that have taken place over the past 10 to 15 years. On the one hand, Modernist Studies has moved considerably from the strictly literary approaches, to encompass engagements with the everyday, the body, the political, while also extending its geopolitical reach. On the other hand, Performance Studies itself could be seen as acquiring a distinct epistemology and methodology within Modernism. Indeed, the autonomy of Performance as a distinct aesthetic trope is sometimes located at the exciting intersections between genres and media; intersections that this series sets out to explore within the more general modernist concerns about the relationships between textuality, visuality and embodiment. This series locates the theoretical, methodological and pedagogical contours of Performance Studies within the formal, aesthetic and political concerns of Modernism. It claims that the 'linguistic turn' within Modernism is always shadowed and accompanied by an equally formative 'performance / performative turn'. It aims to highlight the significance of performance for the general study of modernism by bringing together two fields of scholarly research which have traditionally remained quite distinct – performance / theatre studies and Modernism. In turn this emphasis will inflect and help to re-conceptualise our understanding of both performance studies and modernist studies. And in doing so, the series will initiate new conversations between scholars, theatre and performance artists and students.

Published
The Speech-Gesture Complex: Modernism, Theatre, Cinema
Anthony Paraskeva
Irish Drama and the Other Revolutions: Irish Playwrights, Sexual Politics, and the International Left, 1892–1964
Susan Cannon Harris
Modernism and the Theatre of the Baroque
Kate Armond

Forthcoming
Beckett's Breath: Anti-theatricality and the Visual Arts
Sozita Goudouna
Russian Futurist Theatre: Theory and Practice
Robert Leach
Greek Tragedy and Modernist Performance
Olga Taxidou

www.edinburghuniversitypress.com/series/ecsmdp

MODERNISM AND THE THEATRE OF THE BAROQUE

Kate Armond

EDINBURGH
University Press

Edinburgh University Press is one of the leading university presses in the UK. We publish academic books and journals in our selected subject areas across the humanities and social sciences, combining cutting-edge scholarship with high editorial and production values to produce academic works of lasting importance. For more information visit our website: edinburghuniversitypress.com

© Kate Armond, 2018

Edinburgh University Press Ltd
The Tun – Holyrood Road
12(2f) Jackson's Entry
Edinburgh EH8 8PJ

Typeset in Sabon and Gill Sans by
Servis Filmsetting Ltd, Stockport, Cheshire,
and printed and bound in Great Britain by
CPI Group (UK) Ltd, Croydon CR0 4YY

A CIP record for this book is available from the British Library

ISBN 978 1 4744 1962 8 (hardback)
ISBN 978 1 4744 1963 5 (webready PDF)
ISBN 978 1 4744 1964 2 (epub)

The right of Kate Armond to be identified as the author of this work has been asserted in accordance with the Copyright, Designs and Patents Act 1988, and the Copyright and Related Rights Regulations 2003 (SI No. 2498).

CONTENTS

ACKNOWLEDGEMENTS

I would first like to like to thank Rachel Potter for all the support and advice she has given me over the last ten years, and for her conscientious supervision of my PhD at UEA. I am grateful to her for her patience and insight, for always knowing how to get the best from me, and for introducing me to the work of Djuna Barnes and Wyndham Lewis at Queen Mary many years ago. Thank you also to Andrzej Gąsiorek, Deborah Longworth, Dan Moore, Ross Wilson, Daniela Caselli, Jeremy Noel-Tod, David Trotter, Lyndsey Stonebridge, Paul Edwards and Philip Wilson for their guidance, the benefit of their experience, and their encouragement at various stages of this study. Thanks also go to my students at UEA, in particular Tim Anderson, Will Parker and Stephanie Young, for helping to make the teaching and discussion of modernism and critical theory such a rewarding experience. I am grateful to Beth Alvarez at the University of Maryland, for her help in accessing and navigating the Djuna Barnes Archive between 2008 and 2010, at a time when my sight was failing. The three chapters on Barnes' work would not have been possible without this help. Most of all I want to thank my husband Steve, my dad, Sue, Adela and Jean for the love and support that kept me focused and happy in my work.

The author and publisher gratefully acknowledge the following copyright permissions: Quotations and sections of manuscript from the Djuna Barnes' Papers, Special Collections and University Libraries, University of Maryland Libraries, are used with permission from the Authors League Fund and St Brides Church, as joint literary executors of the Estate of Djuna Barnes. All quotes by Emily Holmes Coleman Copyright © 2017 by the Estate of Emily Holmes Coleman and my thanks to Joseph Geraci as Executor of the Estate of Emily Holmes Coleman for copyright permission. Thank you to Amber Kohl and Rebecca Johnson Melvin for their correspondence in securing this permission. I would also like to thank Janet Remmington and Routledge, Taylor & Francis Group, for permission to reproduce text from my article 'Allegory and Dismemberment: Reading Djuna Barnes' *Nightwood* through the forms of the Baroque Traurspiel', first published in *Textual Practice, 6.5*, October 2012. This material appears in Chapter 2 of *Modernism and the Theatre of the Baroque*.

For my late father, Michael Armond

INTRODUCTION

The term 'baroque' has long been troubled by complex associations and a sense of the vulgar and excessive, with analysis of art and literature providing an array of competing terms such as late Renaissance, high baroque, late baroque and Mannerist, all of which attempt to group works together according to era or stylistic similarities. The cultural developments that followed the sixteenth century were seen as a decadent fall into the chaotic, the grotesque, the thoughtless and the overwrought, as the baroque became an aesthetic sitting uncomfortably between the restrained artworks of the Renaissance and the measured, delicately ornamental Rococo of the 1700s. More complex still, in the case of English literary history, the baroque is often further fragmented according to the reigning monarch or style of government – 'Jacobean', 'Commonwealth' and 'Caroline'. A baroque aesthetic is generally seen as formalising in the late sixteenth and early seventeenth century, once Mannerism's self-conscious artifice and defiance of Renaissance harmony and poise fell out of favour. As a stylistic tendency, it evolved as a response to Mannerism, striving to redress the balance of representation in favour of coherence, symmetry and the presence of the subject. While Mannerism used ornament to distort form and to distract from any sense of symmetry, the baroque used the extravagant and decorative to complement the artwork as an integrated whole, and Mannerism's move towards an abstract formal aesthetic was countered by the baroque representation of earth-bound mortal bodies, as man became confined to a realm of immanence and matter. The Rococo period of the eighteenth century, sometimes referred to as 'late baroque', originated in France as a response to the extravagant aesthetic embodied in the Palace of Versailles, and employed a lighter touch, humour, soft muted colours and decorative forms such as shells.

In recent years, critics have brought the baroque and the twentieth century into dialogue several times, and those accounts seem to fall into two categories. In the first, our sense of the baroque is inseparable from a particular period in history, while the second elaborates our understanding of the term through the aesthetic contours of language, form and style. Within critical analysis, the baroque assumed this potential to inhabit periods beyond the seventeenth century, with the art historian Heinrich Wölfflin's analysis in *Renaissance und Barock* (1888; *Renaissance and Baroque* 1971) and his *Kunstgeschichtliche Grundebegriffe* (1915; *Principles of Art History* 1950). Wölfflin rescues the term from the prevailing sense that it somehow represents a degenerate and derivative art-form, a regrettable fall from Renaissance classicism, arguing instead that the baroque can be seen as a counter-principle of classicism in its own right, a parenthesis evolving between the two classical ages of the Renaissance and the Enlightenment. He also argues for the adjective 'baroque' to be applied to a wider aesthetic than that of its original and particular period, while initiating a transfer of the term from architecture and the plastic arts to literature and music. The 1920s and 1930s followed Wölfflin's lead with a succession of studies that acknowledged the baroque as a source of inspiration and a topic of research in its own right, and I mention some of these in my first chapter.

José Antonio Maravall's *Culture of the Baroque: Analysis of a Historical Structure* (1983) defines the baroque as a clearly outlined historical period that falls across the seventeenth century. Rather than providing a formal analysis that seeks to identify specific baroque traits within particular disciplines, he establishes a narrative that is quite at odds with Wölfflin's sense of the baroque as an aesthetic definition, identifiable through style and across a number of accomplishments in the arts. Maravall takes as his premise the idea that each facet of culture, whether art and literature, politics, military strategy, religion or the economy, might share qualities and invite comparison with other facets, but those similarities do not in themselves constitute the baroque. The critical factor and constant behind that definition is a complex historical structure, and each aspect of culture evolves with reference to the whole and is subsumed by it. Maravall may turn to literature in the sources that he cites, but he is interested in these works for the insights into life and experience that they offer, and not in their distinctive artistic qualities.

The baroque of his analysis is a panoramic cultural and social history comprising a guided mass culture, urban society under absolute rule, the Catholic Church, political spectacle, the arts, fiestas, costume, fashion and psychological tendencies. He suggests that, during this epoch, madness became a phenom-enon of collective experience rather than individual diagnosis, a state of mind fostered by change and instability and resulting in a pervasive consciousness of crisis. While Spain is at the heart of this study, his baroque is not exclusive to one nation, nor is it a self-contained concept. Instead, his subject remains intimately connected to the historical narratives that surround it. Maravall's Spanish baroque evolves from the Italian artworks of the Renaissance and Mannerism that are so often used as points of contrast, and its boundaries often expand to include other European countries. The Spanish culture that he describes is 'guided' by the monarch's self-interest and determination to manipulate, subdue and entertain their potentially unruly subjects. He associ-ates the baroque with a return to aristocracy, privilege, absolute authority and bonds of dependency, all of which contradicts the democratic ideal that had been fostered during the Renaissance. Maravall's accounts of the seventeenth-century culture industry, its reproduction of thousands of sonnets, theatrical works, lampoons and paintings, and his description of baroque kitsch are all particularly fascinating as they gesture towards links between contemporary production or consumption and baroque entertainment long before Omar Calabrese and Angela Ndalianis formalised these similarities in their respective studies. Throughout the seventeenth century, established class relationships were unsettled by demographic changes, economic upheaval and the Thirty Years War, and more of the rural population moved to the cities creating a large population of bandits, vagabonds and beggars. Wherever authority and privileges were felt to be under threat the public looked to absolute monarchy and a system of customs and traditions to preserve their status as part of an essentially conservative culture. The result of Maravall's study is a baroque world-picture that transcends discrete elements of practice, personality, obser-vation and event, presenting human experience as regulated, phenomenal and transient.

Studies that have brought the baroque to terms with contemporary culture have tended to focus on the visual arts and postmodernism. Mieke Bal's *Quoting Caravaggio: Contemporary Art, Preposterous History* (1999) inves-tigates the significance of baroque artworks for late-twentieth-century culture, following and reviewing the 'Going for Baroque' exhibition (1995–6) in Baltimore and the 'Baroque Revisions' (1996) conference in Vienna. She for-mulates the analytical term 'preposterous' history, whereby earlier art-forms are placed behind the revisions of the present day to create a dialogue between historical periods. Within preposterous history the value of past artworks is conferred in the present moment, with the contemporary example offering a considered and informed perspective, a lens through which past aesthetic practice is reconsidered and reworked. In describing this aesthetic position, she refers back to Deleuze's use of Leibniz's philosophy, and having disrupted

linear time by making its boundaries ambiguous Bal proposes a similar instability or fluid exchange between subject and object. This leads not to the
consolidating of identities, but to an event that Bal terms 'entanglement'. The
premise of this definition and of preposterous history is that we are inseparable from the historical narratives that we envisage, we not only interpret them
we become their authors. Using contemporary paintings and installations by
artists such as Andres Serrano and Ken Aptek, works that inhabit the baroque
through their techniques of multi-dimensional representation, trompe l'oeil,
mirror reflections and their attendant ideas of scale, perspective, exteriority
and display, Bal proposes an epistemological position that transcends the
traditional distinctions between subject and object in relation to the artist's
canvas, suggesting instead a co-dependency. The contemporary work displaces
the original as source and inspiration, and the intervention of the former
becomes an essential stage in the assimilation of both by the modern viewer
and artist.

In his *Neo-Baroque: A Sign of the Times* (1992) Omar Calabrese claims
that 'many important cultural phenomena of our time are distinguished by a
specific internal "form" that recalls the baroque', and his term, 'neo-baroque',
becomes synonymous with postmodern culture.[1] Using contemporary sources
such as video games, music, architectural designs, television programmes and
literature, Calabrese examines culture as a constellation of signs using either a
classical or a baroque definition, with only one able to assume ascendancy at
any particular time. Neo-baroque defines the responses and interpretations of
the consumer, as well as the design, presentation and manufacture of particular cultural objects and images. Angela Ndalianis's *Neo-Baroque Aesthetics
and Contemporary Entertainment* (2004) uses the same term and extends the
period of analysis to include the twenty-first century. Rather than borrowing
from or recreating the historical baroque, the technologies behind entertainments such as theme park amusements and computer games are shown by
Ndalianis to have sensory affinities with the sculpture, magic lanterns and artworks of the seventeenth century, while articulating a uniquely contemporary
experience.

Giles Deleuze's *The Fold: Leibniz and the Baroque* (1993) opens by introducing his reader to the image of the labyrinth as a multiple form, and the
smallest and most enigmatic unit of matter within that multiple is the fold.
The fold itself is not secondary to any point within the artwork and it takes its
power from inflection as it is always folded within another fold. For Deleuze,
art becomes philosophy as practice, and Leibniz's baroque philosophy aligns
itself with modern configurations of pictorial space, offering definitions that
gesture beyond the tired conventions of representational painting to create an
aesthetic of mass and immanence. *The Fold* includes examples of artists from
the twentieth century whose work is non-representational – the Expressionist

and Der Blaue Reiter painter, Paul Klee, and the French sculptor, painter and founder of the Art Brut movement, Jean Duffet – and Deleuze claims their work as part of a baroque legacy that returns abstraction to a fundamental materiality grounded in force and motion.

These artworks of the historical baroque and their twentieth-century counterparts are innovative creatures of cloaking, twists, convolutions, drapes, rich heavy costume, turbulent movement and excessive ornamentation, but Deleuze's fold is not held by human or visible forms alone: 'the Baroque differentiates its folds in two ways, by moving along two infinities, as if infinity were composed of two or floors: the pleats of matter, and the folds in the soul'.[2] It is as if the fold echoes the movement of the fabric, going on to produce an aesthetic that exceeds mere form, combining sensation and abstract figuration to produce a layering of matter, surface, textures, textiles and depth. The motion of the material in turn succeeds in exciting equivalent intensities of movement within the mind or the soul. The baroque edifice of Deleuze's definition, with its two floors or levels, entails first the consolidating of matter through the artist's brushstrokes and then a corresponding resonance or pulse that lies beyond the material artefact, and yet is still somehow a part of the realm of matter. The aesthetic is one of becoming through multiplicity of exchange across the two storeys of the house. Although Deleuze refers repeatedly to the baroque philosophy of Leibniz, the suggestion that there is a fundamental affinity between matter and soul, and a lack of separation between organic and non-organic worlds, formed part of Baruch Spinoza's theory of *conatus* as set out in Chapter 5 of my own study of baroque philosophy and modernism. Like Calabrese and Bal, Deleuze counters definitions of the baroque that narrow focus to particular times, places or disciplines, in fact the term seems to suggest an aesthetic that consistently ruptures expected boundaries as architecture engages with its surroundings, paintings spill from their frames or extend into sculpture, while sculpture insinuates itself into the designs of architecture.

Christine Buci-Glucksmann's *Baroque Reason: The Aesthetics of Modernity* (1994) argues that the philosophy of modern art began with the seventeenth-century baroque play as a self-conscious drama of spectacle. This study is of particular significance not least because, like Djuna Barnes and Walter Benjamin, Buci-Glucksmann sees the world of the nineteenth-century Paris explored in Charles Baudelaire's *Les Fleurs du Mal* as a critical third point of crisis alongside those represented in the baroque Trauerspiel (play of mourning) and in the artworks of the twentieth-century avant-garde. She argues that the enigmatic fragments of language and image through which the baroque allegorist sought to capture their world deserve attention as the precursors of modern aesthetic techniques involving shock, shattered and distorted forms and montage. My own study will examine the influence of allegory within modernist literature rather than the visual arts. As she studies Baudelaire's

Parisian landscape through images of exhibitions, architecture, crowds, fashions and photographs, Buci-Glucksmann argues that unconscious modes of seeing are disturbed by industrialised mass production and in turn this resurrects the great female myths attendant upon allegory – the prostitute, the lesbian, the androgyne, the sterile woman and the angel. The author stretches the idea of 'baroque reason' beyond postmodernism to include social theory and feminist critique, while the poet of her analysis becomes prey to the vagaries of the capitalist marketplace and new expressions of time and the uncanny emerge. Perhaps the most important baroque image for her vision of modernity comes with the figure of Salome in Gustave Moreau's *Salome Dancing Before Herod*, Oscar Wilde's 1890 play *Salome*, and Richard Strauss's 1905 opera of the same name, as the fragmented body of Jokanaan takes the destructive principle of modern allegory to its extreme.

So the baroque had enjoyed a long-established fascination for writers concerned with analysis of postmodern theory and culture, and with art and technology media in particular, until Mary Ann Frese Witt's *Metatheater and Modernity* (2014) nudged that sense of aesthetic affinity closer to the modernist canon and to a world of baroque theatre that extended far beyond Shakespeare. In 1963, Lionel Abel coined the term 'metatheatre' with his book of the same name, referring to performance that reflects on its own practices of artifice and illusion, and the conventions of audience and actor in which both are complicit. For Abel, this term first appears with the baroque topos of the *theatrum mundi* or 'all the world's a stage' and the play within the play in Shakespeare's *Hamlet* and *The Tempest* and in Calderón's *Life's a Dream*. He also suggests that this dramatic form has reappeared more recently in the work of Pirandello, Brecht and Beckett. *Metatheater and Modernity* revisits this sense of affinity, locating the ascendancy of metatheatre in the baroque and 'neobaroque', with the latter interpreted as a postmodern period that Witt extends to include modernists such as Luigi Pirandello. She analyses Tony Kushner's pastiche of Corneille's baroque tragicomedy *L'Illusion Comique* as Kushner's *L'Illusion* (1988) had boasted of its derivative origins, emphasising the acts of intervention or metatranslation and forsaking the discreet presence of the translator. She also takes the baroque sculptor Gian Lorenzo Bernini's scripted play dating from 1644, now lost and untitled, and a small section of text from Bernini's *L'Impresario* as blueprints for Pirandello's *Sei Personaggi in cerca d'autore* (*Six Characters in Search of an Author*). Both baroque and modern works share the comedy that arises when individuals strive to create theatrical illusion, and the result is a self-conscious spectacle tracing the production of a baroque stage aesthetic. While the theatre of the historical baroque adopted technological developments that would enhance the illusions and fantasies made possible by stagecraft, neobaroque theatre responds to rival media and technologies by celebrating effects that are possible only on the stage. By bringing the twentieth century and the seventeenth century to terms in this way, Frese Witt opens a new approach to comparative studies in theatre, highlighting defining similarities and differences.

My own study shifts the terms of that engagement yet again to focus almost exclusively on modernism rather than the postmodern. As my title suggests, the text will return to the baroque theatre, but will extend the dialogue between the twentieth century and the seventeenth century to include the modernist novel, critique, archival research, and dance and stagecraft as both theory and performance. My argument identifies an alternative baroque aesthetic that runs counter to the dominant modernist values promoted by T. S. Eliot and James Joyce, and that challenges our understanding of modernist creativity. The chosen writers and performers are not passive recipients of tradition, but are innovative, playful and even irreverent in their reworking of original sources. Baroque theatre offered modernism far more than the gravitas of historical detail, the violence of court intrigue and the mischief of the harlequin, and Isadora Duncan, Djuna Barnes, Wyndham Lewis and Edward Gordon Craig made the original seventeenth-century aesthetic their own. Each chapter introduces key characters, forms or definitions that allow the baroque to be used as a framework for analysing modernist achievements, showing how readily ideas and practices translate across genres, but at the same time acknowledging that my own choices and analysis are by no means intended to be exhaustive. *Modernism and the Theatre of the Baroque* is necessarily selective and modernism's many debts to the seventeenth century are only just beginning to be addressed, with studies such as Deborah Longworth's forthcoming *The Sitwells: Ornamental Modernism*.[3]

In extending the influence of seventeenth-century drama beyond the postmodern and modern stage, I am following the baroque's own sense of theatre as an art-form that was applied to a whole constellation of social, political, technical and aesthetic roles. Theatre went hand in hand with the selling of remedies in the Italian piazza during the early commedia dell'arte performance, combining folk medicine with political comment and robust physical comedy; it enforced monarchy as part of court pageant and procession, and it was as integral to the rituals and excesses of carnival as to the architecture and spectacles that displayed state authority, wealth and power. Baroque theatre was never confined to the stage, so to rediscover its influence within the fiction, polemic, theory and stagecraft of modernism is quite in keeping with the spirit of the original.

In his *Late Modernism: Politics, Fiction and the Arts between the World Wars* (1999), Tyrus Miller provides a detailed cultural context for a number of neglected late-modernist works with a study that has done much to bring both authors and texts to the fore in terms of critical attention. He argues that Samuel Beckett's *Murphy*, Mina Loy's *Insul*, Wyndham Lewis's *The*

Childermass and *The Apes of God* and Djuna Barnes's *Ryder* and *Nightwood* are all in dialogue with technological media such as advertising, broadcasting techniques, cinema, and popular vogues such as jazz music. Rather than view an established literary canon from the perspective of high modernism and assume that postmodernism follows modernism by disrupting the latter's formal unity with parody, ambiguity and disorientation, Miller rethinks our vantage point. He places the reader at the end of modernism, caught between the two World Wars, troubled by economic depression and an awareness of changing relationships between popular and literary culture. The late-modernist tendencies that he identifies across this selection of novels include self-reflexive laughter, dismemberment, corporeal automatism and a loosening of symbolic unity. *Late Modernism* is significant for my own study, not just because I have also chosen to focus on Barnes's *Nightwood* and Lewis's *The Apes of God*, but because Miller briefly introduces the idea of Benjamin's 'allegorical optic', a vision that contains the ruin of an entire modernist aesthetic, and one that I develop in some detail in my analysis of *Nightwood*. In my conclusion, I return to his suggestion that later texts turn away from high modernism's concern with somehow ordering and unifying an unruly contemporary world through formal mastery, while their late-modernist counterparts forsake the authority offered by large symbolic forms, mediated narratives structured through many perspectives, ironic detachment, and the dramatisation of states of consciousness. Barnes and Lewis may have left behind their peripheral position in modernist studies with Oxford University Press's decision in 2013 to publish the entire works of Lewis, and with events such as the first international Djuna Barnes conference held in 2012, but as writers they remain notoriously difficult to place and interpret. *Nightwood* and *Apes of God* have continued to perplex, with questions about Lewis's defence of satire and the extravagant and unusual language of both texts. This present study aims to suggest at least one way to interpret these novels – as examples of late modernism and baroque modernism that are astonishingly detailed in their recreation and their unravelling of the original seventeenth-century works.

My discussion does not attempt to formulate a single, unified style for either modernism or the baroque, but to examine individual works and genres from the seventeenth century alongside close readings of high and late-modernist writing to provide sustained engagement on both sides of the comparison. I make no apology for the detailed engagement with Djuna Barnes's novel *Nightwood*, as I believe it to be the most detailed baroque vision captured by any modernist writer. In Isadora Duncan and Edward Gordon Craig, I have chosen two theorists who were convinced that their particular seventeenth-century sources would transform modernist performance, and in their desire to redeem culture, and in the timing of their theories, they fall within the period and the preoccupations of high modernism. In the case of Isadora Duncan, I set her theories of dance against the monist philosophy of Baruch Spinoza and his controversial treatise *Ethics* (1677), exploring identity and movement through Spinoza's definitions of matter and the universe. The two baroque performance genres that have held my interest are the German Trauerspiel (play of mourning) and the Italian commedia dell'arte. They are intriguing, not least because so little remains of their original performances in terms of written record, and they have only been recaptured in authentic, accurate form for modernism through pains-taking research and scholarship and within performance tradition. For Walter Benjamin, the Trauerspiel's extravagant lament and brutal scenes captured the essence of baroque history, and he spent the years of his Habilitation qualifica-tion for the University of Frankfurt working through examples of these dramas that combined butchered human corpses with allegory, eschatology and court intrigue. The Trauerspiel dramatists were Martin Opitz, Andreas Gryphius, Daniel Caspar von Lohenstein and Johann Christian Hallmann, names and plays that were all too easily eclipsed by the elegant expression, formal sophis-tication and less graphic violence found in the plays of William Shakespeare and Pedro Calderón de la Barca. The result of this research was formalised as the text *The Origin of German Tragic Drama*, available in its original language between 1928 and 1931, and in English translation from 1977. Knowledge of the Trauerspiel came to Djuna Barnes through her familiarity with German Expressionism's baroque heritage and through her extensive knowledge of sev-enteenth-century aesthetics across the arts. Edward Gordon Craig immortalised the Italian commedia dell'arte in the many articles and sources that he included in his journal *The Mask*. Just as the Trauerspiel had been eclipsed by less difficult and offensive plays, the authentic Italian commedia had been long overlooked in favour of more refined French adaptations of the genre and its characters or masks. Craig's research, his collaboration with established academics, and the publishing of his journal, represent a timely intervention in the history of com-media, rescuing and restoring the Italian drama in all its coarse vigour from the later elegant French tradition that had found favour with the Symbolists, the Romantics and modernists of his own time. Wyndham Lewis's fascination with the commedia tradition predates *The Mask*, but his writing reveals that he was familiar with the journal and Craig's ambitions for the theatre, and with the Sitwell's commedia aesthetic. Chapter 1 will continue this introduction to the three baroque sources that form the basis of my study.

NOTES

1. Calabrese, *Neo-Baroque: A Sign of the Times*, trans. Charles Lambert (Princeton: Princeton University Press, 1992), p. 15.
2. Deleuze, *The Fold: Leibniz and the Baroque* (Minneapolis: University of Minnesota Press, 1993), p. 3.
3. Deborah Longworth, *The Sitwells: Ornamental Modernism*, forthcoming with Oxford University Press.

I

BAROQUE EUROPE

This chapter aims to offer an overview of those resurgences of the baroque that are most significant for my study – Germany's rediscovery of the Trauerspiel and allegory, the colourful legacy of the Italian commedia dell'arte and the monist philosophy of Baruch Spinoza that informs Ernst Haeckel's evolutionary science at the turn of the century. Anglo-American modernism's debt to the baroque has already been discussed in some detail in the context of English metaphysical poetry, and this interest stemmed from T. S. Eliot's essay 'The Metaphysical Poets' (1921). The essay is a review of Herbert J. C. Grierson's anthology *Metaphysical Lyrics and Poems of the Seventeenth Century: Donne to Butler* (1921), and between them the two works were responsible for a reappraisal of the poetry of John Donne, George Herbert, Andrew Marvell, Richard Crashaw, Henry Vaughan and Abraham Cowley during the 1920s and 1930s. As with the term 'baroque' in the early 1900s, the adjective 'metaphysical' was largely pejorative when applied to poetry, but Eliot's celebration and Grierson's anthology encouraged the canonising of these forgotten poets, while acknowledging the difficulty of offering single defining qualities or methods within their verse. They used striking and unexpected contrasts, elaborate similes and word associations that demand a particularly attentive reader. The essay is also at pains to register a degree of continuity with the Elizabethan aesthetic of Shakespeare, Webster, Middleton and Tourneur. For Eliot, the metaphysical poets display an informed, philosophical sensibility and an analytical turn of mind, and he has a particular admiration for their ability to blend thought and feeling, a talent that he believes modernist poets should emulate as they too are called upon to attain a similar complexity of expression. Rather than attempting to identify this form of seventeenth-century verse through the apparent flaws detailed by Dr Johnson, Eliot offers the definition of a 'unified sensibility', one that is able to form composite images and phrases from contradictory experiences, displaying sentiment qualified by erudition. In order to capture the convoluted, manifold essence of modernity, the contemporary poet must become more allusive and more indirect 'in order to force, to dislocate if necessary, language into his meaning', and in so doing, they will arrive at something like the striking word pictures of the seventeenth-century conceit, a form with intricate or cryptic words and yet uncomplicated phrasing.[1]

Eliot was not the only writer of the early 1900s to turn to the seventeenth century in their pursuit of innovation and formal difficulty. In Germany, Expressionist writers also plundered and researched the controversial poetic language of predecessors such as Andreas Gryphius, Martin Opitz and Johann Christian Gunther. In the same year that Grierson published his English anthology, Rudolf von Delius published his equivalent volume, *Die deutsche Barocklyrik* (*German Baroque Lyric Poetry*), and baroque verse began its own revival in modern Germany. The poets of the German baroque were considered the kindred spirits of the nation's own brand of modernist, the Expressionist. The two shared a jagged, war-torn language and a disdain for classical standards and decorum. The baroque offered August Stramm, Georg Heym, Jakob van Hoddis and Georg Trakl iconoclastic and jarring figurative devices, radical contradictions and reversals, and a forsaking of lyric beauty, while the Expressionists, in turn, initiated a change in literary tastes that made the baroque popular and relevant once again. English metaphysical verse will not be the focus of my study, as this subject has already occupied critical attention following the publication of Eliot's essay, while Genevieve Taggard's *Circumference: Varieties of Metaphysical Verse, 1456–1928* (1929) has extended the parameters of the anthology to include the poetry of Hart Crane, Emily Dickinson, Marianne Moore and many others.[2] Anglo-American modernism has seldom been studied in the context of German influences for obvious reasons. German Expressionism is recognised as an influential avant-garde movement of the 1910s and 1920s, but its impact on English-language writers is rarely discussed. Much critical analysis has placed the movement outside the concerns of European counterparts. Breon Mitchell's study views literary Expressionism as a phenomenon peculiar to the despair of post-war Germany and the social and political crises that followed military defeat.[3] Narratives of modernism interpret the hostilities of the First World War as a point at which English-speaking modernists had to distance themselves from their German peers, regardless of talent and achievement. My analysis of

Djuna Barnes's writing will address that sense of distance and dissimilarity by placing her work in the context of both Expressionist stagecraft and its baroque heritage. While I acknowledge affinities between her late-modernist aesthetic and baroque poetry, the focus of this comparative study will remain the Trauerspiel of the German baroque and its preoccupation with allegory as opposed to symbol and myth. Germany's renewed interest in the baroque verse of writers such as Andreas Gryphius and Martin Opitz should not eclipse the fact that these men were also the authors of the seventeenth-century Trauerspiel, a tradition that passed down to Expressionism through the Sturm und Drang movement of Germany's eighteenth century.

Tangled definitions continued to blur the boundaries between Renaissance and Counter Reformation culture, and yet when Djuna Barnes wrote of a 'baroque sentence' in a draft of her 1936 novel *Nightwood*, she used the word 'baroque' with a confidence that suggests the adjective enjoyed a particular scholarly currency at the time of her writing.[4] While in European countries such as France, the baroque as a reference in critical studies did not appear until the 1950s, in Germany and Italy it made its way into scholarship as early as the late nineteenth century. By 1888, the academic and architectural historian Cornelius Gurlitt had published his entire three-volume *Geschichte des Borockstiles, Rococo und Klassicismus* (*The History of Baroque Style, Rococo and Classicism*). This text placed him at the forefront of Germany's new respect for, and interest in, the art of the baroque and Middle Ages, establishing Gurlitt as one of the first effective champions of baroque art and architecture in Germany. He was also an influential figure in the education of Die Brücke (The Bridge) artists, and so the seventeenth century loomed large during the formative years of Germany's earliest Expressionist painters and architectural designers.

The term was introduced to a critical study for the first time in Jacob Burckhardt's *Der Cicerone* (1855), effectively rehabilitating the baroque as a style of some merit in its own right. 1908 saw the first publication of Wilhelm Worringer's theoretical treatise on modern art, *Abstraktion und Einfühlung* (Worringer 1997), a seminal work in the evolution of Expressionist aesthetic forms. Here, and in Worringer's earlier *Formproblem der Gotik* (1888; Worringer 1927), the seventeenth century found an advocate. He claimed that only the Gothic and baroque periods were worthy of study by modern scholars and artists, thanks to their mystical tradition and spiritual discontent, and he laid claim to the baroque as a fundamentally German phenomenon, a late flowering of Gothic power. In 1916, the German critic Fritz Strich uses the word in his analysis of seventeenth century lyric poetry, and he proposes that the rhetorical figure of the asyndeton, the omission of a conjunction, characterised German baroque verse, while scholars such as Herbert Cysarz seemed to welcome the magnitude and inexactness of the term.[5] In 1923, Erwin

Panofsky and Fritz Saxl published a study of Albrecht Dürer's 'Melencolia, I'.[6] This publication was the seminal work of the Warburg Institute's approach to Renaissance and baroque allegory, and was indicative of the importance of the baroque in general, and allegory in particular, within academic research across Europe during the 1920s. In Germany, the art historian Werner Weisbach considered the Expressionist movement in the context of a baroque art-world with his *Der Barock als Kunst der Gegenreformation* [Baroque as an Art of Counterreformation] (1921) and *Die Kunst der Barock in Italien, Frankreich, Deutschland und Spanien* [Baroque Art in Italy, France, Germany and Spain] (1925). The baroque thus became both a topic of academic research and a stylistic and thematic resource during the decades in which Expressionism held sway in modern Germany, while in Italy the idealist philosopher and historian Benedetto Croce's *Storia della età barroca in Italia* (*History of the Baroque Age*) (1925) provided a certain continuity of interpretation with his disdain for the baroque as a base, practical style, crude in its execution, and dulling to the mind and senses.

Barnes's arrival in Berlin during the late summer of 1921 coincided with the baroque's ascendency as a fashionable term of analysis; René Wellek notes that 'the enormous vogue for the baroque as a literary label arose in Germany only about 1921–2'.[7] Her novel *Nightwood* was published in 1936 at least a decade after the demise of Expressionism. At this particular point in time, Barnes not only had the complete Expressionist legacy to consider, but was also engaging with a particular form of European modernism that was still controversial and of consequence within Marxist debate. Chapter 4 of my study will examine *Nightwood* in the context of Expressionism's Schrei performance techniques, a particular legacy of the German baroque, but my first two chapters on Barnes will discuss other baroque qualities in her work. In her 2005 study, 'The Neobaroque in Djuna Barnes', Monika Kaup argues that both formalist and feminist critics of Barnes's work have repeatedly, but casually, remarked on her use of 'seventeenth century expressive forms'.[8] Eliot laid the foundations of this response in his 1937 Introduction to the novel, discovering 'a quality of horror and doom very nearly related to that of Elizabethan tragedy'.[9] Graham Greene's review in *The Catholic Tablet* of 1936 discovered *Nightwood*'s final chapter to be quite 'as horrible as anything conceived by Webster and Tourneur', while the novel's language was found to closely resemble that of the Jacobean dramatists.[10] Kaup closes her article by noting Benjamin's emphasis on the contrast between the silences of Greek tragedy and the ostentatious lamentation of the Trauerspiel. She suggests that the latter spectacle of suffering links *Nightwood* with the baroque plays, making a passing reference to Benjamin's study as 'yet another trace that links *Nightwood* with the seventeenth-century baroque', while Daniela Caselli has noted strong similarities between Barnes's play *The Antiphon* and the Trauerspiel's ostentation and exaggerated gesture.[11] Caselli has placed this author firmly in the context of an English-language baroque using references to volumes of seventeenth-century prose, drama and verse that Barnes owned, and to the sermons of John Donne in particular. More recently, Deborah Parsons' 2007, 'Djuna Barnes: Melancholic Modernism', reminded readers of F. R. Leavis's dislike of 'the baroque exhaustion of high modernist principle in *Nightwood*', while Peter Nicholls' *Modernisms* makes reference to the 'darkly baroque underworld of Djuna Barnes's *Nightwood*'.[12]

In his prologue to the Trauerspiel study, *The Origin of German Tragic Drama*, Benjamin discovers the strongest link between the baroque dramatists and Expressionism to be their use of language. He argues that the two literary styles share a linguistic extravagance and exaggeration.[13] Susan Buck-Morss believes that these aesthetic and rhetorical similarities can be traced to a shared historical consciousness linking the crises and aftermath of the Thirty Years War in baroque Europe with the decades following the First World War:

> Baroque allegory was the mode of perception peculiar to a time of social disruption and protracted war, when suffering and material ruin were the stuff and substance of historical experience – hence the return to allegory in his [Benjamin's] own era as a response to the horrifying destructiveness of World War One.[14]

Ernst Schürer also argues that the Expressionist's love of striking visual or pictorial images led them back to the seventeenth century's use of allegory: 'with their proclivity for graphic imagery the Expressionists gravitated to allegory, and, in their adoption of this literary device, borrowed from yet another period of German literature, namely the Baroque.'[15] Barnes's arrival in Europe also coincided with a renewed theatrical interest in the baroque spectacle, with dramas such as Max Reinhardt's *Jederman* (*Everyman*) and *Das Grosse Welttheater* (*The Great Theatre of the World*). *Everyman* was first staged at the Circus Schumann in Berlin in 1911, and by 1920 the play had achieved world renown as Reinhardt's Salzburg Festival production, appearing annually from 1926 to 1937.[16] These plays were allegories and descendants of the medieval morality plays, in which Trauerspiel itself had its roots. With their fantastical, elaborate baroque images, their vast audiences, their use of allegory and the sheer scale of their production, these were modern versions of the seductive visual spectacles used to manipulate and entertain the potentially disruptive masses during the seventeenth century.

THE BAROQUE LEGACY OF EXPRESSIONISM AND BARNES'S EXPRESSIONIST BACKGROUND

The Trauerspiels were dramas of extravagant melancholy that showed the monarch or prince of seventeenth-century absolute rule as simultaneously victim and martyr. This sovereign's style of rule was irresolute, dream-like and abject, and their stage properties were the crown and robes of office, and the dismembered bodies and decapitated heads of their victims. These bodies and heads were to become the stock-in-trade of Expressionism's category of the grotesque. In Frank Wedekind's play *Frühlings Erwachen* (*Spring Awakening*) (1910) a young student, Moritz, is haunted by the story of a headless figure. This decapitated queen is conquered by a king with two heads – an allegory of the German education system and its tendency to restrict girls while privileging boys. Moritz also claims to see attractive girls without their heads, and later shoots himself, reappearing at the play's conclusion with his head under one arm. Walter Hasenclever's Expressionist drama *Die Menschen* (*Humanity*) (1918) presents a decapitated body as its principal character, opening with a dead man as he rises from the grave to receive a severed head from a murderer. The play's brief and disjointed scenes and speeches provide a formal analogy for the dismembered body of the protagonist Alexander. In Hans Henny Jahnn's *Pastor Ephraim Magnus* (1919), the Dance of Death scene, itself an allegorical representation dating back to the Middle Ages, features four dismembered bodies – a castrated man, a decapitated man, a crucified figure and a man with no hands. Hermann Scheffauer summarised what he termed 'the essence of Expressionism': 'Dismemberment of nature is the first phase in the fury of a new creation – the organic is shown petrified into formal or geometric figures' – a definition that recalls exactly allegory's repertoire of mutilated, reified and fossilised forms during the seventeenth century.[17] This general definition also translates easily into the rigid, angular poses of the Expressionist actor, as the body's plastic, semiotic quality eclipsed its role in consolidating individual agency and psychological realism. By the time that Barnes arrived in Berlin in 1921, the Expressionist actor's body had become an empty, allegorical signifier, while the playwright, and more importantly, directors such as Jessner and Martin Fehling had assumed the role of allegorist, and I will explore these techniques of performance in more detail in Chapter 4.

There has long been a tendency to view Expressionist drama in terms of heightened subjectivity, emotionally charged communication and a rejection of objective reality. As early as 1924, in *The New Vision in the German Arts*, Scheffauer attempted to speak for the movements' artists across the disciplines:

> The Expressionist says: 'I will not let the outer world impinge upon me and use me as a recording or interpreting instrument. *I* am the recorder, the interpreter of my own inner feelings, thoughts, moods and emotions; and these I express directly, abstractly, free of the thraldom of the object'.[18]

In his *Über den Expressionismus in der Literatur und die neue Dichtung*, Kasimir Edschmid also declared an end to the artist's dependence on external factual or perceptual reality – the empiricist languor that characterised the Impressionist and Naturalist representations of the object: 'They did not look/ They envisioned/ They did not photograph/ They had visions)'.[19] This experience of cognition suggests a degree of independence, originality and innovation on the part of the subject, reducing the external world to a mere catalyst in the process of expression. Like the baroque allegorist in his search for truth, the Expressionist appeared to hold the object's inherent meaning and its organic context in contempt, as the subject's projected soul states and emotional tensions eclipsed his material surroundings. Sokel's study of the movement claims for this powerfully productive subjectivity that 'thoughts become events. The most brutal desires are acted out in dreamlike scenes'.[20] In Kaiser's *Von Morgens bis Mitternachts* (*From Morn To Midnight*), for example, as the guilty cashier sets out across the snow-covered countryside with 60,000 marks that he has embezzled from the bank, a sudden squall of wind blows his hat from his head. His guilt and his apprehension of approaching death, are projected into, and overwhelm, the existing landscape – 'Snowflakes, shaken from the branches, stick in the tree-top and form a skeleton with grinning jaws. A branching arm holds the lost hat'.[21] The cashier tells the deathly figure to envelop him, but then decides that his quest for higher values and salvation is not at an end, and continues his journey. This hypersubjectivity on the part of baroque and Expressionist protagonist is offset by an unsettling power on the part of the object, a dialectic that I explore further in Chapter 2.

Barnes may have arrived in Berlin to witness innovative ideas in stagecraft and acting, but her introduction to Expressionism and its baroque heritage predated this trip to Europe. In 1914, Mary Heaton Vorse and her husband Joseph made an unlikely purchase, transforming Lewis Wharf, an area that had been part of Provincetown's cod-fishing industry, into an artistic haven. Vorse was instrumental in gathering Barnes and other Greenwich Villagers together for the new theatre in Provincetown, and the wharf proved an ideal venue for their stage. Under the leadership of George Cram (Jig) Cook, this theatre group became known as the Provincetown Players, and even when Kenneth MacGowan and Robert Edmond Jones reorganised the group in 1922, the public continued to use the original name. Barnes's companions in this artistic community included Alfred Kreymborg, Eugene O'Neill and Susan Glaspell, with O'Neill becoming the most influential dramatist in developing Expressionist forms for the American stage. Provincetown's artistic community dominated Barnes's social and creative life between 1915 and 1920, and its members were not restricted to playwrights and actors – American artists such as Marsden Hartley and Charles Demuth joined the group in 1916.

First-hand accounts of new developments in Expressionist theatre and art would have reached Barnes from many sources within Provincetown. In an interview dating from 1963, Mary Heaton Vorse recalls how impressed she had been by the European theatres of this period.[22] During a trip to the continent, she had met the Expressionist playwright Ernst Toller, and remembers discussing German Expressionist dramatists with the Provincetown Players on her return to Massachusetts in 1920. Between 1913 and 1914 Robert Edmond Jones travelled to Germany to spend a season at Max Reinhardt's Deutsches Theatre, thanks to funding from Jack Reed and Jones's patron Vorse. Reinhardt's productions during this period are considered seminal works, instigating the transition from Naturalistic stagecraft to Expressionist performance techniques. Edmond Jones's experiences of Expressionist theatre framed the German movement's period of innovation in drama and performance, as his second visit to Europe was in the spring of 1922, when he and Kenneth MacGowan spent ten weeks touring the theatres of the continent, documenting their experiences for the publication *Continental Stagecraft*. Opening with a review of Realism in the Moscow Art Theatre, this account of the European stage lingers over the details of German theatres such as Berlin's Freie Volksbühne, the new breed of directors including Leopold Jessner and Max Reinhardt, and Expressionist productions such as Toller's *Masse-Mensch*. Robert Edmond Jones contributed painstaking illustrations of notable scenes and stagecraft, while MacGowan argues that their account is both pertinent and broadly representative: 'luck and the repertory system found us at various German theatres in time to witness the most characteristic and significant work of the past few years'.[23]

The playwright Eugene O'Neill was the most influential figure to produce Expressionist drama for an American audience, and Cook staged many of his plays during the five-year period when Barnes was a member of the Provincetown group. It was not until 1920, however, with the premiere of *The Emperor Jones*, and then with the 1922 production of *The Hairy Ape*, that O'Neill's writing seems to engage in any developed sense with Expressionist forms and stagecraft. A second, lesser-known, Provincetown dramatist would have proved more influential in introducing Barnes to the innovative Expressionist style before she left for Europe. Alfred Kreymborg joined the Provincetown circle during their first season, and was already a close friend of Marsden Hartley. While O'Neill was intent on denying the influence of Georg Kaiser in his work, Kreymorg's affinity with the German movement appeared stronger and more explicit. He became editor of magazines such as *The Glebe* and *The Others*, where his admiration for proto-Expressionist and Expressionist work led him to publish translations of plays by Frank Wedekind and Leon Andreyev. The Provincetown Players performed Kreymborg's early play, *Lima Beans*, in 1916. With its repetitive Telegrammstil language, and abstract, stilted gestures this drama about a husband's desire to eat lima beans every evening, is already Expressionistic in its characterisation, speech and movement: 'Husband and wife might be two marionnettes'.[24] *Manikin and*

Minikin, a dramatisation of the dialogue between two bisque aristocratic figu-
rines on a mantelpiece, employs the same mechanical, clipped Telegrammstil
exchanges, but the awkward, unnaturalistic movements have been taken to the
extreme of inertia, as the ornaments discuss their own paralysis and the change
and modulation apparent in the animated humans that pass before them. This
play proved too experimental for the Provincetown group, so Kreymborg
joined forces with Edna St Vincent Millay to found a second theatre company,
'The Other Players', and successfully produced this drama. He returned to the
Provincetown stage with the February 1920 performances of *Vote the New
Moon*, an Expressionistic representation of the electoral campaign between
the Red and the Blue parties, where votes are cast by the Burgher and Burgess
of the town, each popping out of their doors like jacks-in-the-box, to embark
on a heavily ritualised and violent campaign. Here Kreymborg breaks the
automaton-like progression of the election by introducing the new idea of
a purple candidate with a corresponding purple moon, combining the two
opposing colours.

Another member of the Provincetown Players was particularly well placed
to inform and interest Barnes in the Expressionist movement. The American
painter Marsden Hartley had spent a great deal of time in Germany and had
come to see Berlin as his creative and cultural home before the outbreak of
war forced him to leave. He had visited Munich on his travels, familiarising
himself with *Der Blaue Reiter* group, and developing contacts with Wassily
Kandinsky, Franz Marc and Gabriel Munter. Kandinsky's influence is apparent in the title and forms of works such as Hartley's 1912–13 *Musical Theme
(Oriental Symphony)*. When the Expressionist Herwarth Walden staged his
1913 *Erster Deutscher Herbstsalon (First German Fall Salon)* in Berlin's Der
Sturm gallery, these friendships were to prove valuable, as Kandinsky and Marc
were instrumental in persuading Walden to exhibit four of Hartley's paintings
alongside the leading European avant-garde artists of the time. At this stage in
the American's career, his work had strong German affinities in both its style
and subject matter. *The Warriors* and *Military* illustrate Hartley's keen interest in the German armed forces, while paintings such as *Pre-War Pageant* are
Expressionist in their use of abstracted forms and emblems that present the
artist's intuitive response to a stimulus rather than offering a mimetic representation. Hartley arrived back in America full of enthusiasm for the art-world
he had reluctantly left behind, and this Expressionist influence continued into
the *Movements* series of paintings that he worked on while in Provincetown.
Barnes would have seen Hartley's work in the 291 Gallery in New York, where
Alfred Stieglitz hosted solo exhibitions for him in 1909, 1912, 1914 and 1916.
He and Barnes were reunited when she arrived in Berlin in 1921.

The Lukács–Bloch Debate

Scholarly debate on the significance and relative merits of Expressionism reached an unprecedented level of intensity during the years that framed the publication of Barnes's novel *Nightwood* (1936). The polemic formally began in January 1934 with the appearance of Georg Lukács's article 'Grösse und Verfall des Expressionismus' [The Significance and the Decline of Expressionism] in *Internationale Literatur*, and this particular version of Marxist theory soon gained in popularity and influence. The responses and counter-attacks that followed Lukács's essay have in many ways defined the terms in which Expressionism is discussed to this day. In 1937, as part of this retrospective approach, the journal *Das Wort* began a systematic critique of the German Expressionist movement initiated by Alfred Kurella, himself an acolyte of Lukácsian anti-Fascist views. This hostility towards Expressionism was countered by individuals such as Herwarth Walden, a critic and early champion of Expressionist literature, in his avant-garde magazine *Der Sturm*.

Walden and Kurella aside, some of the most important and defining exchanges within this debate on modernism in general, and Expressionism in particular, were those between the Marxist philosopher Ernst Bloch and Lukács himself, as the latter's passion for realism and all things classical provoked Bloch to defend avant-garde modern art. This dialogue is largely responsible for placing Expressionism at the heart of discussions of modernist literature during the mid-1930s. The cornerstone of Lukács's literary theory, as it appears in his anti-Expressionist essay, 'Realism in the Balance', is the Marxist assertion that capitalism constitutes an objective totality of social relations. As a result of the comprehensive and unified nature of capitalism's ideological, social and financial structure, a closed integration or 'totality' exists, an objectified reality that transcends modern representations of a fragmented society. This led Lukács to criticise Expressionism's fondness for abstraction and for shattered images of the world, notably those of capitalism, dismissing such techniques as acts of destruction and a fall into decadence. Using the examples of trade and money, Lukács acknowledges that, under capitalism, elements of our society assume a remarkable autonomy that results in financial crises, and my analysis of allegory and the commodity in Chapter 2 discusses this sense of self-determination and independence on the part of objects. Denying that these crises highlight the disintegration and independence of capitalism's component parts, Lukács insists that 'the crisis thus makes manifest the unity of processes which had become individually independent'.[25] He believes that at such a time human consciousness experiences a kind of inverse apprehension of this phenomenon: 'in periods of crisis, when the autonomous elements are drawn together into unity, they [the wider population] experience it as disintegration'.[26]

Returning to the subject of literature, Lukács's 'Realism in the Balance' describes an apparent contradiction or dialectical tension between the 'appearance' of events and the 'essence' of an objectified totality of capitalism, an uneasy relationship that is successfully navigated by the exemplary realist. The modernist writer, meanwhile, penetrates no further than appearances due to his rigid reliance on subjectivity. Such individuals overlook the cohesive totality that lies beyond, while literary realism is praised for its ability to relate social and psychological details to this wider historical totality. Modernism's literary schools are presented as fleeting, unstable artistic endeavours, taking reality just as it appears to both writer and character. The form of this immediate manifestation changes as society changes, hence such movements are quickly superseded by new avant-garde counterparts, Naturalism, Impressionism and Expressionism, and finally Surrealism. The realist meanwhile seeks to 'uncover the deeper, hidden, mediated and not immediately perceptible network of relationships that go to make up society', producing, Lukács implies, a more profound, considered and authentic representation.[27] Despite the fact that many Expressionists considered themselves to be politically left-wing, Lukács insisted that the movement's literary forms had an irrational foundation. This gave rise to a hypersubjectivity, and a pernicious form of academic and spiritual elitism.

Bloch, meanwhile, opens his essay 'Discussing Expressionism' (1935) by challenging the very ground upon which Lukács bases his argument – the quality and breadth of his knowledge of Expressionist works. 'Discussing Expressionism' defends the movement against charges of élitism and exclusivity by stressing its humanist stance and its strong connections with the nation's cultural heritage: 'As the *Blue Rider* proves, it [Expressionism] ransacked the past for like-minded witnesses . . . in primitive art and even in the Baroque'.[28] The most important point at issue between the two theorists is the nature of the relationship between Expressionist and modernist art and social reality. While for Lukács, Expressionism was easily dismissed as a decadent by-product of the imperialist phase of capitalism, Bloch interprets the movement as a historically pertinent and valuable response to a particular period of crisis and transition. He goes some way towards acknowledging the transience of Expressionism's authority, its tendency to unduly subjectivist breakthroughs and chaotic forms, but nevertheless champions its fracturing, idealising and imaginative representations, reluctant to locate Lukács's definition of totality solely within the realm of objective representation. He asks: 'What if Lukács' reality – a coherent, infinitely mediated totality – is not so objective after all? What if authentic reality is also distorted?' and suggests that the sites of genuine novelty and innovation to be excavated by a modernist artist are the '*real* fissures in . . . surface inter-relations'.[29]

The inaugural essay for this Marxist discourse on modernism is Lukács's

1934 essay, 'Expressionism: Its Significance and Decline'. His analysis of the movement's creative methods draws attention to the anonymous, allegorical stage figures of Expressionist theatre, actors who 'become in their form mere silhouettes', while the writer himself appears as the play's central character.[30] These silhouettes are the actors of Schrei performance and they influenced Barnes's interpretation of the human body. Lukács goes on to regret 'the unconcealed hollowness and vacuity' of these representations and the resulting 'deliberate impoverishment of the reality portrayed'.[31] Expressionism becomes synonymous with a particular definition of 'essence', one which severs all links between an object and the processes of the external world, our customary causal connections of time and space. It is for this reason that Lukács finds Expressionist artworks incapable of producing the vital syntheses of a realist totality.

By pausing the debate here, in the early and mid-1930s, I want to reconsider Expressionism in more detail. Rather than setting Lukács's critique of the movement's chaotic, fragmented forms against later counter-attacks by Bloch or Brecht, my analysis will look backwards to Benjamin's pre-Marxist text, *Ursprung des deutschen Trauerspiels* (*The Origin of German Tragic Drama*), first published in 1928, some years before the essays and correspondence of the Marxist debate. I interpret this text as a significant articulation of German Expressionism's transgressive forms and the movement's debt to Germany's baroque past. Benjamin's study of the seventeenth-century German Trauerpsiel and its dominant aesthetic form, allegory, is considered by Adorno and Lukács as central to the understanding of modern art. While I will examine the post-war re-emergence of allegorical forms in more detail in Chapter 2, it is important to note, in the context of this Marxist consideration of modernism, that Benjamin's interpretation of allegory contradicts Lukács's ideal of the closed totality of a world represented by symbol, and the paradigms of nature and civilisation within classical antiquity. The organic unity of the symbol is undermined by Benjamin's counter-image, allegory, with its fractured forms and inherent sense of despair and isolation. For Benjamin, the unconcealed hollowness of forms noted in Lukács's essay becomes the only apposite quality of expression during a period of catastrophe and spiritual desolation. Towards the close of the 'Epistemo-Critical Prologue' to this study, Benjamin identifies Expressionism as the modernist movement in which allegory assumes its greatest significance, as its artists struggle to articulate the conditions of post-war Germany. While his immediate concern appears to be a baroque world-picture and aesthetic forms, the subtext of *The Origin of German Tragic Drama* can be seen as an acknowledgement of Expressionism's representation of immediate, limited and alienated experience, and its failure to reconcile this subjectivity with a wider social and economic objective reality.

Benjamin's study of Trauerspiel evolved from his sense that Expressionism owed a considerable debt of influence to the seventeenth century, but also from a conviction that this particular modernist movement had proved a catalyst for exploring and reworking the baroque. In the prologue to his text, Benjamin claims:

> The lack of autonomy manifest in the present generation has for the most part been overwhelmed by the compelling force it encountered in the baroque. Hitherto there have been no more than a few isolated cases where the revaluation which began with the emergence of Expressionism ... has led to a genuine insight which reveals new relationships within the material itself.[32]

His study aims to address this paucity of critical writing, focusing his comparisons and analogies on language, a sense of shared spiritual anguish and the historical context of war. Expressionism was characterised by its desire to shatter the resistant but superficial surface of existence in order to attain a more elusive, essential core of reality. As with the writers and artists of the baroque, the Expressionists turned to allegory in this endeavour, and allegory as a detailed aesthetic will remain at the centre of my analysis of Barnes's work.

Baruch Spinoza and Evolutionary Theory

Baruch Spinoza spent his youth living as part of a Hebrew community in seventeenth-century Amsterdam. As a young man he studied Latin and Divinity, but soon found himself ostracised from the Jewish church and repeatedly censured for his unorthodox and deductive account of a universe defined by one single compound substance. *Ethics* was by far his most significant and controversial work, and its challenge to established religion and morality prevented its publication until his death in 1677. He was dismissed as an atheist whose ideas undermined orthodox spiritual beliefs such as revelation, free will, absolute definitions of good and evil, and the existence of a providential God who has created and ordered the world. Contradicting anthropocentric interpretations of man as an exceptional being who presides over a less sophisticated realm of nature, *Ethics* describes a profound continuity and parity between these two states of being, based on the conviction that we differ from other life forms in quantitative but not qualitative terms. Spinoza subsumes matter, mind and energy under one universal substrate that has neither genesis nor an immortal soul in the Christian sense of that word. He also establishes animation and subjectivity as inherent within all matter, a claim that becomes possible by interpreting sensation and consciousness in terms of physical energy. His repetition of the phrase '*Deus sive Nature*' (God or Nature) suggests that he recognised no distinction between God and the natural world, with matter becoming essential to a Deity who is infinite, material but not transcendental. So while his treatise could be argued to set out a reductive pantheism, he nevertheless dismisses the religious convictions that determine any construction of theism. *Ethics* takes as its premise the weakness in Cartesian definitions of substance and agency that place thought and human consciousness apart from the realm of matter, with each remaining separate and irreconcilable and yet able to interact and influence one another. Chapter 5 explores this interrogation of Descartes' ideas in more detail but here, by way of introducing Haeckel's work, it is enough to note that perhaps the most important legacy of *Ethics* for evolutionary science was the idea that the creation and development of organic and inorganic entities is inherent in the essence of nature itself and not in teleology, linear progressivism or the intervention of a hidden God.

Just as Benjamin intervened in the narrative of literary modernism to research and theorise the Trauerspiel and allegory as a pertinent baroque world picture, so Ernst Haeckel intervened in the narrative of Darwinian evolutionary science by assimilating and theorising the vision of baroque monist philosophy. Haeckel was a philosopher, physician, zoologist and professor of comparative anatomy at the University of Jena from the mid 1860s until 1909. He read *On the Origin of Species by Means of Natural Selection* (1859) before he met Darwin in person in 1866, and was at once convinced by its propositions and inspired to extrapolate the laws of evolution out into the wider cosmos, far beyond Darwin's original thesis. Haeckel's scientific discourse had developed from his own interest in cell biology and morphology, and from longstanding monist convictions that were grounded in Spinoza's original treatise. To this blend, Darwin added the belief that life had originated spontaneously from entirely natural causes, with individual species evolving in a directionless, unforeseeable way that he termed 'natural selection'. Darwin's open, materialistic description of the evolutionary process lacked a theory to account for the changes involved and, while Haeckel followed Spinoza in dispensing with a providential God, Darwin was far more circumspect, investigating a world in which the existence of a deity was neither insisted upon nor denied. Haeckel's intervention in evolutionary science locates itself at precisely this point, and his skill in crafting a compelling narrative for both academic and popular consideration lay in the way that he combined his own philosophical beliefs with Darwin's claims, completing gaps in the existing argument and giving *The Origin of Species* a bold monist spin. Spinoza's philosophy had already argued that mind and body, and man and animal, are one and the same thing, and Haeckel now consolidated his argument by presenting the world as a chain of connections cohering through mechanistic forces and a continuity of life from man down to unicellular or molecular levels. Haeckel's law of biogenetics stated that ontogeny repeats phylogeny, that is to say that the stages of an embryo's development are said to recapitulate the morphology or modifying forms of its predecessors within that species, and this allowed him to plot a comprehensive genealogy of all evolutionary organisms.[33] In his determination to establish an unbroken continuum of life-forms that would substantiate his monist vision, Haeckel speculated that the lowest of these creatures had developed spontaneously through combinations of basic elements such as oxygen and carbon, and he insisted on the existence of formless microorganisms without nuclei from which single-cell bodies had evolved. These 'monera' were catalogued to support his research but were discovered to be fictitious, as were certain geological periods that he had invented to accommodate these transitional forms without fossil evidence.

For all the religious and scientific hostility that his philosophy and its attendant scientific claims generated, Haeckel became a hugely influential figure within late nineteenth- and early twentieth-century European culture. Popular science writers and laymen such as Wilhelm Bölsche gave a particularly ecstatic and flamboyant interpretation of Haeckelian monism in texts such as *Love-Life in Nature* (*Liebesleben in der Natur*) (1931), a rather lyrical account of the sex lives of all creatures from amoeba through to man, that emphasised progress and perfection as inherent in evolution. Artists and architects such as Paul Scheerbart, Bruno Taut and Hermann Finsterlin applied his monist principles to building design, architectural fables, literature and sketches.[34] Not all responded to Haeckel's reworking of Spinoza's *Ethics* with such utopian and optimistic creativity, and the artists Gabriel von Max and Alfred Kubin engaged with his ideas in more guarded and unsettling ways. Their monist vision of man trapped within nature inspired representations of the human–animal boundary that range from the mocking to the macabre. Haeckel had claimed man's descent from the apes before Darwin and von Max's paintings, such as *The Toast* and *Monkeys as the Judges of Art* play uncomfortably with that sense of intimacy and shared identity. Alfred Kubin's sketches and artworks show strange transitional organisms that combine a primitive creature with more sophisticated forms such as his *Verwandlung* [Transformation], or the octopus fused with the fragments of spines, shell and limbs belonging to a less evolved marine crustacean in *Praparats* [Preparation].

Critical accounts of Isadora Duncan's work have certainly acknowledged the influence of philosophy on her ideas, with the most developed focusing on Friedrich Nietzsche.[35] The Austrian writer and translator Karl Federn helped her to understand and analyse texts such as Nietzsche's *The Birth of Tragedy*, and this intense period of study allowed her to follow the debates of artists, philosophers and musicians in the Munich Künstler Haus. Other academic studies of Duncan's ideas have briefly acknowledged her debt to the work of Ernst Haeckel, noting that her proposals for the evolution of dance echo the vocabulary of Haeckel's theories of recapitulation, and drawing attention to Haeckel's own use of the term 'dance' as a metaphor for cosmic evolution and development within individual species.[36] Duncan read with enthusiasm translations of Haeckel's *The Riddle of the Universe*, *The Evolution of Man* and

The History of Creation, and her subsequent correspondence with the scientist establishes their mutual admiration and the suggestion that they meet and that she dance for him in Bayreuth during the summer of 1904. Their meeting took place at the Festspiele that year and Haeckel enjoyed her performance, but for all this familiarity and esteem, Duncan's engagement with Haeckel's texts differs fundamentally from that of the artists mentioned above. Although she does not shy away from borrowing images and phrases from *Riddle of the Universe*, *Anthropogeny* and *The History of Creation*, signalling that her ideas are progressive and of-the-moment, Duncan's philosophy of dance seems much closer in its concerns and its exposition to the original monist thought of Spinoza. At first glance there appears little to connect the two – Duncan was a twentieth-century performer, whose theories envisaged dance as a catalyst for regeneration across the arts, while Spinoza was a seventeenth-century heretic, whose speculative philosophy overlooked the category of aesthetic experience almost entirely. There is no doubt that the particular definitions and ideas from Spinoza's *Ethics* that Duncan came to best understand and adapt are those that Haeckel appropriated for his evolutionary science, and that later sections of Spinoza's text that discuss morality, reason and virtue interest both Haeckel and Duncan far less than the baroque theories of substance, motion, and the relationship between mind and body. Chapter 5 will argue, however, that Duncan's ideas are often closer to the original baroque definitions with their focus on movement and the principle of *conatus*, rather than the scientific mediation of *Ethics* developed by Haeckel, and my analysis will address the fact that existing scholarship has yet to explore the seventeenth-century origins of her rhetoric.

Edward Gordon Craig and the Commedia dell'Arte

Without doubt, the commedia dell'arte's most conscientious champions within Anglo-American modernism were the theatre director and theorist Edward Gordon Craig and his fellow researcher Dorothy Nevile Lees. The articles and documents that they unearthed and published in their journal *The Mask* from 1910 onwards provided modernism with its most detailed and authentic account of this genre, from its beginnings in the sixteenth century through to its eighteenth-century revival in the dramas of Carlo Gozzi and his arch-rival Carlo Goldoni. Although the commedia players were performing in the sixteenth century, with troupes such as I Confidenti and I Comici Uniti coming together in the late 1500s, the commedia came into its own during the seventeenth century, a time when the mask of Arlecchino replaced Brighella as first zanni and developed the defining qualities of wit and athleticism that we recognise today. The early commedia actors acted in pairs or small groups and travelled relentlessly to find new and appreciative audiences and to avoid hostility from both church and state. They set up their high trestle stages in piazzas across Italy and from these humble beginnings they went on to form established companies with representative names. The Gelosi performed mainly in Milan and were one of the first to band together, boasting the learned Francesco Andreini, a skilled improviser who made the mask of Capitano Spavento his own, and the actor and writer Flaminio Scala, who played the role of a young Inamorato called Flavio. The Gelosi were among the first to take the commedia dell'arte to France in 1577 at the invitation of Henry III. I Comici Confidenti – so-called as they were confident their performances would be well received – performed during the first part of the seventeenth century and Scala went on to become the company's director. The Accesi acted together during the late sixteenth and early seventeenth century and their Arlecchino was the acclaimed Tristano Martinelli. Each region of Italy had its own native mask and dialect, and Craig claims to be the first commedia scholar to catalogue these in their entirety. The principal masks were the two vecchi (old men) and the two zanni (servants or buffoons). The vecchi were the old Venetian merchant Pantalone, or Magnifico, and his friend and sometimes rival Il Dottore, or Gratiano, an academic from the University of Bologna. Il Dottore wore a black mask with red daubs on the cheeks and was inclined to deliver pompous speeches peppered with esoteric knowledge and Latin phrases. Pantalone wore a brown bearded mask with a large nose and he was varying degrees of lecherous, foolish, greedy and self-indulgent. The two did battle and negotiated intrigues with the two zanni, Brighella and Arlecchino, and the latter played servants with no permanent master. Brighella was a cynical manipulator of the other masks, ruthless, untrustworthy, and initially more intelligent and devious than the hapless Arlecchino. As Arlecchino's wit and abilities grew, enhancing his acrobatic skills and bawdy offences, he replaced Brighella as the principal zanni. The commedia Captain began life as Capitan Matamoros during the Spanish ascendancy in Italy and he sported a mask, ruff and flamboyant hat. His Italian counterpart Spavento was equally cowardly and conceited and was soon joined by a French equivalent, Captain Rodomont. Pedrolino, the youngest and most naive of the characters, became Pierrot as the commedia became popular in France, retaining the wistful, guileless qualities of the young Italian rustic. The lovers or inamoratos, Isabella, Flaminia and Flavio, did not wear masks and were invariably engaged in romantic intrigues and flirtations, and Arlecchino's beloved was a maidservant called Columbine.

The origins of the commedia dell'arte have always been the subject of disagreement among historians and academics. The ancient Roman Atellanae, improvised popular comedies and political satires performed by masked actors, are favoured by Pierre Duchartre and Maurice Sand, with other more diverse sources explored by Dr Michele Scherillo and Winifred Smith.[37] Although a quickening of interest in the Italian commedia is often traced to Maurice Sand's *Masques et Bouffons* (1860) the quality and breadth of research offered by Edward Gordon Craig's *The Mask* was unprecedented and it undoubtedly inspired the flurry of books on this genre that appeared between 1910 and the 1930s. Craig reviewed the most significant of these texts, alongside primary sources from the baroque period and accounts of performance and technique written by commedia actors themselves. Winifred Smith's *The Commedia Dell'Arte – A Study in Popular Italian Comedy* was published in 1911, and Craig expresses his admiration for her work along with the hope that she will in future offer more detailed individual studies of celebrated commedia actors such as Francesco Andreini of the Comici Gelosi.[38] Alongside English-language accounts of the genre, *The Mask* also reviewed Professor Luigi Rasi's *I Comici Italiani* (1905), praising Rasi's discriminating research and expressing Craig's delight at being the first to introduce such remarkable work to English readers.[39] There were also reviews of translated studies such as Angelo Constantini's *The Birth, Life and Death of Scaramouch* (1924), a biography first published in 1695 in Florence by F. Lumach, and translated for the modern audience by the dance historian, publisher and translator Cyril W. Beaumont.[40] This account of the life of Tiberio Fiorilli, commedia actor, vagabond and thief, is full of anecdote recounted by his fellow performer Constantini, and Craig's review looks forward to more commedia projects from Beaumont. The latter was soon to oblige with *The History of Harlequin* in 1926, a book-length study of the Arlecchino mask, for which Sacheverell Sitwell wrote an introduction. Then, in 1928, Beaumont translated, edited and published a selection of commedia dance drawings, Gregorio Lambranzi's *New and Curious School of Theatrical Dancing* after Craig had issued a plea for information on this mysterious text in a 1923 edition of *The Mask*. The extent to which commedia dominated Craig's vision of baroque theatre in its entirety is clear in his review of C. C. Stope's study *Burbage and Shakespeare's Stage*, where he cannot help but ask the reader how such a text can be complete without mention of Tristano Martinelli's Arlecchino, a celebrated Italian performer who made the Harlequin role his own, and who apparently visited London during the period that Stopes discusses.[41]

Craig and Lees did not content themselves with analysis and translations from the 1920s, but took particular delight in introducing their readership to the accounts and advice offered by the baroque actors and coragos behind the commedia performances. Craig considers Evaristo Gherardi's *Le Théâtre italien* (*The Italian Theatre*) to be the most important baroque text for the commedia actor. Gherardi was an Italian actor and playwright who took the mask of Arlecchino and travelled to France to perform in the commedia during the 1670s. Lees offers *The Mask's* readers an introduction to this text and a translation of the Preface. Craig also values Andrea Perucci's 1699 *Dell'arte rappresentativa premeditata ed all'improvviso* (*A Treatise on Acting from Memory and by Improvisation*) as the most comprehensive discussion of the commedia dell'arte during the seventeenth century. Perucci was a Neopolitan librettist, actor and playwright and he offers advice and insights on the use of masks, improvisation, gesture, the roles of different characters and the corago and manager. He also promotes the use of notebooks (zibaldoni) to record jokes, stock routines and lazzi. Finally Craig introduces Luigi Riccoboni's *Histoire du Théâtre italien* (1730), with his advice to actors printed in the April 1911 edition of Craig's journal. Riccoboni was one of a troupe of commedia actors invited to Paris by Philippe d'Orleans in 1716, later to become an expatriate writer and director of the Comédie Italienne.

Craig proved unsuccessful in his attempts to establish a school of experimental theatre in England, but in February 1913, The Gordon Craig School for the Art of Theatre was finally established in Florence at the Arena Goldoni. *The Mask* was the school's sister venture and the two projects were interdependent, with the journal publishing research and prints that would have formed part of the school's extensive archive and teaching on the history of theatre. Craig's colleague in both undertakings, and co-editor of *The Mask*, was Dorothy Nevile Lees, a young woman who had moved to Florence in 1903, remaining there for many years before the school opened its doors to students. Although it suited Craig to be the figurehead for both projects, neither would have been possible without Lees' constancy and support, and as an accomplished translator of Italian, a gift that Craig lacked, her involvement ensured the smooth running of all practical undertakings at the Arena Goldoni. She and Craig haunted the archives at the Marucelliana Library and the Biblioteca Nazionale discovering prints, documents and commedia scenarios to fill the pages of *The Mask*, research that had never been published in translation before. They were not alone in contributing articles on the commedia, but were joined by Italian academics whose scholarship in this genre had already been established by their monograph publications. Dr Michele Scherillo's *La Commedia Dell'Arte in Italia* was published in 1884 and the journal made this standard of academic research accessible to an English readership for the first time. Scherillo wrote a lengthy genealogy of Pulcinella in 1910, and the following year a history of Capitan Fracassa, the commedia's vainglorious Spanish soldier.[42] He also penned more discursive articles, such as 'The Scenarios of Della Porta', in which he takes issue with existing scholarship to suggest that the Italian scholar and cryptographer Giambattista Della Porta elaborated Plautus's *Pseudolus* to create the complex scenarios of his *Trapolaria*.[43]

THE MODERNIST COMMEDIA

The tradition of the commedia dell'arte was never captured in full by the records of baroque performers or their coragos but has made its way to us from prints, collections of brief scenarios, autobiographies, contemporary accounts and subsequent interpretations. Without prescriptive records it lent itself to many modernist incarnations. In October 1912, Arnold Schoenberg's melodrama *Pierrot Lunaire* enjoyed its first performance, setting a German translation of Albert Giraud's poems to music and following Pierrot through his defining expressions of desire, jest, buffoonery and melancholy. Igor Stravinsky's 1911 ballet *Petrushka* tells of the showman in a Russian fairground who bewitches three puppets so that they come to life, in a tale taken from the tradition of puppet or burattini theatre that remained home to commedia characters long after they had been outlawed from streets, piazzas and courts. The Petrushka puppet assumes Pierrot's role as the slighted, lovelorn suitor, while the object of his desire, a beautiful ballerina, falls in love with the character of the Moor. Stravinsky's second ballet to borrow from the commedia dell'arte is his 1920 *Pulcinella*, a work commissioned by Sergei Diaghilev, with Pablo Picasso designing the costumes and sets. The story is taken from an Italian canovaccio called *Quatre Polichinelles Semblables (Four Identical Pulcinellas)*, and combines the expected commedia elements of jealousy, violence and resurrection. As was the case with Craig, Diaghilev's passion for the Italian comedy led him to study and research in Italy's libraries where he discovered the early eighteenth-century manuscript and persuaded an initially hostile Stravinsky to use it as the blueprint for the ballet. The commedia was an evocative reference again and again in the Cubist paintings of Pablo Picasso, Gino Severini and Juan Gris, in the Expressionist artworks of Paul Klee and in the poetry of Guillame Apollinaire, but however keen these modernists were to adopt the genre's recognisable figures and stereotypes, there was little of the original spirit of improvisation, spontaneity and accessible popular culture in any of their stylised representations, sophisticated musical adaptations or scripted rehearsals. I have chosen to discuss the work of Edward Gordon Craig and Wyndham Lewis because they engage with the commedia by acknowledging and assimilating its original forms and significance, and in ways that go far beyond the nostalgic associations of individual masks.

No study of the baroque in English language modernism can overlook the Sitwell siblings and their extensive engagement with the art and culture of that period. The term 'baroque' had been gathering a charm of its own and a critical momentum for some years before the publication of Sacheverell Sitwell's *Southern Baroque Art* (1924), but the Sitwells' unique achievement was to somehow consolidate its appeal by appearing to preside over its many incarnations and rediscoveries all at once within English culture. While Barnes, Lewis and Duncan engage in great detail with baroque writing and performance, shaping their modernist aesthetic with one eye always on a precise understanding of the original creativity, the Sitwells did not assimilate the baroque in quite the same way. While their knowledge of the period's key figures and cultural achievements is impressive and well documented, and, in the case of Sacheverell, almost encyclopaedic, the baroque served their flair for predicting and promoting cultural vogues rather than providing them with particular works of literature or drama that could be given a developed and authentic recreation. As was the case with so many modernist artists, the commedia dell'arte that enchanted them owed far more to the elegant interpretations of Jean-Antoine Watteau, Gilles Callot, Romanticism and Symbolism than to the original baroque performances that preoccupied Craig and Lewis. The baroque as it was introduced to cultured modernist society by Sacheverell in 1924 was a creature of intriguing architectural and artistic discoveries, subversive aesthetic statement and long-forgotten genius that challenged the neat, classical turn of high modernism with shameless excess and a defiant, decorative strangeness. It was Sir George Sitwell who first introduced his children to the baroque architecture and art of Southern Italy, but Osbert and Sacheverell made their own tours in these lands as young men in the early 1920s, gathering names and images in Apulia's Lecce, Naples and Noto, while its narrative of baroque absolutism and ornament delighted their appetite for privilege, exclusivity and excess. The brothers were introduced to the paintings of the Italian baroque at an exhibition held in Florence's Palazzo Pitti in 1923, and in their native England they formed the Magnasco Society with the Finnish art historian Tancred Borenius. The society was intended as a vehicle to promote and publicise themselves, their knowledge, and the artworks that they championed, and the painters celebrated included Guido Reni, Carlo Dolci and the society's namesake Alessandro Magnasco.

For all the detailed descriptions and scholarship contained in the spectacle of the baroque that they set before their public, it was also a world of fantasy and freedom, not least because its subjects were so little known. In *Southern Baroque Art*, Sacheverell tells of a lavish court ceremony in Naples where Spanish and Italian splendour combine.[44] The reader sees the king's state descent of a staircase, fireworks, flights of glittering birds, archways full of zanni waiting to begin their commedia buffoonery, and fiery harlequins. The enigmatic bird actors of Naples have arrived by water, Neapolitan Punchinellos with their full white trousers and the barbed white bird masks that were to become the famous bauta, as commedia costumes merged with those of the eighteenth-century masquerade. In *Cupid and the Jacaranda*, Sacheverell offers his reader a layering of worlds and sensations as the baroque and modern blend seamlessly in his imagination. The book opens with a scene at Renishaw, and Sacheverell is fourteen years old as he encounters the commedia figure of Mezzetin. Mezzetin was a singer and musician, a less ruthless version of Brighella, and a particular favourite of the French artist Jean-Antoine Watteau, although when Watteau arrived in Paris and began to paint the commedia masks, the players themselves had been banished from the city for some years. Such facts link the present and Sacheverell's allusive engagement with Watteau's painting 'L'Embarquement Pour Cythère', but they are absent from the text which glides instead between Mezzetin as a shadowy childhood acquaintance and as one of the commedia subjects identified on Watteau's canvas. Watteau's technique is to project the commedia players into a setting that is not their own, and once they have forsaken the pace and athleticism of improvisation in piazzas and theatres they find themselves grouped by the lake of a chateau and intent on courtship. Watteau's suggestion that the figures are staying at the chateau is incongruous and provocative, not only because they are far removed from the setting of commedia performance, but because the commedia dell'arte, by definition, only allowed professional actors to attempt the masked roles – guests, courtiers and aristocrats would not have done so. Sitwell explains that he takes the characters up at precisely the point that Watteau leaves them, and that the painting offers him a label for his own art as 'the perpetual explorer of the rose-hung island'.[45] In texts such as *Southern Baroque Art* and *Cupid and the Jacaranda*, Sitwell does indeed use a similar technique whereby the paintings, costumes, buildings and texts of the baroque are significant only as the starting point for his aesthetic, while his metaphor of the rose-hung island seems to suggest a desire to pursue the after-life of images captured within these original baroque sources through a series of strong emotional responses, memories, fantasies and lyrical fictions. The Sitwell baroque was about straying far beyond the original forms, patterns and devices, and by rewriting the period in this way the youngest sibling believed he improved upon historical fact and artefact and brought the baroque to life for his reader. When he continues the narrative of 'L'Embarquement Pour Cythère', those embarking alight on a Venetian quay, and we are quickly among the bird actors of the city, men and women captured with their heads bent in thought. We walk on to encounter more black-cowled figures watching a charlatan on a platform, and finally we glimpse a black mask, bright colours and a glint of mischief – the reader does not need to be told that they have exchanged glances with the company's Arlecchino.

Lewis was a satellite of the Sitwell's social and cultural world for long enough to learn from their knowledge of the commedia, facts and experiences that would have consolidated his own well-documented interest in its forms and cultural significance. His writing also reveals that he was familiar with Craig's research into this particular performance style and his plans for the future of the theatre.[46] The painter Augustus John makes the bold claim that Lewis's entire vision of life evolved with the commedia dell'arte at its heart.[47] He apparently relished the spontaneous inventions, the vulgar humour and the clowning, and delighted in watching amateurs take up their masks, their lazzi and their stock phrases, in an attempt to revive this tradition. John insists that diffidence alone prevented his friend from joining these would-be Pulcinellas and Harlequins in their exuberance. For those familiar with Lewis's critique of modernist culture these observations, and the suggestion that such improvisations allowed the rather shy Lewis to relax and drop his own mask, are surprising and somewhat ironic. In texts such as *The Art of Being Ruled*, the commedia revival and its host of enthusiastic amateurs who dabble in extemporisation beyond the footlights, present an image that is anything but pleasurable and liberating. My analysis of Lewis's polemic, and his novels *Mrs Duke's Million* and *The Apes of God* will pursue these contradictory responses to the commedia and the implications for Lewis's writing.

In 'Wyndham Lewis: The Transformations of Carnival', Alan Munton uses the above excerpt from John's *Finishing Touches* to focus on Lewis's love of theatre and to work backwards from commedia dell'arte to the theatrical elements of carnival from which it evolved.[48] Munton and Green both mention the uninhibited world of Munich's bohemian Schwabing quarter, where art and carnival excess came together on a regular basis throughout the year, and where Lewis enjoyed himself a great deal during his visit to Germany.[49] Munton links Lewis's comedy, as a form of writing grounded in the human body, with Bakhtin's views on Rabelais, and he and Green follow the tradition of commedia and carnival through the short stories of *The Wild Body*. Paul Edward's chapter on *The Apes of God* returns to carnival in a discussion of the novel's affinities with Roman Saturnalia, with Zagreus as a version of Dionysus, and Julius Ratner as the figure subjected to mock execution.[50] My own analysis aims to separate the commedia from its carnival roots, as this sense of difference or modification informs the particular examples of Lewis's work that I have chosen to study.

NOTES

1. Eliot, 'The Metaphysical Poets', in *The Norton Anthology of Theory and Criticism*, p. 1104.
2. Kuna, 'T. S. Eliot's Dissociation of Sensibility and the Critics of Metaphysical Poetry', *Essays in Criticism*, 1963, 13.3, p. 241; Matthews, *T. S. Eliot and Early Modern Literature*; Matthews, 'T. S. Eliot's Chapman: Metaphysical Poetry and Beyond', *Journal of Modern Literature*, 2006, 9.4, pp. 22–43.
3. Mitchell, 'Expressionism in English Drama', in *Expressionism as an International Literary Phenomenon*, pp. 181–3.
4. See Chapter 2, opening quotation.
5. Nelson, 'Baroque' in *The New Princeton Encyclopaedia of Poetry and Poetics*, p. 122; Cysarz (1924) *Deutsch Barockdichtung*.
6. Erwin Panofsky and Fritz Saxl, *Durer's Melencolia 1: eine quellen- und typengeschichteliche Untersuchung* (Leipzig: Teubner, 1923), later extended with Raymond Klibansky to become *Saturn and Melancholy: Studies in the History of Natural Philosophy, Religion and Art* (1964).
7. Wellek, 'The Baroque', in *Concepts of Criticism*, pp. 74–91.
8. Monika Kaup, 'The Neobaroque in Djuna Barnes', *Modernism/Modernity*, 12.1, January, 2005, p. 85.
9. Eliot's introduction appears in the Faber publication of Djuna Barnes, *Nightwood* (London: Faber and Faber Publishing, 1949), p. xiv.
10. Greene, 'Fiction Chronicle', *The Catholic Tablet*, 14, November 1936, pp. 678–9.

11. Kaup, p. 105; Caselli, *Improper Modernism: Djuna Barnes's Bewildering Corpus*, p. 244.
12. Deborah Parsons, 'Djuna Barnes: Melancholic Modernism', in *The Cambridge Companion to the Modernist Novel*, p. 175; Peter Nicholls, *Modernisms: A Literary Guide*, p. 222.
13. Benjamin, *The Origin of German Tragic Drama*, p. 55.
14. Buck-Morss, *The Dialectics of Seeing – Walter Benjamin and the Arcades Project*, p. 178.
15. Quoted in Schürer, 'Provocation and Proclamation, Vision and Imagery: Expressionist Drama between German Idealism and Modernity' in *A Companion to the Literature of German Expressionism*, p. 148.
16. Styan, *Max Reinhardt*, pp. 86–107. *Everyman* was staged on a platform in front of Salzburg Cathedral, with an audience of 5,000.
17. Scheffauer, *The New Vision in the German Arts*, p. 7.
18. Ibid. 105.
19. Kasimir Edschmid, *Tribune der Kunst und Zeit Eine Schriftensammung – Uber den Expressionismus in der Literatur und die Neue Dichtung* (Berlin: Erich Reiss, 1919), p. 52, trans. in Walter H. Sokel, *The Writer in Extremis – Expressionism in Twentieth-Century Literature* (Stanford: Stanford University Press, 1959), p. 51.
20. Sokel, *The Writer in Extremis – Expressionism in Twentieth-Century German Literature*, p. 44.
21. Kaiser, *From Morn to Midnight*, p. 22.
22. Interview with Mary Heaton Vorse, 3 August 1963, quoted Valgemae, *Accelerated Grimace: Expressionism in the American Drama of the 1920s*, p. 28.
23. MacGowan and Jones, *Continental Stagecraft*, p. viii.
24. Alfred Kreymborg, 'Lima Beans – A Scherzo-Play', *Plays for Poem-Mimes*, p. 43.
25. Georg Lukács, 'Realism in the Balance', in *Aesthetics and Politics*, p. 32.
26. Ibid. p. 32.
27. Ibid. p. 38.
28. Ernst Bloch, 'Discussing Expressionism', in *Aesthetics and Politics*, p. 23.
29. Ibid. p. 22.
30. Georg Lukács, 'Expressionism: Its Significance and Decline', pp. 106–7.
31. Ibid.
32. Benjamin, *The Origin of German Tragic Drama*, p. 54
33. For an account of Wyndham Lewis's engagement with the work of Ernst Haeckel and monist philosophy see Armond, 'Cosmic Men – Wyndham Lewis, Ernst Haeckel and Paul Scheerbart', *Journal of Wyndham Lewis Studies*, 4, 2013, pp. 41–62.
34. For a discussion of these architects and Haeckel, see Armond, 'A Paper Paradise: Ernst Bloch and the Crystal Chain', pp. 259–73.
35. LaMothe, *Nietzsche's Dancers – Isadora Duncan, Martha Graham, and the Revaluation of Christian Values;* Preston, 'The Motor in the Soul: Isadora Duncan and Modernist Performance', in *Modernism/Modernity* 12. 2, April 2005, pp. 273–89.
36. Simonson, *Body Knowledge: Performance, Intermediality, and American Entertainment at the Turn of the Twentieth Century.*
37. See Duchartre, *The Italian Comedy*, pp. 24–9; Smith, *The Commedia Dell'Arte – A Study in Italian Popular Comedy*, pp. 21–30.
38. *The Mask*, 5.3, January 1913, p. 272.
39. *The Mask*, 3.10–12, April 1911, p. 187.
40. *The Mask*, 10.4, October, 1924, p. 188.
41. *The Mask*, 6.2, October 1913, p. 175.

42. *The Mask*, 3.1–3, July 1910, p. 22; *The Mask*, 3, 1911, p. 149.
43. *The Mask*, 6.1, July 1913, p. 33.
44. Sitwell, *Southern Baroque Art*, pp. 83–96.
45. Sitwell, *Cupid and the Jacaranda*, p. 42.
46. Lewis, *The Art of Being Ruled*, pp. 175–6.
47. John, *Finishing Touches*, pp. 119–20, in Munton, 'Wyndham Lewis and the Transformations of Carnival', p. 141.
48. Munton, 'Wyndham Lewis: The Transformations of Carnival', p. 141.
49. Green and Swan, *The Triumph of a Pierrot – The Commedia Dell'Arte and the Modern Imagination*, p. 31.
50. Edwards, *Wyndham Lewis: Painter and Writer*, pp. 348–57.

2

MODERN ALLEGORY: READING *NIGHTWOOD* THROUGH THE FORMS OF THE BAROQUE TRAUERSPIEL

'In the twilight they had spoken in baroque sentences that were as the flower and fall of their palaces, a honeycomb of despair.'[1]

A Commodity appears, at first sight, to be a trivial and easily understood thing. Our analysis shows that, in reality it is a vexed and complicated thing, abounding in metaphysical subtleties and theological anxieities.[2]

The first opening quotation forms part of a discarded fragment from Djuna Barnes's manuscript for *Nightwood*, text that was intended for the novel's second chapter 'La Somnambule'. We find Felix Volkbein in conversation with Robin Vote, describing to her the lives of past generations of courtiers and aristocracy as they talk and play cards. The passage was perhaps discarded because it shows Robin momentarily interested in Felix's account, asking questions, engaging with another character in a way that does not correspond with the enigmatic and almost silent protagonist that Barnes ultimately creates. The quotation itself, however, offers an illuminating insight into Barnes's writing, as it introduces the idea of a 'baroque sentence', a form of expression characteristic of a particular era, with associated ideas of aristocracy, courts and palaces, a sense of inevitable fall and ruin, and a quality of melancholy and hopelessness. While Barnes did not include Felix's sentence or the surrounding text in her final draft of the novel, this chapter and Chapter 3 will argue that it suggests a hidden blueprint for *Nightwood's* development as a modernist counterpart of a particular form of seventeenth-century drama, the Trauerspiel or play of mourning. In Chapter 4, I will discuss in detail Barnes's debts to Expressionist drama and its rediscovery of baroque gesture and sound.

BENJAMIN'S THEORY OF ALLEGORY

For Benjamin and Barnes, the baroque sentence takes as its premise an unmistakeable hostility towards symbolic forms and their context of myth and both writers take inspiration from the seventeenth-century passion for allegory, and its particular significance within the aesthetic of Trauerspiel. According to our familiar sense of this term, a sentence or image that uses allegory brings together an object and an abstract meaning, one thing denoting the other. Following this definition, Goethe concludes that allegory is the result of 'the poet's seeking the particular from the general'.[3] Benjamin finds accomplished writers and artists such as Yeats guilty of practising under this flawed interpretation, while only those versed in the literary and visual emblem-books of the seventeenth century experienced the full power of its aesthetic. Its devalued form is the legacy of the Romantic and Classical traditions within Germany and other nations, wherein allegory was rejected as an archaic, mechanically repetitive and arbitrary form, while the symbol was seen to offer ontological wholeness as an eternal unity of form and content that cannot be fractured. This conviction persisted during the sixteenth century. Contained within the mythic movement of tragedy, the symbol provides a teleology that reconciles the visible, sensuous form and the transcendental ideal. It is a unity that Benjamin feels he must deconstruct:

> The unity of the material and the transcendental object, which constitutes the paradox of the theological symbol, is distorted into a relationship between appearance and essence … As a symbolic construct the beautiful is supposed to merge with the divine in an unbroken whole.[4]

While Benjamin does not challenge the spiritual significance of the theological symbol, he discredits the mythic character of symbolic expression as it passes from a religious context to a secular, literary representation. He cannot countenance the symbol's paradoxical sensual immediacy of phenomena and Eidos in the realm of the beautiful, turning instead to allegory to shatter and correct this apparent unity. Allegory acknowledges that there can be no unbroken whole combining the transcendent realm of meaning and truth with the world of object and form. It recognises that the phenomenal world is separated from any pre-Edenic or transcendent truth by an irremediable gulf, and that this void is the direct result of Adam's guilt. Truth, as such, exists only through a sense of its absence – the melancholy subject contemplates a world that has been drained of all original truth valuations and all objective or inherent meaning. Once this loss has been acknowledged the allegorist is faced with the devaluation of his existence and surroundings as the world of mere appearance becomes a transient period before death.

Benjamin's account of antiquity and the fate of the pagan gods can be used to illustrate his sense of the close relationship between myth and symbol, and the way in which these forms became vulnerable to, and dependent upon, reinterpretation through allegory. The gods of the pantheon were symbols of a mythologised nature. Each deity represented a powerful and formidable divinity, anthropomorphised within the human figure and with this blend of the material, sensual form and the sacred they captured precisely the paradoxical qualities of symbol that Benjamin calls into question. The goddess Venus, for example, combined exquisite beauty, mortal passion and divine love. Christianity later dismissed these deities as heathen and they were rescued from obscurity in their hollow, demythologised forms by baroque allegory. Benjamin writes that 'the deadness of the figures and the abstraction of the concepts are therefore the precondition for the allegorical metamorphosis of the pantheon into a world of magical conceptual creatures'.[5] Since antiquity, these devalued forms had survived as 'cosmic demons' or astrological figures. Allegorical representation reduced Venus to the profane, mortal embodiment of erotic love, Dame World. The mythical symbols from the animal kingdom that had existed alongside the gods of antiquity suffered a similar fate. The faun, the centaur and the harpy were just three such examples that only survived into the seventeenth century as allegorical figures in the circle of Christian Hell. Without this humbling reinterpretation through allegory, the pagan gods and creatures would have no place within the Christian world.

For Benjamin, the accomplished allegorist takes the emblem books of the seventeenth century as his inspiration. Barnes's imagination was strongly anchored in this period of history through her affection for Robert Burton's *The Anatomy of Melancholy*, a treatise on the subject of melancholy, and one of her favourite books. Burton had consulted the words and pictures of the baroque emblem books throughout his study, but most notably during his analysis of love-melancholy, and refers his readers not only to Albrecht Dürer's 'Melencolia I', but to the emblems of Andrew Alciat, Otto van Veem, Daniel Heinsius and Joachim Camerarius.[6] Barnes's library also suggests a sustained interest in analysis of figurative language, containing texts such as Wallace Fowlie's *Love in Literature – Studies in Symbolic Expression*, Mircea Eliade's *Mephistopheles and the Androgyne – Studies in Religious Myth and Symbol*, Bernard Berenson's *Aesthetics and History* and Benedetto Croce's *Aesthetic As Science of Expression and General Linguistic*. Her opposition to symbolic writing becomes clear in her correspondence with Emily Coleman: in a letter dated 14 December 1935, she admits to a marked dislike for Ibsen's work. Having read his plays once, Barnes explains to Coleman that she has no desire to return to these texts. Her criticism is clearly focused on the dramatist's use of symbolism: 'His plays annoyed me because they are symbolic (I do not like symbolism), sort of matrimonial symbolism – always throwing itself off high mountains or getting wind-blown at some fjord.'[7] At the time of writing and correcting *Nightwood*, therefore, Barnes's correspondence suggests considerable hostility to symbolic form, and while she did not provide a detailed theoretical critique of myth and symbol, with *Nightwood* she creates a creative, fictional assault on these devices through the medium of baroque allegory.

Benjamin's *The Origin of German Tragic Drama* evolves from the premise that the genres of Trauerspiel and Greek tragedy are distinct and dissimilar, as are their related forms of allegory and symbol. An early discarded draft of manuscript called 'Run, Girls, Run' suggests that *Nightwood* may also have evolved through a desire to set the two genres in opposition by alternating chapters of allegorical forms with chapters that inhabit tragedy's world of myth and symbol. Barnes's experiment with the world of Greek tragedy is made explicit within this fragment of writing: 'tragedy must come from all points of the compass. The Hellenic gesture, Epic injustice, were in those days things that did not seethe in the brains of scholars alone' and she documents the 'undoing' of three young women, each 'ducked in mythology', 'under a mythically roving moon'.[8] The fate of the ruined girls follows the metamorphoses of Ovid's tales, their souls combining with the elements. Just as Callisto was turned from one of Diana's nymphs into a bear, and from a bear into a constellation, after she gave birth to Jupiter's illegitimate son, so Barnes's Nell, holding the hand of her illegitimate daughter, takes her own life, rising up to the heavens as vapour and descending as rain. Her daughter, meanwhile, ascends to the heavens as a funnel of smoke where her name is linked with Leda, yet another victim of Jupiter's attentions, once he has transformed himself into a swan to seduce her. Here Barnes's characters join the gods of the pantheon by becoming symbols of a mythologised nature – an identity that seems crucial to her own and Benjamin's sense of tragedy and symbolic form.

Later drafts of *Nightwood* juxtapose the worlds of Trauerspiel and tragedy using more subtle techniques, as skirmishes of interpretation between symbol and allegory become focused within the details of individual images. Our introduction to the character Robin Vote begins this process:

> The woman who presents herself to the spectator as a picture forever arranged is, for the contemplative mind, the chiefest danger. Sometimes one meets a woman who is beast turning human. Such a person's every movement will reduce to the image of a forgotten experience; a mirage of an eternal wedding cast on the racial memory; as insupportable a joy as would be the vision of an eland coming down an aisle of trees . . . a hoof raised in the economy of fear, stepping in the trepidation of flesh that

will become myth, as the unicorn is neither beast nor man deprived, but human hunger pressing its breast to its prey.[9]

Robin becomes the enigmatic central signifier in the text, and her relationships with Nora Wood and Felix Volkbein take place in a field of tension between symbol and allegory, where allegory ultimately proves the stronger form of cognition. The opening sentence can be read as a reference to this point of restlessness or strain between the two aesthetic forms. As a picture 'forever arranged', Robin tends to the permanence and fixity of symbol, an eternal quality repeated later in the image of 'an eternal wedding cast on the racial memory'. She seems to embody the indivisible, privileged temporality of symbol. She is also represented as an 'image', 'a mirage', a 'vision' and a 'picture' set before a spectator – Barnes appears to allow the visual and the eternal to dominate this interpretation in a way that recalls Benjamin's definition of symbol as a form that reconciles the visible with the transcendent, allowing it to pass out of history and into myth. Robin, presented as a picture forever arranged, is 'for the contemplative mind, the chiefest danger' because any interpretation of her that pretends to the instantaneous revelation of symbol undermines the process of allegorical signification. Allegory proceeds through a mournful, repetitive rhythm of contemplation, a temporal quality that Benjamin refers to as 'progression in a series of moments'.[10] Within allegory truth is endlessly deferred, as one fragment or image after another is liberated, allegorised and discarded in favour of another. Any knowledge of Robin that pretends to be absolute in the metaphysical sense works against, and is therefore the 'chiefest danger' to, the restless, meditative approach of allegory.

While the vocabulary of Robin's introduction as a picture forever arranged at first seems to claim her as a symbolic signifier, the structure of this passage is serving another pattern of interpretation entirely. The static, enduring quality of 'forever arranged' is soon contradicted by a succession of transformations, each set out in a separate clause or sentence. Robin becomes 'beast turning human' – the apparently fixed female form is soon complicated by a transition across species, and further unsettled by the present continuous tense, registering that the 'turning' of this metamorphosis is not yet complete. We then lose the material body of the signifier, focusing on the more abstract quality of 'movement', which is in turn 'reduced' to something 'forgotten'. This loss of clarity and presence is repeated with the suggestion that signification is now taking place through 'mirage' and 'memory', and then through the more abstract medium of emotion with 'joy'. Throughout this introduction to Robin, Barnes appears to engage with the process of allegorical composition, which cannot repeat or build images so as to consolidate and give permanence of form, but which must progress through many disconnected fragments, as the impulse to subjectively bestow meaning intensifies. The image of the eland, a large horned antelope, becomes a unicorn, which in turn is 'neither beast nor man deprived', and so fails to stabilise the earlier image of a beast turning human. Just as in the pantheon of the gods, where the human form merged with the sacred to produce the deities of myth, so this passage seems to combine the natural form of the eland with immortal qualities, to produce the unicorn: 'flesh that will become myth'. The anxiety and dismay registered in 'trepidation' and 'economy of fear' checks the 'insupportable joy' of this symbolic transformation. Here, the reader may recall the fate of other celebrated mythical creatures, such as centaurs, that were claimed by baroque allegory for the circle of Hell, after the fall of the gods of antiquity. 'Flesh that becomes myth' is vulnerable to mortification through allegory.

Images, Metaphors and Emblems of the Baroque Sentence

Allegory's presentation of nature, without recourse to the transcendent, takes place through images of collapse and degeneration. For Benjamin, baroque nature becomes significant only through the intervention of death, rot and petrifaction: 'death digs most deeply the jagged line of demarcation between physical nature and significance'.[11] Decay bestows significance in this way because nature shares man's fallen state, and is used by the baroque allegorists to represent history as the passage of time towards death and not salvation. Forms that had been beautiful and vital under the symbolist's gaze were betrayed as registers of human arrogance and delusion. Without their divine significance, these images could only confirm a condition of mortality that is denied God's grace. Barnes seems to share this baroque passion, as the images of *Nightwood* are always working the living towards death and decomposition. For Barnes, love itself partakes of this dynamic of decay, it is reduced to 'the deposit of the heart, analogous in all degrees to the "findings" in a tomb . . . In Nora's heart lay the fossil of Robin'.[12] Dr O'Connor describes his own wisdom and his attempts to enlighten *Nightwood*'s characters as a descent into putrefaction:

> like a rotten apple to a rotten apple's breast affixed we go down together, nor is there a hesitation in that decay, for when I sense such, there I apply the breast the firmer, that he may rot as quickly as I.[13]

Barnes withers and rots the forbidden fruit of Eden that represents the original Fall into flawed subjective knowledge, continuing the momentum of that descent as the hypersubjectivity of the doctor's allegorical discourse contaminates and rots his listeners. The nature-history of *Nightwood* and baroque allegory is losing vitality through its immanence and decay, and it is here that Barnes seems to ally herself most closely with the German baroque dramatists as opposed to their Jacobean or late Elizabethan counterparts. Benjamin notes that, while the rejection of eschatology was characteristic of the baroque dramas across Europe, the descent into a nature deprived of grace is a peculiarly German phenomenon.

If the baroque sentence unfolds through the forms and details of allegory, then what led Barnes to complete her own description with the words 'honeycomb of despair'? Benjamin's text examines seventeenth-century theology, and suggests an answer to these questions with his claim that the baroque knows no eschatology. This does not mean that the Trauerspiel and the world of *Nightwood* are already secularised world pictures, but that allegory is at once the cognitive, creative and expressive medium of a century haunted by an inescapable immanence and spiritual despair. Benjamin explains that

> The hereafter is emptied of everything which contains the slightest breath of this world, and from it the baroque extracts a profusion of things which customarily escaped the grasp of artistic formulation . . . in order to clear an ultimate heaven, enabling it, as a vacuum, one day to destroy the world with catastrophic violence.[14]

The existence of God and heaven are not called into question, but rather the baroque subject is shown to be completely alienated from the transcendent realm. The immediate and material world is emptied of all meaning, and humans forfeit the possibility of capturing and expressing truth. Rather than reproducing the tenets of a particular church, Barnes recreates the all-encompassing spiritual emptiness that results from the eschatological void of baroque theology and this is nowhere more apparent than in the life of Robin Vote as she visits five different churches in Paris, failing to find solace in any of them.

While this spiritual wretchedness may account for the note of despair that characterises the baroque sentence, Barnes also uses the word 'honeycomb' to describe the technique of the allegorist faced with this world of devalued phenomena. Benjamin's allegorist proceeds by collecting these hollow, debased objects and images as fragments liberated from their literal meaning, and attempting to bestow a new allegorical significance upon them:

> In the field of allegorical intuition the image is a fragment, a rune . . . the false appearance of totality is extinguished. For the eidos disappears, the simile ceases to exist, and the cosmos it contains shrivels up. The dry rebuses which remain contain an insight which is still available to the confused investigator.[15]

The 'insight' available to him is his sense that the fragment is encoded with an occluded divinity, a redemptive, pre-Edenic meaning, and he collects them so as to offset the vision of fallen nature as a melancholy and empty realm. That Barnes should describe the baroque sentence as a 'honeycomb of despair' captures precisely the ultimately hollow structure of each fragment or cavity of lost meaning, joined to its neighbours in a pattern of empty cells through the determined endeavours of allegory. As the novel's narrator, Barnes uses the technique of structuring images through contradiction to ensure that each of these cells within the honeycomb structure remains hollow or uninhabited.

In our introduction to Robin Vote, she writes that

> the perfume that her body exhaled was of the quality of that earth-flesh, fungi, which smells of captured dampness and yet is so dry, overcast with the odour of oil of amber, which is an inner malady of the sea.[16]

This sensual representation of Robin emerges through the allegorical layering of images, none of which are strictly cumulative in the sense or values they confer – they do not work to corroborate a truth about her. The smell of 'captured dampness . . . [which] is so dry' offers two obviously contradictory qualities, but the image is one of movement between contraries in other less obvious ways. Fungi, with their associated ideas of rot and decay, are presented as earth-flesh, and the juxtaposing of flesh and decay suggests a corpse and so a smell of putrefaction that is at odds with the often subtle and pleasant smell of fungi. With the word 'amber', the yellow fossil resin, Barnes presents the archetypal allegory of transient nature – the fossil. Amber is as translucent as the fungi are opaque, and as hard and petrified as the fungi are soft and yielding. She contradicts these qualities with the next image, 'inner malady of the sea', which suggests that the amber is in fact ambergris, a wax-like substance formed in the intestines of the sperm whale, and often found floating in tropical seas. Wax is more like the original fungi in its softness, but the image of the sea is at odds with the solid, static qualities that seem to define Robin as 'earth-flesh', and the smell of ambergris is as potent (it is used in musky perfumes) as the dry smell of fungi is subtle. Barnes's use of contradictory images sustains allegorical movement as our sense of Robin is never allowed to 'settle' with any degree of permanence. No one individual cell within the honeycomb structure can be said to contain a defining quality, its content is always negated or contradicted by subsequent and preceding cells. As the doctor explains 'an image is a stop the mind makes between uncertainties'.[17] This hesitant, polarised structuring of sentences fulfils the baroque theory that opposites are contained within a single being or idea. If Wölfflin's texts argue for the translation of categories of style between artistic media, then this vocabulary of movement finds a parallel within his definitions of baroque art. He writes of the change from a linear Renaissance form to a painterly baroque composition wherein 'the whole takes on the semblance of a movement ceaselessly emanating, never ending'.[18] Such artworks register a subtle depreciation in line, and an open rather than closed organisation, all of which can be readily applied to the contradictory and inconclusive images, and lack of stable identity, so characteristic of *Nightwood*. Richard Samuel acknowledges that, for

Expressionist writers, this rhetoric of paradox and contradiction was the most important legacy of the baroque aesthetic, while for Wellek, Expressionism was responsible for overcoming the public's distaste for these baroque conventions of violent contrast.[19]

Maravall adds the baroque topoi of the world upside-down or back-to-front to this catalogue of reversals. This sense of inversion also finds its way into the doctor's repertoire of images through a sense of instability between genders. Lamenting his lack of soprano voice and womanly features, Dr O'Connor asks 'And what do I get but a face on me like an old child's bottom – is that a happiness do you think'?[20] The upside-down body with its face like a bottom is coupled with an oxymoron, 'old child', in an image of multiple contradictions. Philosophising on the experience of melancholy, he inverts the laws of gravity, claiming that 'a man's sorrow runs uphill', while later curses include 'May you die standing upright! May you be damned upward' and he talks of confessing to a priest while upside-down.[21] Dr O'Connor's conclusion is that 'there is no direct way. The foetus of symmetry nourishes itself on cross-purposes, this is its wonderful unhappiness'.[22] Beyond the baroque figurative devices – the oxymoron of 'wonderful unhappiness', and the concretising of the abstract idea of symmetry as it takes on an embryonic form – this image contains an inescapable truth about the baroque sentence. Language that evolves through opposition and paradox cannot work towards an exact meaning or conclusion, and thereby creates its own balanced or equilibrated structure. It is for this reason that Dr O'Connor and the baroque allegorist have their quest for original meaning deferred into the afterlife, while their images and ideas remain trapped between contradictions and ultimately incomplete.

Barnes's preoccupation with a night-world setting can be related to the crucial role that night plays in distinguishing the baroque drama from the daylight setting of tragedy. From the original baroque dramas, Benjamin names Lohenstein's play, *Agrippina*, and *Carolus Stuardas* by Gryphius, as Trauerspiels that begin at midnight, while others such as *Cardenio* offer scenes that take their poetic quality from the night, a tradition continued by Dr O'Connor's speeches in the novel's fifth chapter, 'Watchman, What of the Night'. While the doctor's outbursts may take the night as their subject, they take their shape from the peculiarities of allegorical form. Writing structured by allegory follows random collections of dislocated images that fail to offer any clear sense of progression or resolution. Dr O'Connor summarises the allegorist's suspicion of the identities, definitions and conclusions drawn by reason – 'we who are full to the gorge with misery [the allegorist in his melancholy] should look well around, doubting everything seen, done, spoken, precisely because we have a word for it and not its alchemy'.[23] The allegorist doubts the 'word' with its literal meaning because it is profane and devalued, preferring to transform it from its base element into more precious configurations with other words that may reveal its prelapsarian significance. This process is the doctor's alchemy and its premise is an ontological doubt that undermines all rational thought.

A large part of this linguistic alchemy is the result of the baroque allegorists' love of objects and their subsequent obsession with concrete nouns. Benjamin explains that this, coupled with their love of antithesis, means that 'when an abstract word (or idea) seems quite unavoidable, a concrete word is added to it with quite uncommon frequency so that new words are invented' and he offers examples from the original Trauerspiels, such as 'the cedars of innocence', 'the blood of friendship' and 'the lightning of calumny'.[24] Dr O'Connor creates images according to a similar law of reification: 'that priceless galaxy of misfortune called the mind, harnessed to that threadbare glomerate compulsion called the soul, ambling down the almost obliterated bridlepath of Well and Ill'.[25] The abstract qualities of 'Well' and 'Ill' have found concrete form in a bridlepath, while the mind has taken on a stellar scale and complexity with 'galaxy', and the soul has acquired a tattered and clustered material form. The doctor elaborates the abstract image of death with similar concrete extensions: 'death lies couched on a mackerel sky, on her breast a helmet and at her feet a foal with a silent marble mane', and he describes 'remorse . . . sitting heavy like the arse of a bull'.[26] With each of these examples, the underlying idea of the sentence evaporates in a succession of images, frustrating our sense that metaphors should overcome apparent disparity or discontinuity at the level of meaning by revealing latent similarities between images and objects.

The Trauerspiel stage was also characterised by certain emblems or visual images that Barnes appropriates in her reworking of the baroque form. The most important of these appear in the apotheosis scenes of the Trauerspiel, climactic scenes of cruelty and anguish where the corpse assumes its full allegorical significance. For Benjamin, the human body was no exception to the baroque compulsion to fracture organic form in the pursuit of meaning: 'Only thus, as corpses, [can Trauerspiel characters] enter into the homeland of allegory'.[27] Martyrdom, dismemberment and decapitation thus prepared the body of the protagonist for emblematic purposes, and it is for this reason that the Trauerspiel was the resting place of severed limbs and heads. This led to the 'Todtenmahlzeit' (Banquet of Death) in the first or last scenes where rows of heads or fractured bodies were served up as a feast. This spectacle was reported as happening off-stage in the early plays, but later came to be represented in front of the audience, as actors' heads appeared through a hole in a table while their bodies were hidden by a cloth, and the corpse in turn became this drama's most significant emblematic property.

Barnes also appears determined to build her sentences around such emblems, following the Trauerspiel's framing technique by focusing the doctor's first and last monologues on the theme of decapitation. His first lengthy discourse at the Count Altamonte's party is preoccupied with the subject of the guillotine and his own encounter with a headsman, while his final scene recalls a quack medicine man who promises to behead a small boy. In between these two passages, the doctors' stories continue this obsession – we learn of Mademoiselle Basquette, a girl without legs, while the doctor threatens Nora: 'I would instigate a Meat-Axe Day and out of the goodness of my heart I would whack your head off, along with a couple of others'.[28] It is perhaps fitting that Dr O'Connor, who has described the balanced contradictions inherent in allegorical language as the 'foetus of symmetry', is an accomplished practitioner of both back-street abortion and allegory. He presides over the birth of fragmented and mutilated corpses, and the creation of dead and fractured figurative language, providing the modern Trauerspiel of *Nightwood* with its grisly baroque emblems and its dominant aesthetic form. Like the baroque allegorist, Barnes believes that the first step to recovering original, pre-Edenic truth is the destruction of the organic and beautiful whole that lends itself so readily to symbol.

The baroque sentences of *Nightwood* can also be described as scatological. Dr O'Connor refers to his house as a pissing port, and his night haunts are the female toilets and the pissoirs of the Paris underworld. It is a preoccupation that translates into his repertoire of metaphors as he argues that his generation's legacy for the next will be 'not the massive dung fallen from the dinosaur but the little speck left of the humming-bird'.[29] Felix recognises this obscene quality in the doctor, but is able to excuse it. When the doctor refers to kings and emperors who 'may relieve themselves on high heaven ... the Baron who was always troubled by obscenity, would never in the case of the doctor, resent it; he felt the seriousness, the melancholy, hidden beneath'.[30] It is this conviction that the doctor's shocking speech has its foundations in 'seriousness' and 'melancholy' which allow us to trace this obscenity back to its source in baroque allegory. First, the allegorist is concerned with liberating the vile, degraded elements of the baroque world with new associations and significance – it is the alchemy of allegory that can transform the excrement of the hummingbird into the medium of historical legacy for future generations to examine. The doctor's scatological preoccupations are further excused by the 'serious' and 'melancholy' practice of allegory if the definition of the Trauerspiel corpse is examined. Benjamin explains that: 'It is not only in the loss of limbs ... but in all processes of elimination and putrification that everything corpse-like falls away from the body'.[31] It is therefore as part of the fragmented body of the corpse, the most important Trauerspiel emblem, that these bodily functions are dignified and excused as essential to the process that allows the Trauerspiel character to enter the homeland of allegory.

FROM BAROQUE TO MODERN – BAUDELAIRE AS ALLEGORIST

Barnes and Benjamin may have turned to the baroque period, and to allegory in particular, as they offer a perspective that is peculiarly relevant to a modern commodified society. Although Chapter 4 will examine the legacy of the baroque through Expressionist stagecraft, Benjamin's earlier choice of modern allegorist was the poet Charles Baudelaire. There were few socio-economic similarities linking the flourishing capitalist conditions of nineteenth-century Paris with the post-war context of the Trauerspiel, but Benjamin's sense of continuity between the modern and the baroque becomes clear in his collection of notes published as *Zentralpark* (*Central Park*) and in the 'Convolutes' of *Das Passagen-Werk* (*The Arcades Project*). These texts are all that we have of his proposed studies 'Baudelaire as Allegorist' and 'The Commodity as Poetic Object', and his intended theory of modern allegory. While the formal project remained unwritten, the reflections and quotations that have been published present Baudelaire and the poetry of *Les Fleurs du Mal* in the tradition of baroque Trauer and its figurative devices. As Barnes fashions her modernist aesthetic from baroque detail, Baudelaire's poetry also seems to offer her stepping-stones, images that mediate the modern and the baroque and that cannot be overlooked, suggesting that, without having read Benjamin's *Arcades Project*, she too has interpreted *Les Fleurs du Mal* as a crucial part of the Trauerspiel tradition. For Baudelaire, the female anatomy provides the allegorical impulse with its finest material, and his poems linger over the fractured anatomy of lover and prostitute alike, the sculptural leg of an unknown woman in *A Une Passante*, or the heavily scented, blue-black hair that envelops the poet in *La Chevelure*. Recalling the final scenes of suffering in the Trauerspiel, *Une Martyre* shows a headless corpse with the head placed beside it on the bedside table, while a putrefying carcass lies with its legs in the air, inviting comparisons with lewd women in *Une Charogne*. If the seventeenth-century mortification of nature and the object evolved through Christianity's distance from pagan antiquity, in the case of Baudelaire's poetry, Benjamin discovers the mortification of the material world in the urban dreamscapes of 1850s Paris. Allegory is used in *Les Fleurs du Mal* to expose and fracture the mythical unity of the capitalist marketplace, using images of Second Empire Paris, rebuilt and reconfigured by Prefect Haussmann through the grand boulevards, World Exhibitions and arcades of nineteenth-century consumerism. Here, the emblem-books of the seventeenth century have been replaced by collections of wish-images – private anthologies of consumer icons and sought-after articles that feature in the arcades and exhibitions. The mythic form of these objects, heavy with their promise of abundance, fashion and novelty, and the mythical appearance of Haussmann's newly configured Paris, are then shattered by the poem's allegorical interpretations.

If Baudelaire allegorises Haussmann's new Paris with a succession of images that recall classical antiquity and the ruins of the old city, then the objects themselves as commodities and wish-images are allegorised by the process of production and advertising within a consumer society – 'the devaluation of the world of things in allegory is surpassed within the world of things itself by the commodity'.[32] Here they become distanced from their place of origin and from the human labour force involved in their creation. These original values and connections are replaced by price – a new significance that is bestowed in apparently random fashion – and by the context of display and advertising. Benjamin writes that 'The wrenching of things from their familiar contexts – as is normal for commodities when being exhibited – is to Baudelaire a very significant procedure. It is connected to the destruction of organic contexts in allegorical intention.'[33] The successive stages of marketing, costing and exhibiting therefore constitute a process that in many ways repeats the work of the allegorist.

ALLEGORY AS FETISHISM AND THE ALLEGORIST IN HIS DEN

The connection between allegory and commodification is also a significant one for Barnes. In his analysis of the night-world, Dr O'Connor offers Nora a rather bewildering explanation: 'a high price is demanded of any value, for a value is in itself a detachment'.[34] The reference to cost and value may indicate that the doctor's discourse acknowledges both baroque allegory and the world of the commodity. As allegory translates from a baroque to a modern context, 'detachment' becomes the sheer distance between the object's inherent worth, in real terms, the production process and the social labour this entails, and its significance and desirability within the market. Barnes's sense of this random and irrational assigning of value or price appears again in the doctor's description of an ermine stole. He draws attention to the vagaries of female fashion, suggesting that the expensive and much-coveted ermine furs derive their prized colour from something as vulgar as urine or tears. It is through the character of Jenny Petherbridge, however, that Barnes is able to develop this relationship between allegory and the commodity, and to apply it to human relationships.

Barnes creates Jenny as the novel's failed allegorist and through her we come to understand how the allegorist's accumulated objects stand in relation to their owner. She is a widow, whose physical body itself seems the result of allegorical endeavour poorly executed: 'she had a beaked head, and the body, small, feeble and ferocious, that somehow made one associate her with Judy, they did not go together. Only severed could any part of her have been called "right"'.[35] Those fragments that have been pieced together do not connect or belong, Jenny needs to be fractured, and reassembled at the hands of a more skilled practitioner such as the doctor. In her passion to become an allegorist, Jenny fully understands that history is the necessary medium of her art, and she has tried to force her unfortunate husbands into this identity. Barnes describes their fate: 'Each husband had wasted away and died; she had been like a squirrel racing a wheel day and night in an attempt to make them historical; they could not survive it'.[36] She seeks the allegorist's title because she must find a meaning or significance for the spoils of her plundering. Jenny has certainly mastered the first part of the allegorical process: magpie-like, she collects the objects and details of other peoples' lives; passionate and covetous, she acquires other people's marriage rings, photographs and book selections. In other words, she successfully completes the allegorist's task of liberating the object from its original or inherent meaning in the life of its rightful owner, or, in Benjamin's terms, the destruction of organic contexts. She also exhibits the allegorist's tendency to give concrete form to abstract ideas – 'she speaks of people taking away her faith in them as if faith were a transportable object'.[37] Allegory, however, is a twofold undertaking, as once the object has lost its original meaning, it remains hollow, incapable of emanating any meaning or significance on its own. The allegorist must now confer new meaning on his or her hoard of fragments by arranging them in unexpected combinations and patterns in the hope of discovering their encrypted knowledge. This, Jenny cannot do. She lacks the doctor's intellectual knowledge, the wisdom of the melancholic scholar. In the hands of such a collector, allegory becomes an imperfect and sterile process. The now meaningless items become insignificant and almost invisible as Jenny's

> Own quivering uncertainty made even the objects which she pointed out to the company, as, 'My Virgin from Palma' or 'the left hand glove of La Duse' recede into a distance of uncertainty, so that it was almost impossible for the onlooker to see them at all.[38]

In Baudelaire's poetry, the emblems of allegory return as commodities, as the object's meaning becomes its price, an exchange value that is as arbitrary and abstract in its origin as the significance conferred by the allegorist. Jenny's mania for removing the object or person from their familiar context could also be seen as an interesting distortion of this interpretation of allegory as commodity fetishism. In capitalist economies, material items succumb to commodity fetishism as certain qualities and powers are imputed to them, forming the basis of their exchange value. None of these qualities are intrinsic to the objects, but are peculiar to conditions of the market economy. For Jenny, the objects and loves of other people's lives appear to possess particular qualities esteemed by their original owners, and she expects such significance or value to withstand the transfer between parties. Barnes uses the vocabulary of the marketplace to describe Jenny as she falls in love with these objects or individuals: 'she became instantly a dealer in second-hand and therefore incalculable emotions'.[39] The corrupt and capricious premise of the fetish relation between subject and object, however, prevents the newly acquired possession or relationship from achieving the desired objective reality. Regardless of whether Jenny buys or steals the items or lovers that have been so treasured by those around her, once outside their organic context they cannot but disappoint, as Dr O'Connor diagnoses: 'she has a longing for other people's property, but the moment she possesses it the property loses some of its value, for the owner's estimate is its worth'.[40] Just as the wrenching of things from their familiar contexts comes to define Baudelaire's poetry, so the violence and brutality of this initial stage in allegorical intention becomes the sole momentum of Jenny's existence 'her present is always someone else's past, jerked out and dangling' – life as a rhythm of constant evisceration.[41]

While the allegorist may attempt to fill the void between image and significance with his collection of objects, within the Trauerspiel drama such items exist in a particular relation to their subject and occupy a particular setting. This may be one reason why Barnes allows the reader access to Dr O'Connor's tiny, cluttered attic room. Martina Stange has interpreted this scene as a modern version of Albrecht Dürer's 'Melencolia I'.[42] For Benjamin, Dürer's study was one of the most influential engravings bequeathed to seventeenth-century allegory by the Renaissance, and depicts the melancholy scholar surrounded by the utensils of life. As Klibansky, Panofsky and Saxl's study of the engraving notes – 'the essential characteristic of Dürer's Melencolia is that she is doing nothing with any of these tools for mind and hand, and that the things on which her eye might rest simply do not exist for her.'[43] The saw lies at her feet, the whetstone, rhomboid and instruments of geometry are untouched. This is the fate of the object of allegorical attention which seems to promise wisdom while remaining detached and without a spontaneous, creative relationship with the allegorist. The doctor's water-stained, dusty medical books, and some of his neglected medical instruments, share the same fate. While Stange examines these belongings in the light of Julia Kristeva's study of abjection, both the objects and the room can also be referred back to their origin in baroque allegory. Benjamin lays great emphasis on the particular setting for the objects of allegory: 'it must not be assumed that there is anything accidental about the fact that the allegorical is related ... to the fragmented, untidy and disordered character of the magician's den or alchemist's laboratories familiar to the baroque'.[44] He goes on to list attics and lumber rooms among these chaotic hideaways. Not only does Dr O'Connor occupy the attic home of the objects of allegory, it is also confirmed as the scene of his alchemy when Nora acknowledges that she has discovered him 'in the grave dilemma of his alchemy'.[45] Among the disorder of allegorical objects, Benjamin stresses that 'the extravagant distribution of instruments of penance and violence is particularly paradoxical'.[46] Barnes has provided the doctor with just such an inconsistent display, a pair of rusty forceps, a broken scalpel and other surgical apparatus as the Trauerspiel's machinery of violence, and an abdominal brace and ladies' corsetry as the instruments of penance.

The Baudelaire Convolutes of *The Arcades Project* focus attention on two consecutive poems from *Les Fleurs du Mal* – 'La Destruction' and 'Une Martyre'. For Benjamin, the two combine to present a sequence of destructive allegorical method and its distinctive setting, an arrangement that closely resembles Dr O'Connor's own den of iniquity. In 'La Destruction', the instruments of bloodshed and the evidence of their vile practice are introduced to the poet by the devil, who 'Jette dans mes yeux plein de confusion/ Des vêtements souillés, des blessures ouvertes/ Et l'appareil sanglant de la Destruction (Throws into my eyes, filled with confusion/ Soiled garments, open wounds/ And the bloody implements of destruction).[47] These implements are similar to Dr O'Connor's surgical instruments, the tools of the abortionist's trade glimpsed by Nora as she enters his room. As we move to Baudelaire's 'Une Martyre' the results of this destruction become apparent – in a room that was once the setting for passion and intimacy, a headless corpse pours blood over the pillow of a bed, while the decapitated head of the poet's lover languishes on the bed-side table. As to the results of the doctor's baleful work in *Nightwood*, we are left with the contents of his swill-pail 'brimming with abominations'.[48] Barnes describes a room in which 'every object seems to be battling its own compression', while Baudelaire creates 'Une chambre tiède où, comme en une serre/ L'air est dangereux et fatal' ('A room where, as in a hothouse/ The air is terrible and fatal') – in both cases, the atmosphere is heavy and oppressive with the practice of allegory.[49] The reader's eye must navigate its way through a cluttered array of objects in each room, before finally discovering the body in the bed. For Baudelaire, this place is occupied by the victim of allegorical violence, while in *Nightwood* we discover the practitioner himself beneath the sheets. The body of *Une Martyre* lies in the midst of bottles, spangled fabrics and scented dresses, while the doctor, clad in a woman's nightgown, is surrounded by perfume bottles, ribbons, stockings, laces and ladies undergarments. Fragrance and a wealth of ornate, feminine visual detail combine to intensify the decadent, sultry medium in which subject and object encounter one another. Benjamin concludes that of all Baudelaire's poems

> 'La Destruction' comprises the most relentless elaboration of the allegorical intention. The 'bloody retinue', which the poet is forced by the demon to contemplate, is the court of allegory – the scattered apparatus by dint of which allegory has so disfigured and so unsettled the world of things, that only fragments of that world are left to it now.[50]

The objects that surround Dürer's figure of melancholy are instruments of constructive physical toil and practical scholarly application; they are slighted, but remain creative in their original and intended use. The objects within the modern court of allegory are degraded, forgotten, and the context in which they vie for attention is above all destructive, connected to the baroque through the Trauerspiel's instruments of torture and murder.

The melancholy of baroque 'Trauer' becomes the 'Spleen' of Baudelaire's *Les Fleurs du Mal*, but as allegory passes from the seventeenth century to a modern context, something happens to the experience of subjectivity. Baroque melancholy acknowledged the dialectical relationship between subject and object through its emblem of the corpse, as in death man was reduced to the status of object. *Les Fleurs du Mal* continues to use the emblem of the corpse in its severed or decomposing forms, but the dialectic intensifies as the object or commodity itself becomes human in the guise of the prostitute. The same synthesis of subject and object within allegory allows the prostitute to evolve, not only as commodity, but as mass-produced article, with Benjamin citing the mask-like, professional uniformity achieved by the women's cosmetics and their dance-hall costumes as the catalysts of transformation. As poet and flâneur, collecting his images of Paris street-life for the attention of wealthy patrons, Baudelaire had also experienced the descent into the creaturely realm of the object, empathising with the soul of the commodity. More unsettling still, as allegory made its transition to a nineteenth-century setting, its preferred home became the inner world of the subject rather than the shattered and decaying cityscape. Modern allegory concerns itself less with the suffering and decline of the human body or material artefact, and more with the subject's own spiritual and emotional torment – 'baroque allegory sees the corpse only from the outside. Baudelaire sees it also from within'.[51] In Baudelaire's poem *La Morte Joyeux*, for example, this peculiarly intimate witnessing of death, deterioration and anguish leads the poet to ask nature to begin the process of decomposition while he is still alive, and for his own pleasure: 'Vivant, j'aimerais mieux inviter les courbeaux/ A saigner tous les bouts de mon carcasse immonde . . . /O vers . . . /A travers ma ruine allez donc sans remords' (Still living, I would rather invite the crows/ To bleed the extremities of my foul carcass . . . /O worms . . . /Pass through my ruin then without remorse).[52] Benjamin identifies a combination of sadism and fetishism in Baudelaire's imagined 'assimilation of the living to dead matter'.[53] Modern allegory's extension of the realm of death focuses once again on the figure of the prostitute – for Baudelaire, she becomes 'the life which signifies death', and in *Nightwood*, the Tupenny Upright whores of London Bridge are also as silent and passive as the dead.[54] While continuing the Trauerspiel's repertoire of limbs and corpses, Barnes subjects other characters to this internalised torture and living decay – when Nora strikes Robin awake, we learn that 'no rot had touched her until then and there before my eyes I saw her corrupt all at once and withering', while Dr O'Connor says of the experience of ecstasy and love that 'we do not "climb" to heights, we are eaten away to them'.[55] Barnes goes beyond the Trauerspiel's use of the dismembered corpse as a visual emblem – her characters experience emotions that imitate in agonising severity the allegorical compulsion to fragment. As Nora watches Robin in the arms of another woman, she is described as 'experiencing a sensation of evil, complete and dismembering'.[56]

THE ANTIPHON AND THE BAROQUE TRAGEDY OF FATE

Just as Baudelaire empathised with the object or commodity, assuming its guilt as his own, so the baroque subject and object appear as one in their culpability. Within the Trauerspiel's context of fallen nature, both the objects and creatures of the profane world share in man's exile from the original state of Creation. A form of Trauerspiel known as the Tragedy of Fate allows objects as stage properties to assume a certain power over the fallen subject. Benjamin explains that

> destiny is not only divided among the characters, it is equally present among the objects ... The passions themselves take on the nature of stage-properties. In a drama of jealousy the dagger becomes identical with the passions which guide it.[57]

Trauerspiel stage properties refer back to prelapsarian Eden and a time when man instinctively named the creatures and material objects of his world. With God's grace, the language used in the act of naming bore an exact relation to truth, until the moment of the Fall, when knowledge of good and evil, and the exercise of will and deliberation, led man to overlook the particular essence or expression of creatures and things: I return to this degeneration of language in Chapter 4. In the baroque Tragedy of Fate, these neglected objects are allowed to exact their revenge at the moment of the subject's downfall.

The stage of Barnes's play *The Antiphon* bears many of the hallmarks of Trauerspiel. Beewick, a manor house that has belonged to the Burleys since the late seventeenth century, is a baroque ruin, and many of the stage properties, statues, a gilt crown and costumes, are suitably decayed. The play opens in England, 1939, and the dread of war that pervades the play recalls the sense of imminent catastrophe so characteristic of the Trauerspiel. Miranda, the daughter of Titus and Augusta, has come to Burley Hall from Paris as a refugee of the war. She travels with a coachman, Jonathan, who is revealed at the final curtain to be her brother Jeremy. Jeremy has summoned Augusta and Miranda to Beewick in the knowledge that the remaining two brothers, Dudley and Elisha, will follow, intending to harm their mother and sister. This gathering is the occasion for the family's history to unfold, and at the centre of this history lies Miranda's betrayal by her father. Miranda points to the moment of her conception, and then her birth, as a loss of innocence: 'The cock crew, the spur struck and Titus Adam/ Had at you with his raping-hook ... / A door slammed on Eden, and the Second Gate/ As I walked down your leg.'[58]

Here, the Fall of man has become the dissolution of a particular family. The guilt of postlapsarian knowledge has become the wickedness of a father who prostitutes his daughter to an ageing Cockney, and the disgrace of a mother and brothers who stand accused of acquiescing to, or at the very least ignoring, Titus's abusive behaviour.

Daniela Caselli's analysis of *The Antiphon* notes a striking autonomy in the play's objects or stage properties: 'these props do not psychologically or economically determine the status of the dramatis personae by signalling property or propriety, but point back to themselves'.[59] Unclaimed and somehow independent, these objects may not preside over the character's financial identity or emotions, but I would suggest that one prop in particular determines the fate of both mother and daughter. It is with the figure of the gryphon that Barnes gives her most faithful reproduction of the Trauerspiel concept of fate. As the play opens Barnes describes a 'single settle facing front, at either end of which is set the half of a gryphon, once a car in a roundabout'.[60] It is Miranda's father, Titus, who has cut the gryphon in two, and, using stage direction and dialogue, Barnes draws her characters to this stage property eleven times during the course of the play. Louis Kannenstine has interpreted the creature as a mythic figure, half-eagle, half-lion, sharing the symbolic qualities of Dante's gryphon in Canto 31 of his *Purgatorio*. This beast was not only a symbol from the world of myth, but a symbol of 'incarnation, duality resolved, divine and human nature made one' – in other words, it represents that combination of the transcendent and the phenomenal that Benjamin is so critical of in his Trauerspiel study, a union that allegory deconstructs.[61] Having placed the gryphon in the world of myth and unity, Kannenstine cannot see the end of the play, where mother and daughter fall to their death across the gryphon, as anything other than a paradox. He has ignored the fact that Barnes allegorises the creature – it is removed from its original setting in the carousel, and is therefore liberated from its initial or inherent meaning, and, by splitting the creature in two, it joins the allegorist's world of fragmented objects. In Act Three, the gryphon becomes synonymous with the destructive vanity and arrogance that led Titus to betray both daughter and mother; like the doll that signifies Robin's betrayals, it has become the emblem of his guilt: 'he became so sure of his sufficience/ Blew his own horn, composed his own libretti – / Sawed the gryphon up; the what-not down . . . '.[62]

Within the Tragedy of Fate, guilt is not only inherited by families in their entirety, but comes to be associated with a particular stage property. Having established the link between the father and a particular stage object, Barnes seems to adhere to the laws of the Tragedy of Fate by expanding the context of sin across the entire family. Titus's guilt therefore continues to haunt his family even after his death, and that culpability remains focused within the gryphon. Benjamin notes that 'the effectiveness of the object where guilt has been incurred is a sign of the approach of death'.[63] Barnes signifies the 'effectiveness' of her fatal stage-object as Augusta draws attention to its identity as a stage property, establishing it as a solid and exemplary theatrical device, and then suggesting that the object has a power or agency of its own: 'I think the gryphon moved. We have a carriage!'[64] Once the 'effectiveness' of the object has been established, it is not long before the fatal stage property claims both mother and daughter as they fall across the gryphon. This baroque interpretation of the final scene explains why both mother and daughter fall, when only Miranda has been struck by the curfew bell – both have inherited the curse of their father's guilt. Barnes takes to its ultimate baroque conclusion a quality of resistance that she had earlier identified in the allegorist's den of *Nightwood*, where objects seem to battle a force of compression; the material world, having quietly retained a power of its own, defies allegory's flawed process of identifying and assigning meaning. *The Antiphon* allows the stage property to resume its baroque significance and to complete allegory's modern dialectic between subject and object.

THE GREAT DEPRESSION

This independent and formidable agency also has its modern counterpart in the capitalist marketplace. In the 'Exhibitions, Advertising and Grandville' section of his *Arcades Project*, Benjamin includes a quotation from Otto Rühle's *Karl Marx*, in which the commodity seems to return to the baroque stage at precisely the point where the subject forfeits mastery and the object's power increases:

> Once escaped from the hand of the producer and divested of its real particularity, it ceases to be a product and to be ruled over by human beings. It has acquired a 'ghostly objectivity' and leads a life of its own . . . Cut off from the will of man, it aligns itself in a mysterious hierarchy, develops or denies exchangeability, and, in accordance with its own peculiar laws, performs as an actor on a phantom stage.[65]

As the above quotation continues, just as the gryphon develops the ability to execute effective and self-determining action, so within a market economy cotton 'soars', copper 'slumps', corn is 'active' and petroleum 'displays a healthy trend'. Inanimate objects have gained autonomy, and they take on human qualities. The gryphon is refashioned by Titus, and then Miranda and Augusta reclaim it as a carriage, but within the laws of allegory and the Trauerspiel, the stage property ultimately presides over the fate of the protagonists. For Benjamin, a similar law governs the relationship between subject and object in the world of nineteenth-century commerce and the arcades – 'the commodity has turned into an idol that, although the product of human hands, disposes over the human'.[66]

While capitalism as a definition is too general and its implications too wide-ranging to relate to the resurrection of allegory in European literature, certain periods of modern history witnessed events that re-focused attention on the implications of free-market capitalism. As writers examined socio-economic conditions and human relationships, these moments of scrutiny witnessed a return to favour of allegorical representation. While Barnes's night-world may be set within 1920s Europe and post-war desolation, the decade in which the novel was written suggests another significant context for the return to allegorical form. If Benjamin puzzled initially over the use of allegory in the midst of capitalist wealth and splendour, he might have wondered less at its use during the Depression of the 1930s, the time of *Nightwood*'s composition. The Great Depression started in October 1929 with the United States' stock-market crash, but spread rapidly to most countries, and its consequences were felt until the late 1930s or early 1940s. The causes of this economic crisis are still a matter of debate and controversy – individuals from the Monetarist school of economics, such as Milton Friedman, argue that the decisive factor was monetary contraction exacerbated by the policies of the American Federal Reserve System. While Friedman argued that economic policy could have prevented the crisis, the Keynesian school of thought dismissed the efficacy of this particular form of intervention, with Keynes himself focusing on counter-cyclical public spending. This episode of economic history was the first to be given the title 'depression', marking a transition in the typical context and severity of the downturn. As accumulations of capital increased, and productivity and exchange rates became inextricably linked to market conditions, periods of financial exigency could no longer be traced simply to single events such as wars or natural disasters.

Marxist theorists saw this point of crisis as the third stage in the evolution of capitalism, following on from the initial post-war difficulties and subsequent recovery of the 1920s. Not only was this third stage considered inevitable, but it was seen to be indicative of the system's eventual demise, forcing increased class conflict and revolutionary change within society. As productivity consolidated the economy's innate tendency to concentrate wealth and control in the hands of a privileged few, the industrial-commercial system translated from a national to an international stage, the imperialist stage of capitalism, serving both industrial and military strengths. For Lenin and Bolshevik theorists, there was a clear correlation between this fiercely administered capitalism and the ascendancy of finance capital. This transition in the role of government came to prominence during the world wars, with the need to galvanise production and the labour force, but was most notable during the Great Depression. A centralised and undemocratic political directive replaced the capitalist class with heavily interventionist state authority, and Tyrus Miller draws attention to the links between this form of capitalism and Fascism: 'This greater degree of intervention also entailed a re-organised, intensified state power, of fascism, Stalinism, and the New Deal welfare state represented alternative forms.'[67] During the 1930s and 1940s, therefore, with the consolidation of state-organised capitalism, the identity of the subject presiding over the production and fate of the commodity appeared to have reached a particularly extreme and powerful configuration. The significance of the object within industrial-commercial society, however, cannot be overlooked. As suggested by the opening quotation for this section on modern allegory, Marx's *Das Kapital* and subsequent Marxist theorists presented the enforcing of an exchange value as a catalyst for the illusory realisation of a metaphysically autonomous object. Once alienated from the stabilising, social context of its production, the object of free-market capitalism assumes an agency or counterforce of its own. The commodities such as copper and cotton that have been argued to 'slump', become 'active' and assume human features within this metaphysical freedom, encounter a dominant, rigorously executed human subjectivity in the form of the state, giving rise to the allegorical dialectic of 1930s capitalism. With Barnes's knowledge of the Trauerspiel, baroque and Baudelarian allegory, and her familiarity with *Das Kapital* – her library contains an edition of the text – it becomes possible to suggest the economic context in which *Nightwood* was conceived and written as another reason for the return to allegorical form and detail. The object of 1930s allegorical intention, whose predecessors were once implicated in the baroque Tragedy of Fate, now presides, not over the death of the individual, but over the downfall of the human subject within his world of capitalist growth and prosperity. Barnes's apparent fascination with allegory can be seen as in part due to her sense of the Great Depression as a critical point in the dialectic between the human subject and their commodity counterpart.

Nightwood's text suggests not only that Barnes was familiar with the details of Trauerspiel and baroque allegory, but that her interest in allegorical method may also have drawn her towards Baudelaire's modern reworking of the form in *Les Fleurs du Mal. Nightwood*'s aesthetic, however, retains a closer relationship with the original baroque details of the Trauerspiel and its figurative devices, perhaps because, unlike nineteenth-century Paris, Barnes night-world shares the historical context of post-war suffering and desolation to which allegory first responded in the seventeenth century. As Barnes's sought to refashion allegory for the modern novel, she may have discovered in *Les Fleurs du Mal* a troubled heightening of allegory's synthesis of subject and object, as the modern writer internalises the harrowing exchange of identities first introduced through the baroque emblem of the corpse. Baudelaire's poet and the characters of the night-world and *The Antiphon* encounter creatures and objects alike under the conditions of modern allegory – a stifling and antagonistic dialectic, charged with the hypersubjectivity of the protagonist and the object's own counter-force.

How does Barnes's fondness for this aesthetic affect her place in the modernist tradition? In his study of late-modernist fiction, Tyrus Miller has focused his chapter on Djuna Barnes around the themes of rescue and redemption. He suggests that Eliot used his preface in *Nightwood* to intervene between reader and text, forestalling criticisms and difficulties that might place the text outside his own sense of the modern literary canon. Eliot felt 'that a great deal was at stake in these points of difficulty: the formal unity of the work . . . the accessibility of the text to a totalising synthesis in reading or interpretation'.[68] Without his intervention, *Nightwood* might be lost to the symbolic and moral cosmos of Eliot's modernism. Miller suggests the 'mythic' or literary analogues within *Ulysses*, and the dominant psychological agent used by Henry James and Joseph Conrad, as examples of the overarching symbolic unity of modernist texts. He feels that Barnes was determined to deconstruct this unity or redemptive impulse assigned to artistic form.

In her analysis of the boundaries of modern and postmodern writing, Donna Gerstenberger also argues that writers such as Eliot, Joyce and Woolf 'seek in myth a coherence that contemporary culture and history could no longer afford'.[69] Miller claims that *Nightwood* focuses the metaphor of rescue on both plot and interpretation. In terms of plot, Barnes questions whether her characters can 'save' themselves or one another from self-destruction. Robin senses and resists Nora's desire to rescue her, while many of the doctor's discourses aim to console and rescue Nora from the grief of Robin's betrayal and loss. In its hermeneutic form, 'rescue' is seen by Miller as a matter of identifying ways in which the seemingly meaningless sufferings of the characters can be redeemed and given significance. Genealogy is the hermeneutic device favoured by Felix, memory is favoured by Nora, and religion by the doctor. Miller concludes that Barnes 'consistently emphasises *failures* of rescue, the futility of redemptive strategies in keeping her characters together, whole, and credibly personlike'.[70] I would suggest that Barnes's use of allegory and Trauerspiel carries the idea of frustrated redemption beyond the character's individual strategies noted by Miller, and into the aesthetic valuations and signifiers of the text itself.

Using the forms and ideas inherent in baroque allegory and Trauerspiel, it becomes possible to interpret *Nightwood* as a dialectical presentation of modernity and signification, a dialectic created through the tension between myth/symbol (created by Nora and Felix) and allegory (the voice of the narrator and Dr O'Connor). The night-world has, in fact, become Barnes's ontological project. It undermines the pretensions of modernist subjectivity discovered by Miller within Eliot's 'tradition', pretensions rooted in idealistic claims to coherence and unity. Barnes has made full use of the dual definition of the term Trauerspiel, with its merging of aesthetic and historical significance. She uses allegory to question our accustomed ideas of perception and cognition – it deconstructs our framework of metaphysical and referential truth. Her repetition of the disruptive force of figural language encourages the reader to see the disjunctive nature of allegory as an aesthetic valuation in its own right, and not simply as a device that makes the text of *Nightwood* difficult to understand.

NOTES

1. Barnes, '"La Somnambule", Nightwood – Related Drafts', *Djuna Barnes Papers*. Special Collections and University Archives, University of Maryland Libraries, Series III, Box 7, Folder 3.
2. Rühle, *Karl Marx* (1928), quoted in Benjamin, *The Arcades Project*, G5, 1, pp. 181–2.
3. Benjamin, *The Origin of German Tragic Drama*, p. 161. Henceforth cited as *Origin*.
4. Benjamin, *Origin*, p. 160.
5. Ibid. p. 226.
6. The emblems themselves appear in full in Idol, 'Burton's Use of Illustrative Emblems', pp. 19–28.
7. Letter from Djuna Barnes to Emily Coleman, 14 December 1935, *Emily Holmes Coleman Papers*, University of Delaware Library, Newark, Delaware, USA. Folder 12.
8. Barnes, 'Run, Girls, Run', *Djuna Barnes Papers*, Series III, Box 7, Folder 2.
9. Barnes, *Nightwood*, p. 36.
10. Benjamin, *Origin*, p. 165.
11. Ibid. p. 166.
12. Barnes, *Nightwood*, p. 50.
13. Ibid. p. 127.
14. Benjamin, *Origin*, p. 66.
15. Ibid. p. 176.
16. Barnes, *Nightwood*, p. 34.
17. Ibid. p. 93.
18. Wölfflin, *Principles of Art History*, p. 19.
19. Samuel and Hinton Thomas, *Expressionism in German Life*, p. 134; Wellek, 'The Baroque', pp. 75–89.
20. Barnes, *Nightwood*, p. 77.
21. Ibid. pp. 19, 81.
22. Ibid. p. 82.
23. Ibid. p. 72.
24. Benjamin, *Origin*, p. 98.
25. Barnes, *Nightwood*, pp. 124–5.
26. Ibid. pp. 134, 117.
27. Benjamin, *Origin*, p. 217.
28. Barnes, *Nightwood*, p. 108.
29. Ibid. p. 127.
30. Barnes, *Nightwood*, p. 38.
31. Benjamin, *Origin*, p. 218.
32. Benjamin, *Central Park*, in *The Writer of Modern Life – Essays on Charles Baudelaire*, pp. 5, 138.
33. Ibid. p. 148.
34. Barnes, *Nightwood*, p. 76.
35. Ibid. p. 58.
36. Ibid. p. 58.

37. Ibid. p. 83.
38. Ibid. p. 59.
39. Ibid. p. 60.
40. Ibid. p. 82.
41. Ibid. p. 83.
42. Stange, 'Melancholia, Melancholia', pp. 134–40.
43. Klibansky et al., *Saturn and Melancholy*, p. 316.
44. Benjamin, *Origin*, p. 188.
45. Barnes, *Nightwood*, p. 69.
46. Benjamin, *Origin*, p. 188.
47. Baudelaire, *Les Fleurs du Mal*, p. 146; my translation.
48. Barnes, *Nightwood*, p. 68.
49. Barnes, *Nightwood*, p. 68; Baudelaire, *Les Fleurs du Mal*, p. 147; my translation.
50. Benjamin, *The Arcades Project*, J68, 2, p. 349.
51. Benjamin, *Central Park*, 36, 163.
52. Baudelaire, *Les Fleurs du Mal*, p. 102; my translation.
53. Benjamin, *The Arcades Project*, J71, 3, p. 354.
54. Benjamin, *The Arcades Project*, J60, 5, p. 326.
55. Barnes, *Nightwood*, pp. 121, 100.
56. Ibid. p. 52.
57. Benjamin, *Origin*, p. 132.
58. Barnes, *The Antiphon*, p. 105.
59. Caselli, *Improper Modernism: Djuna Barnes's Bewildering Corpus*, p. 229.
60. Barnes, *The Antiphon*, p. 7.
61. Kannestine, *The Art of Djuna Barnes: Duality and Damnation*, p. 149.
62. Barnes, *The Antiphon*, p. 105.
63. Benjamin, *Origin*, p. 132.
64. Barnes, *The Antiphon*, p. 165.
65. Benjamin, *The Arcades Project*, G5, 1, p. 181.
66. Ibid. p. 181.
67. Miller, p. 229.
68. Ibid. p. 124.
69. Gerstenberger, 'Modern (Post) Modern: Djuna Barnes among the Others', p. 33.
70. Miller, p. 151.

3

BAROQUE VIENNA: *NIGHTWOOD'S* LOST ENLIGHTENED MODERNITY

Evil has grown from beauty: art turns it to the flower again. That is what happens. We are frozen to evil. In art we give it back its origin.

(Emily Coleman to Djuna Barnes, 27 August 1935)[1]

Few narratives in history are so tedious and disgusting as that of the Thirty Years War and none a better pointer to contemporary political morality.[2]

Performing Absolute Rule: Viennese Architecture

Modernism's taste for innovative language and forms was not the only factor behind a growing fascination with the baroque during the 1920s and 1930s. By 1922, Benito Mussolini had been appointed Prime Minister and gradually enforced his cult of personality through a one party dictatorship that aspired to totalitarian rule. By the late 1920s, Joseph Stalin was effectively ruling the Soviet Union as a dictatorship, and by 1933, Hitler had become chancellor and was establishing his own absolute rule in Germany. These political trends and crises made the world of baroque absolute rule and its tactics of display and influence pertinent to both scholarship and general interest, and the Trauerspiel sovereign and the kings that he represented were among many examples of authoritarian and imperial rule researched during the modernist period.[3] As Claude Gilbert-Dubois suggests of the writers who explored this world of Europe's authoritarian systems:

Que les auteurs s'inscrivent pour ou contre ces mouvements n'a qu'une importance mineure: l'importance est l'attirance qu'exerce ce terme comme arrière-fond historique d'un horizon d'attente espéré ou inquietant.

(Whether the authors write for or against these movements is of only minor importance: what is significant is the attraction that this term exerts as the historical background of hopeful or disturbing expectation.)[4]

My chapter opens with one such author whose interest lay in the cultural and political achievements of a particular late incarnation of baroque sovereignty, and who views that example of absolute rule as both aesthetically promising and morally unsettling. Sacheverell Sitwell's *German Baroque Art* (1927) is at first glance a mere catalogue of places and artefacts selected from Germany's baroque and rococo past, examples of art and architecture that had hitherto been eclipsed by the music of Mozart, Bach and Handel. Unlike *Southern Baroque Art*, with its imaginative flourishes and desire to mediate historical narrative, the later text's surprisingly clipped, modest prose offers glimpses of the splendour and violence that defined absolute rule in the Germanic countries after Europe's Thirty Years War. This series of conflicts occurred between 1618 and 1648 and was finally brought to a close with the Treaty of Westphalia, an agreement that undermined Germany's international status and resulted in lack of unity, territorial losses, the creation of many petty abso-lutisms and the fracturing of German national identity. The military leader and politician Albrecht von Wallenstein had planned to combine north-east Germany with Habsburg lands to form one powerful Germanic Imperial State but the Emperor's power within the Holy Roman Empire was ultimately weak-ened by the treaty. All hopes of Habsburg hegemony in Europe were dashed as the German princes secured their independence from the Emperor, and the Treaty 'meant that in the future Germany was to be an artificial conglom-eration of two hundred and thirty four states, lacking national consciousness, varying in size and power, ruled by selfish men'.[5] The selfish men of Green's definition exercised their power and political freedom through absolute and often despotic rule, and Leopold I of Austria sought solace for his imperial losses by consolidating the hereditary privileges he enjoyed as prince of the Habsburg dynasty and lands.

For Sitwell, this particular incarnation of Habsburg Vienna supplied wealth, political power, talented artists and enthusiastic aristocratic patronage, a unique combination that financed and promoted the creation of a cosmopoli-tan baroque city to surpass even Bernini's Rome. While *German Baroque Art* lingers over a wide range of artworks – Giambattista Tiepolo's frescoes at Würzburg are cited as the artist's finest work, we learn of the accomplished Dresden sculptor Balthasar Permoser, the churches of Salzburg and the palaces of Nymphenburg and Potsdam – it is with the Vienna of Leopold I, his son Joseph I, and the architect Johann Bernhardt Fischer von Erlach that Sitwell discovers the real authors of Austria's theatrical baroque. This period of intense rebuilding and artistic ascendancy began after the Turkish siege of the city in 1685 as Leopold celebrated victory and Vienna regained confidence as a European power. Sitwell writes that the monarch's Caesarean pretensions and desire for adulation reveal many 'facts about how absolute rule can be applied and to what limits may be carried'.[6] Marriages were decided according to aristocratic pedigree alone, and, following the Emperor's example, all German princes became prodigal in the grandeur they demanded from both artist and architect. Leopold himself was an accomplished musician and composer and his translation of theatrical baroque into an aesthetic of power focused on court performance, artistic excellence, festival parade and lavish architecture. The most influential figure in this grand rhetoric of spectacle and pageant was Fischer von Erlach, a young designer who had studied art and architecture at Rome's papal court and at Bernini's studio. He designed the Palace of Schönbrunn for Leopold as a residence to rival the court of Louis XIV, an extravagant vision that was sadly not executed during his lifetime. His strong sculptural but fluid architecture with its desire to encircle and preserve vast areas of space combined Rome's high baroque forms with classical influences to fashion a unique Austrian style. Fischer designed garden palaces, belvederes, votive columns and churches across Vienna, and his work culminated in the spectacular Hofbibliothek and Karlskirche completed during the reign of Charles VI. Perhaps the best example of this architecture's performative role came with the festival buildings that he constructed for the Imperial family's return to the city in 1690 after the coronation of Joseph as king in Frankfurt am Main. The procession passed under a celebratory archway depicting Leopold as Hercules and the young king as Apollo, while victory over the Turks was emphasised with statues of captive slaves. Lit by fireworks, these buildings showed different perspectives and images to all those who passed through them or viewed them as spectators, embodying street theatre at its most august.

Such majesty came at a price, and Germany's princes were not always able to meet the costs of war or celebration. While the city's Jewish population had faced sporadic hostility since the 1300s, Leopold's reign represented a particular point of crisis in the fate of the Viennese Jew, as cultural enlightenment descended into persecution and suffering. When Leopold became Emperor in 1658, he had renewed his promises of protection and jurisdiction over Vienna's Jewish community as they represented a valuable financial resource, and by the mid-seventeenth century, the Hofjud, or Court Jew, had become a prominent figure in Viennese court life, with Samuel Oppenheimer engaged as Leopold's most privileged financier. The Jewish quarter became a tourist attraction and one of the largest Jewish centres in the Holy Roman Empire, with Jews allowed restricted access to the city by day. The marriage of Leopold to the Spanish princess Maria Theresa introduced a reversal of fortunes, as a strong anti-Judaic influence was introduced to court life, one that augmented existing hostility from rival Viennese merchants. Leopold finally withdrew his support, handing the Jewish community over to the Council of Vienna. Attacks on their ghetto outside the city walls followed, and in March 1670 all Jews were expelled from Vienna, their synagogue claimed for Christian worship, their bodies hung unceremoniously during times of plague, and their civil privileges revoked as part of a programme of persecution that lasted until the late eighteenth century. Sitwell notes the irony of a regime that was 'a kind of restful paradise of intrigue' boasting elaborate artistic refinement offset by evil and suffering with endless public executions, sadistic military practices, corporal punishments, and 'the most brutal bull-fights, and animal contests of more than Spanish cruelty'.[7]

The political and social upheavals of the Thirty Years War and the myriad autocracies that followed define the Trauerspiel's relation to historical time, and the princes of Germany's absolute states were represented as the sovereigns and tyrants of these dramas. The ruler was represented not only as a tyrant but also as a martyr, and cruelty and anguish became no less a matter for ostentatious display than cultural achievement and wealth. By definition, the Trauerspiel's extravagant externalised expressions of melancholy and torment countered the quiet world of Tragödie's heroes. In his account of this period of German history, J. H. Greene notes the similarities between the baroque conflict and the First World War: 'the Thirty Years War gave rise to atrocities which Europe was not again to experience until the twentieth century'.[8] This chapter will continue Greene's analogy by exploring similarities between the baroque court of the Trauerspiel and the post-First World War vision of Barnes's *Nightwood*, and by concentrating on the figures of the sovereign, the Jew and the court intriguer.

Nightwood and the Jew in Pre-war Vienna

On 1 August 1935, Emily Coleman wrote to tell Djuna Barnes that Peggy Guggenheim had read the early manuscript of *Nightwood*: 'She doesn't like the beginning, it is of course the Ryder world, and not in the same streets of the imagination', and in the same letter, Coleman expressed her own concerns that the opening chapter was somehow disconnected from the main body of the text: 'it is not as profound as the rest of the book, it is on another plane'.[9] On 27 August she focused her criticism on the character of Felix – 'Felix should be proportionate, not really important', and in November of the same year she proposed asking T. S. Eliot whether the book could be improved by omitting 'Bow Down' altogether: 'the first part, fine though it is, all about Felix – has nothing to do with the main theme of the book'.[10] The fact that Barnes resisted these changes suggests that the early pages of *Nightwood* are very much in 'the same streets of the imagination' as the rest of the novel, and that it is for the reader to link the world of Felix and Guido Volkbein to the seven remaining chapters.

In her essay 'Laughing at Leviticus: *Nightwood* as Women's Circus Epic', Jane Marcus contradicts Kenneth Burke's reading of the novel as a non-political text that has nothing to do with the Nazis. She focuses her argument on Barnes's treatment of 'the non-Aryan, non-heterosexual body [as] a book inscribed with the modern failure to understand or assimilate the difference of race, class or gender', placing Barnes herself in a 'sisterhood under the skin with the victimised'.[11] Marcus's conviction that the novel remains anti-Judaic seems to exclude the figure of the Jew from this sisterhood, and she concludes that *Nightwood*'s 'anti-fascism is apparent only when it triumphs over its own anti-Semitism, when we realise that its characters – Jews, homosexuals, lesbians, transvestites, gypsies, blacks and circus performers – were all to perish in the Holocaust'.[12] The novel therefore becomes anti-Semitic some years after its publication, when the events of the Second World War had confirmed the fate of the Jew within Europe. My chapter suggests an alternative reading in which *Nightwood*'s anti-Fascism, and Barnes's identification and empathy with the figure of the Jew, begin with its opening paragraph, as Barnes asks her reader to recall a particular part of Europe at a specific time in history. While Marcus describes a modern failure to assimilate racial difference, Barnes's starting point is a city where the economic, political and social conditions augured well for an extensive assimilation of the Jew.

Six years before the publication of *Nightwood*, on 4 November 1930, Barnes had mailed an application for research funding to John Simon of the Guggenheim Memorial Foundation. The original form in the Maryland University Archive reveals a research proposal of two halves. One part of the Guggenheim fellowship funds was to be used for a trip to Poitiers, to study the French nunneries of the Middle Ages. The second half of the proposal reads as follows:

> To visit Austria, Vienna, to make a study of pre-war conditions, intrigues and relations then existing between the Jews and the Court, tracing the interweaving of the two, for a book in progress whose chief figure is an Austrian Jew.[13]

Although unsuccessful, the 1930 proposal remains as an indication that Barnes's desire to create a Jewish protagonist as a link to the court and aristocracy had at one time been strong enough to constitute the basis of a novel in its own right. The opening pages that describe Felix Volkbein and his fascination with the world of the court do not represent a distraction, or as Coleman writes, something 'on another plane'. The first paragraph of the published novel reveals that Barnes retained the Viennese court of pre-war Europe, and a Jewish character, as her story's point of origin. We learn that in the year 1880, Hedvig Volkbein gave birth to her son Felix, and that the valance of her canopied bed is stamped with emblems of the House of Hapsburg. *Nightwood* opens, therefore, with the Vienna of Emperor Franz Josef and the Habsburg monarchy, and the date suggests a critical time of transition during this reign.

Franz Josef was crowned Emperor of Austria in December 1848, and during his reign Vienna rapidly became a cosmopolitan centre of political liberalism. In many ways, the economic and cultural ascendancy that had characterised part of Leopold I's reign was restored. The capital's cosmopolitan character and wealth of opportunities meant that by 1891 a mere 35 per cent of the population were Viennese.[14] Thousands of Jewish immigrants from the east came to Vienna, and by 1880, the year Barnes underlines as Felix Volkbein's birth-date, there were more than 70,000 Jews in the city. As Barnes confirms, 'the Jew seemed to be everywhere from nowhere', and Felix's father, a Jew of Italian descent, would rank among this immigrant population.[15] In 1867, Franz Josef ratified a liberal constitution that established the 'Bürgerministerum', Austria's first parliamentary cabinet. Austrian liberalism fostered an inclusive nationalist ideology based on values of enlightenment, humanism, education and responsibility, with the premise that, through knowledge, industry and acculturation, any race could lay claim to a German identity. As part of this desire for assimilation:

> Apostasy, intermarriage with Christians, and Christian baptism, growing in volume among the educated Jews in the western cities of Austria, made heavy inroads into Jewish ranks. It is probable that Jews and 'non-Aryan' Christians formed, as of 1914, the greater part of the cultivated and well-to-do classes of Vienna.[16]

It is this religious and cultural integration of the Jew that Barnes details as Guido takes his Christian bride Hedvig, and attempts to fashion an aristocratic heritage for himself and his family: 'In life he had done everything possible to span the impossible gap . . . he had adopted the sign of the cross'.[17]

Franz Josef undertook to protect his subjects from extremist politics regardless of nationality and religion, and anti-Semitic propaganda was confiscated during this period. In 1867 equality of rights was formally extended to Austria's Jewry, allowing them to attend universities, own property and enter the learned professions such as law, medicine and the civil service. Jews figured prominently in the city's collective of commercial and intellectual genius, as individuals such as the neurologist Sigmund Freud, the astronomer and natural scientist Edward Mahler, the pianist Julius Epstein and Young Vienna's Arthur Schnitzler all achieved international renown. This period of

Jewish accomplishment and influence led Hermann Bahr to suggest a cultural monopoly among Vienna's elite: 'every aristocrat "who is a little bit smart or has some kind of talent is immediately considered a Jew"'.[18]

Such was the Vienna of Guido Volkbein's lifetime, but as *Nightwood* opens, the democratic, artistic and commercial ideal is already vulnerable. The year in which Guido dies and Felix is born, 1880, saw anti-Judaic nationalist candidates, notably those of the Christian Socialist party, come to dominate Vienna's government. During the 1880s, nationalist rhetoric became increasingly exclusive, presenting German identity as innate, rigidly defined and exclusive, while a nationalist discourse of biological and racial difference evolved. Franz Josef attempted to counter Christian Socialist antagonism, blocking the anti-semitic mayoral candidacy of Karl Lueger and earning himself the title of 'Judenkaiser', but Lueger came to office in 1897, and, as Judson notes, 'disagreement over anti-semitism frequently threatened the unity of the German nationalist movement after 1880'.[19] The year in which Hedvig Volkbein gives birth to her son Felix therefore marks a critical time in Vienna's fall from political and cultural enlightenment, and in the creation of restrictive political definitions of German nationalist identity. Barnes's library contains many books that suggest a continuing fascination with, and knowledge of, this period of Austro-German history and its decline, including Joseph Redlich's *Emperor Franz Joseph of Austria: A Biography* (1929), Robert Graf Zedlitz-Trützschler's *Twelve Years at the Imperial German Court* (1924), a text documenting the flatteries, intrigue and exercise of influence at the court of Wilhelm II, Hermann Pinnow's panoramic *History of Germany: People and State Through a Thousand Years* (1936), Abram Leon Sachar's *A History of the Jews*, a partisan narrative that runs from the ancient Israelites to the Holocaust, and Count Conti's *The Reign of the House of Rothschild*, the second volume of Conti's study of an immensely wealthy and influential Jewish family from the Frankfurt Ghetto, individuals who came to exert great power over court finance and intrigue.[20]

The Thirty Years War and Weimar Germany

Although *Nightwood* appears to move away from the world of the Jewish immigrant and Vienna's glorious past after 'Bow Down', focusing on Nora, Robin and Dr O'Connor, this chapter will argue that Barnes's text continues to mourn a lapsed enlightened modernity. *Nightwood* is at once a historically situated text, with clearly defined contemporary dates and events, and a novel that moves across a historical continuum characterised by man's fallen and graceless condition. Having referred her reader to the fall of an enlightened Germanic city, and moved her focus from Vienna to post-war Berlin, its nightclubs and Count Altamonte's party, Barnes seems to look backwards across literary history to a world that is haunted and defined by immanence and postlapsarian suffering, and a sense of foreboding or catastrophe. Her reading of Vienna and the Weimar state continues obliquely through images and associations that have already been used by the baroque Trauerspiel to present a fallen state. If baroque allegory, its emblems and metaphors, suggest the Trauerspiel as a figurative subtext and a critical framework for the novel, then the world of 'Bow Down' can be argued to add the setting and characters of the Trauerspiel to this connection. These similarities between modern Germany and its seventeenth-century counterpart focus on the fallen creaturely condition of the baroque monarch and the figure of the Trauerspiel intriguer with his mastery of postlapsarian knowledge structured through allegory.

One of the first ways in which the Trauerspiel suggests itself as a critical framework for *Nightwood* is through the significance of the court setting within this world-picture. Benjamin explains that 'the image of the setting or, more precisely the court, becomes the key to historical understanding ... In the Trauerspiel the court represents the timeless, natural décor of the historical process'.[21] In *Nightwood*, Felix's life and aspirations are likewise based on the conviction that the court is a defining cultural institution. He has an obsession with what he termed '"old Europe": aristocracy, nobility, royalty ... his rooms were taken because a Bourbon had been carried from them to death'.[22] Calling himself Baron Volkbein and assuming a false aristocratic ancestry, he tirelessly researches the past life of the court, research that can only emphasise his own false claims to recognition: 'with the fury of a fanatic he hunted down his own disqualification, re-articulating the bones of the Imperial Courts long forgotten'.[23] In *Nightwood*'s second chapter, 'La Somnambule', Felix takes Robin back to Vienna and the couple visit the Imperial Palace and Kammergarten where Felix 'laboured under the weight of his own remorseless re-creation of the great, generals and statesmen and emperors'.[24] He talks to Robin of Emperor Francis Joseph and takes comfort from showing her the city's historic buildings, as if summoning up the spectre of the Viennese court will somehow allow him to understand and communicate the historical process, and to insinuate his bride and himself into its particular narrative. In Weimar Berlin of 1920, however, the Vienna of the Habsburg monarchy is a paradise lost for Jew and Christian alike, and Felix's endeavours are in vain: 'he tried to explain to [Robin] what Vienna had been before the war; what it must have been before he was born, yet his memory was confused and hazy'.[25]

ROBIN VOTE – CREATURE AND SOVEREIGN

George Steiner's introduction to *The Origin of German Tragic Drama* makes the link between the world of the Trauerspiel and modern Germany explicit, and my argument will develop this sense of affinity: 'As during the crises of the Thirty Years War and its aftermath, so in Weimar Germany the extremities of political tension and economic misère are reflected in art.'[26] *Nightwood* and the baroque play of mourning do not engage directly with these historical crises through critique or review; instead, the melancholy experience of historical catastrophe becomes part of the momentum and events of the text, shaping character and action, a technique that culminates in the figure of the court sovereign. The baroque concept of sovereignty that had evolved in response to the Thirty Years War gave the prince or Elector dictatorial power to intervene should foreign powers threaten further conflict, and to protect the established hierarchy of status and privilege. The court sovereign therefore represented stability and completion, but his identity was also complicated by a strange sense of foreboding. Benjamin summarises this polarised fear and optimism: 'as an antithesis to the historical ideal of restoration [baroque society] is haunted by the idea of catastrophe'.[27] This catastrophe entails a long period of profound social disruption, in which forces of change were continually overwhelmed or outwitted by conservative powers defending the status quo. By definition it extended far beyond the impact of the Thirty Years War and isolated incidents of unrest. If 'Trauer', or the melancholy response to such catastrophe, is experienced with greatest intensity through the fate of the monarch, then modern forms of Trauer can be said to concentrate and internalise this process further. Chapter 2 has already noted this process as Baudelaire's allegory sees the corpse from within and a comprehensive state of catastrophe and disquiet becomes embodied within the figure of the poet. The modern writer continues and develops the Trauerspiel's distaste for observation and commentary at the moment of historical crisis, offering instead a visceral incarnation as the melancholy subject becomes that catastrophe.

Barnes's character Robin Vote can be read as just such an intricate modern avatar of Trauer. She retains her intimate symbolic identities in relation to her lovers, her enigmatic allegorical significance for the narrator and the doctor, while at the same time embodying the promised restoration of lost unity, and a sense of imminent catastrophe. Her partners, Felix and Nora, look to Robin to restore the lost unity of their own identities, but we also learn that 'people were uneasy when she spoke to them, confronted with a catastrophe that had yet no beginning'.[28] When Jenny hears Robin speak of her love for Nora, the narrator suggests that 'from that moment the catastrophe was inevitable' and two further images repeat this coupling of fear and crisis.[29] Caught between the projected hope and anxiety of his subjects, the figure of the Trauerspiel sovereign is characterised by a strange impotence, as Benjamin explains: 'the indecisiveness of the tyrant, the prince, who is to be responsible for making the decision to proclaim the state of emergency, reveals, at the first opportunity, that he is almost incapable of making a decision'.[30] Despite the extent and privileges of absolute monarchy, the Trauerspiel prince appeared to act without resolve and deliberation as though in a dream, and Robin shares this defining detail of the sovereign's stage presence. She drifts across the pages of

Nightwood, unable to think and act in a considered, incisive or determined way and falls 'into everything like someone in a dream'.[31]

Jane Marcus's political reading of *Nightwood* argues that the text 'figures by absence the authoritarian dominators of Europe in the 1930's, the sexual and political fascists'.[32] She concludes that 'what is absent is the Nazi who will burn this book', discovering in the minor character Hedvig Volkbein, with her goose-step and sentry-like vigilance, a fleeting female representation of German militarism: 'the blond Aryan beast slouching toward Buchenwald is present in this novel only in Hedvig's resemblance to him in 1880'.[33] Marcus's repetition of this absence might indicate the expectation that Barnes would balance her story of the victims of Nazi dictatorship with a more developed reference to Hitler and his regime. I would argue that the authoritarian dominators of 1930s Europe are present in the novel in a more subtle but detailed form, by association with their Trauerspiel counterparts. As Barnes reads the modern Germanic world through the eyes of the baroque, the spectre of Fascist Germany can be said to haunt *Nightwood* through similarities with the despotic regimes of the seventeenth century. The novel uses a second female form to suggest the tyranny of Nazi rule, as Robin's similarities with the baroque sovereign become clear. Intoxicated by the sacrosanct nature of his power, the Trauerspiel sovereign took on the identity of a tyrant. For Benjamin, the privileges of the seventeenth-century autocrat lead inevitably to the cruelty of the dictator. The prince speaks and gestures as a tyrant, but the execution of tyranny becomes an arbitrary process in which provocation and reaction are strangely dissociated. The Trauerspiel

> Makes a special point of endowing the ruler with the gesture of executive power as his characteristic gesture, and having him take part in action with the words and behaviour of a tyrant even where the situation does not require it.[34]

Barnes offers us two very striking pictures of Robin as her relationships with Felix and Nora founder, and her behaviour approaches madness. In the first, Felix enters the room one night to find Robin holding her son Guido up in the air as if she were intent on dashing him to the ground, but instead she gently lowers him. Nora tells the doctor that, when drunk, Robin repeated this gesture with a doll that represented the 'child' whom Nora and Robin would never have: 'I would find her in the middle of the room . . . holding the doll she had given us – "our child" – high over her head as if she would cast it down', and on one occasion she does dash the doll to the floor, crushing it underfoot.[35] Barnes repeats the unprovoked action so that it becomes Robin's characteristic gesture. These scenes link Robin to one Trauerspiel prince in particular – the figure of Herod. Benjamin stresses that demonstrations of passion or violence that far exceed psychological motivation were most notable in the baroque Herod dramas: 'above all it is the figure of Herod, as he was presented throughout the European theatre at this time, which is characteristic of the idea of the tyrant'.[36] Whether the plays in question were the early Herodian epics of Gryphius, or the Spanish Trauerspiel *El major munstro del mundo* (*The Greatest Monster in the World*) by Calderón de la Barca, Herod became the play of mourning's tyrant of choice. Both seventeenth-century dramatists and artists alike represented Herod falling into madness, holding one or more babes in his hands in order to dash out their brains. With the repetition of this gesture, Robin therefore becomes the baroque sovereign in his archetypal Trauerspiel identity, the tyrant, and a tyrant in his original Trauerspiel form: Herod, the slayer of infants.

If Robin resembles the Trauerspiel sovereign through her indecisive, impulsive nature, her embodiment of catastrophe and promised redemption, and her characteristic gesture of tyranny, the baroque and modern identities can be said to coalesce again through their affinity with the animal kingdom. The baroque prince or king became the focal point for references to man's creaturely identity, and Benjamin explains that 'however highly he is enthroned over subject and state, his status is confined to the world of creation; he is the lord of creatures, but he remains a creature'.[37] In Daniel Caspar von Lohenstein's Trauerspiel *Agrippina* (1665), for example, the sovereign figure is the queen Agrippina, described by Anecitus as 'das stoltze Thier/ das aufgeblassne Weib (the proud beast/ the self-important woman)' as she dares to challenge the accepted order of the state.[38]

The Trauerspiel's peculiarly amoral universe, the apparent void that exists between virtue, ethical reflection and historical life on the baroque stage, evolves from man's creaturely identity. Benjamin traces this to the creaturely guilt of original sin:

> The creature is the mirror within whose frame alone the moral world was revealed to the baroque ... Since it was the view of the age that all historical life was lacking in virtue, virtue was of no significance for the constitution of the dramatis personae.[39]

The baroque protagonist is apparently unschooled in matters of conscience and his behaviour neither adheres to, nor rebels against, codes of integrity. Breitinger's 1740 study of the Trauerspiel dramatist Lohenstein notes this tendency to blunt any bias towards considerations of honour, principle and rectitude, and his technique involved 'giving apparent emphasis to moral principles by examples from nature, which in fact undermine them. This kind of comparison acquires its proper significance only when an ethical transgression is justified purely and simply by referring to natural conduct'.[40] In his analysis of *Nightwood* as a late-modernist text, Tyrus Miller highlights T. S. Eliot's concerns about the novel's formal difficulties and the 'degree to which characters manifest moral awareness'.[41] Barnes's characters do indeed appear to inhabit an amoral universe, well illustrated by our introduction to Nora – 'she recorded without reproach or accusation being shorn of self-reproach or self-accusation ... In court no one would have been hanged, reproached or forgiven, because no one would have been accused'.[42] Not only are the principal characters absolved of moral agency, but Barnes's techniques for achieving this bear close resemblance to those of the Trauerspiel dramatists. Just as Lohenstein created metaphorical analogies between history and the cycle of nature, so Barnes can be seen to collapse ethical questions into demonstrations of natural history. Nora's description of Robin leaving to go on her nightly debauches provides one example of this:

> 'If I asked her, crying, not to go out, she would go just the same, richer in her heart because I had touched it, as she was going down the stairs'. 'Lions grow their manes and foxes their teeth on that bread' interpolated the doctor.[43]

Rather than continue the ideas of pity, cruelty and jealousy that arise from Nora's despair and Robin's repeated betrayals, Barnes offers the example of two natural predators where the savage is innate and necessary and so beyond moral valuations. When Dr O'Connor seeks out the small, quiet Church of Saint Merri in which to contemplate his sins and blasphemous acts, he concludes that 'the roaring lion goes forth seeking his own fury', an image that again diffuses any focused consideration of virtue and morality.[44] In *Nightwood*, as in the Trauerspiel, no judgements are made, no burdens of ultimate responsibility are established, and Benjamin's conclusion could be applied to both the modern and baroque text – 'it is not moral transgression but the very estate of man as creature which provides the reason for catastrophe'.[45]

The Court Intriguer

Before comparing Robin's final scene in *Nightwood* with the closing scenes of the Trauerspiel and the demise of the baroque sovereign, a second character from Barnes's night-world seems to draw the reader back into the Trauerspiel court. Denied a Guggenheim scholarship and the research that would allow her to elaborate the figure of a Jewish intriguer, Barnes offers us instead Dr O'Connor. Among the cast of the seventeenth-century Trauerspiel, the figure of the intriguer becomes the pre-eminent courtier, he is the one character who appears to know everything and who becomes confidant to the main protagonists. This individual had many distinguishing characteristics, not least his talent for alchemy and magic, and the Trauerspiels of the German seventeenth century were well known for their conjuration scenes, presided over by this court official. *Nightwood* has its own conjuration scene during the doctor's first encounter with Robin in 'La Somnamble'. Felix notices to his discomfort that Dr O'Connor performs the gestures and movements typical of the man of magic or the dumbfounder, while committing multiple deceptions and sleights of hand as he helps himself to Robin's perfume, her powder and rouge, and finally a stray 100-franc note lying on the table.

The doctor is also described by Nora as practised in the court intriguer's profession; as she visits his room he is discovered 'in the grave dilemma of his alchemy'.[46] I have argued that, as *Nightwood's* alchemist, Dr O'Connor uses allegory to transform base, 'fallen' words or objects into more precious configurations with other words and objects, in the hope of disclosing their occluded prelapsarian significance. Klossowski de Rola's study explains that the alchemist's primary interest was the pursuit of spiritual knowledge and he writes of their 'hermetic philosophy [that] conceals, in esoteric texts and enigmatic emblems, the means of penetrating the very secrets of Nature, Life and Death, of Unity, Eternity and Infinity'.[47] Benjamin likewise argues that the court intriguer, the master of alchemy, dominates the Trauerspiel, because 'the real purpose of the drama was to communicate knowledge of the life of the soul, in the observation of which the intriguer is without equal' and this is precisely the quality of enigmatic knowledge and subject matter that draws the characters of *Nightwood* to Dr O'Connor.[48] His discourses elaborate the fate of the soul as it enters the night-world, lingering over strangely hermetic emblems of life and death: 'Life, the pastures in which the night feeds and prunes the cud that nourishes us to despair. Life, the permission to know death'; and eternity: 'the space between the human and the holy head, the arena of the "indecent" eternal'.[49] An important part of the court intriguer's identity as alchemist was his fascination with the world of matter, notably his experiments with mineral ores. The extraction of minerals from the earth and the practice of transforming them from ore to metal were at the heart of occult science and involved the heating, processing and tempering of metallic ores using furnaces, bellows, and tools similar to those of a blacksmith. It is perhaps for this reason that Barnes gives Dr O'Connor's room a very distinctive smell: 'every object seemed to be battling its own compression; and there is a metallic odour as of beaten iron in a smithy', the objects battling the compression of their 'fallen' identities, as they await transformation by the alchemist's art.[50]

The doctor's allegorical discourses provide the novel's most arcane language, much of which can be traced to the baroque alchemist's use of cryptic pictorial images, each representing a particular stage in an experiment or procedure. The image of the bird was used repeatedly in alchemical writing, as the wing represented the volatile state of liquids, and stages of transmutation associated with sublimation. The pelican denoted techniques of cyclic distillation, the peacock was used to suggest the stage between 'nigredo' and 'albeido', while the dove flying upwards or downwards represented the eternal process of sublimation.[51] This peculiar affection for bird imagery is continued by *Nightwood*'s alchemist, as he uses the image of a sighing widower bird to describe lovers, profligates and drunks as they enter the night-world state, changing their appearance to the anonymity of an 'unrecorded' look. When referring to transformations brought about by love or passion he offers a bewildering image of a thrush: 'Behold this fearful tree, on which sits singing the drearful bird – *Turdas Musicas*, or European singing thrush', and chooses to represent his own changing or volatile sexual identity through the mocking bird – 'I've never been one thing that I am . . . The mocking bird howls through the pillars of heaven'.[52]

Dr O'Connor develops the image of the bird further by internalising its natural instincts and functions. He describes 'the lining of my belly, flocked with the locks, cut off in odd places that I've come on, a bird's nest of pubic hair to lay my lost eggs in' and later asks 'do I wail . . . of every lie how it went down into my belly and built a nest to hatch me to my death there'.[53] The repeated image of the 'belly' as a nest and as a catalyst in the hatching of eggs, also finds a parallel in alchemical texts. One stage in the manufacture of *Ignis Innaturalis*, or natural fire, involves the 'Philosophic Egg', a hermetically sealed vessel that is placed in the alchemist's furnace or 'Athanor'. During the initial stage of the process the heat is compared to a hen sitting on her eggs, and, as a result, hens and other incubating birds came to be included in the alchemical vocabulary of emblems. The doctor's words 'hatch me to my death' could refer to the alchemical state 'death' which precedes 'nigredo', the precursor of decay, the blackest of blacks, that bodes well for subsequent transformations while the volatile element mercury is described as it 'flies through the microcosm of the Philosophic Egg, "in the belly of the wind", receiving the celestial and purifying influences above'.[54] Barnes has taken these details from the baroque alchemist's art and combined them with elements of a profane modern alchemy, the locks of pubic hair and the doctor's own capacious belly, to form the night-world's Philosophic Egg.

The figure of the baroque intriguer is also remarkable for his unfaithfulness, and this too can be traced to an affinity with the realm of matter. Benjamin claims that 'it is not possible to conceive of anything more inconstant than the mind of this courtier as depicted in the Trauerspiel: treachery is his element', and his unfaithfulness to man is matched by a loyalty to material objects such as the crown, the sceptre, courtly robes and royal purple, as he remains 'absorbed in contemplative devotion to them'.[55] Just as the baroque intriguer is characterised by his betrayals of the sovereign and those around him, so Dr O'Connor betrays Nora by introducing Jenny to Robin. He recalls to Nora his sense of misgiving when Jenny asked him to give this formal and fateful introduction, scruples that are soon overcome as the doctor consents. The element of betrayal is quite explicit, as is the doctor's contrasting loyalty to the world of objects and matter, as he continues some lines later, 'for who will not betray a friend, or for that matter, himself, for a whisky and soda, caviar and a warm fire?'[56] He quickly turns from the implications of his betrayal to his fidelity to the world of objects, coveting some leather-bound books in Jenny's house, before moving on to gloat over his spoils from the fair. He even imagines forgiving Jenny for her greed and all the misery that she has caused, but here again, his good opinion is secured thanks only to the elegance of the long black evening gloves that he pictures Jenny wearing. His loyalty is to the elegant accessory: 'Oh the poor bitch, if she were dying face down in a long pair of black gloves, would I forgive her? And I knew I would forgive her, or anyone else making a picture'.[57]

It is here, with this attachment to material objects, that the relationship between the seventeenth-century image of Satan and the court intriguer comes to the fore. The Middle Ages had bound together the material and the demonic in the figure of Satan: 'Above all the concentration of the numerous pagan powers into one, theologically rigorously defined Antichrist meant that this supreme manifestation of darkness was imposed upon matter more unambiguously than in a number of separate demons.'[58]

Benjamin concludes that it is fitting in the Trauerspiel's secularisation of the passion-plays that the court official should replace the devil, and the intriguer's fascination for, and affinity with, material things confirms this. It is knowledge and not action that represents the most characteristic medium in the existence of evil at this time. For this reason the intriguer's role as the master of meanings becomes the most distinctive mark of his alliance with Satan. Within the world of baroque allegory and Trauerspiel, the devil 'initiates men in knowledge' and rules over the abyss of hollow matter that constitutes allegory – 'this confirms once again the significance of the baroque polymathy for the Trauerspiel. For something can take on allegorical form only for the man who has knowledge'.[59] As allegorist and polymath, the doctor stands securely within the realm of Satan, and this connection goes some way to explaining his rule at the heart of the knowledge of the night. This knowledge is encyclopaedic, it spans history itself, and we learn that the doctor has a prehistoric memory, he is a consummate geographer familiar with the night as it unfolds in each different country, and his breadth of knowledge is attributed to the fact that he has been everywhere at the wrong time. It is to the doctor that Felix and Nora turn for answers. He knows the night, and the night is, above all, evil, leading Barnes to conclude that 'the dead have committed some portion of the evil of the night, sleep and love the other'.[60]

APOTHEOSIS AND THE BAROQUE DEVIL

This chapter's opening quotation forms part of Emily Coleman's judgement of *Nightwood*, drawing attention to Barnes's peculiar ability to fashion an aesthetic of evil. She suggests that we are frozen to evil and that *Nightwood* represents evil as our inescapable fate, putting forward the idea that art, and more specifically Barnes's novel, can somehow return this quality of human knowledge to its origin, a preoccupation clearly visible in the Barnes–Coleman correspondence between May and November 1935. When Coleman wrote to Eliot on 25 October 1935, this theme became an imperative for publication in its own right: 'The human truths revealed . . . (the light it sheds on the relation of good to evil in this life) make it a document which absolutely must be published', and on 31 October she again draws Eliot's attention to the novel as a 'document which points the way to the things we most want to know about evil and suffering'.[61] Barnes herself questions the definition, apprehension and influence of evil in these letters, describing her sense of the expansive, fluid properties of benevolence, and a desire to restrict this ex-centric movement and subsequent loss by using 'an evil being' as an obstacle just 'as light is stopped by objects'.[62] Her sense of evil refers to a denser, more focused medium rather than an expansive flow of energy, an influence that leaves the onlooker feeling stifled and uncomfortably complicit:

> An evil person is always too near, and concentrated, no matter how far his evil reaches, it is always in your hands, you even feel that you are dealing it out . . . as a rope is let out by many seamen.[63]

By examining *Nightwood*'s final chapters, 'The Possessed' and 'Go Down, Matthew', against the Trauespiel's closing scenes, Barnes's sense of the proximity and universality of evil can be elaborated. If she has included details that recall the Trauerspiel genre throughout the text of *Nightwood*, then this section of the novel must be examined against the baroque apotheosis and the tyrant's scenes of suffering, the final movement of the allegorical process that underlies the conclusion of these baroque plays. It is here that the doctor's role as the Trauerspiel's court intriguer, and the exact nature of his knowledge, become clear, as his affinity with the baroque originals and with Satan becomes more focused. As he enters the cafe for this final appearance, Barnes draws our attention once more to the intriguer's treachery: 'In great defaming sentences his betrayals came up; no one ever knew what was truth and what was not', and a few pages later, he asks himself 'who says I'm a betrayer. I say I tell the story of the world to the world'.[64] More significantly his discourses become longer and more intense as 'Go Down, Matthew' progresses, and his pursuit of meaning becomes more urgent.

Knowledge and evil establish an intimate creative alliance within the Trauerspiel and Barnes's night-world, and the intriguer's intellectual abilities and particular quality of knowledge allow him mastery over the hesitant sovereign. For Barnes, and for Benjamin's reading of the Trauerspiel, the Fall away from grace and from the unity of man, nature and divinity, is also an epistemological fall; that is, a Fall from truth into knowledge structured by allegory. Once man had consumed Eden's original fruit of contrast, knowledge became divided between good and evil. Our apprehension or experience of evil, therefore, has no object in the world, but must arise within man himself through his appetite for knowledge. Allegory is based on over-interpretation, as the practitioner slowly and determinedly collects fragment after fragment. The discovery of truth is elusive, and Benjamin explains that the sense of loss of totality and cohesion is experienced as a descent into hell. This downward progress of allegory is one possible interpretation of *Nightwood*'s dominant image of bowing down and going down, and the novel's initial title, 'Bow Down'. The baroque allegorist would plunge ever deeper into subjective inwardness without the final movement of baroque melancholy, the startling transformation of the apotheosis scene:

> The allegorical intention [would] fall from emblem to emblem down into the dizziness of its bottomless depths, were it not that, in precisely the most extreme among them, it had so to turn about that all its darkness, vainglory and godlessness seems to be nothing but self-delusion.[65]

While the allegorist looks for the miracle of revelation in the ceaseless accumulating of fragments, the miracle is to be found elsewhere – within that sense of movement or progress through antithesis which defines allegory. At the point of transfiguration, the absolute subjectivity of melancholy contemplation betrays and abandons the objects of material nature that it sought to master through allegory. That subjectivity is then succeeded by an unassailable religious faith. For Susan Buck-Morss, this is how the baroque reconciled the contradictory nature of allegory: 'This is the baroque theological resolution to the paradoxical meanings of objective matter . . . the contradictory meanings of emblems themselves become an emblem, the sign of their opposite: the eternity of the one, true Spirit'.[66] The multiple and arbitrary meanings of transient, decaying matter become allegories of their opposite – resurrection and the Word of God. Mortality and the devil come to signify hope and the innocence of the created world while Golgotha, as the place of skulls, passes over into eternity, and the baroque is ultimately able to confirm the Biblical premise of the non-existence of evil.

Barnes has used the doctor's final scene to emphasise his dissatisfaction with the flawed, satanic condition of allegorical knowledge. Allegory is an attempt to redeem fallen nature, but in the final reckoning of the apotheosis, the guilty world of objects and matter is abandoned without regret. The doctor, however, acknowledges that he can only 'tell the story of the world to the world'– he remains trapped within its profane, phenomenal condition.[67] By acknowledging how much Barnes has drawn from the structure and detail of the Trauerspiel, this final scene of the doctor's despair can be deciphered. Having established him as the novel's allegorist, Barnes can be argued to withhold the final transfiguration of Trauerspiel's apotheosis. Benjamin offers us a quotation from an unnamed Lohenstein play of mourning to illustrate the baroque transformation: 'Yea, when the Highest comes to reap the harvest from the graveyard, then I, a death's head, will be an angel's countenance'.[68] Barnes briefly offers the doctor the identity of an uninhabited angel, but this is only in the hollow form of an allegory, and Nora quickly replaces this with the image of the devil. The uninhabited are the characters whose night-world and identities are ultimately structured through the emptiness of allegory, and the doctor is trapped at the heart of this perception. While Felix and Nora continue to pursue the eternal through religion and love, the doctor knows that this hope of redemption has passed, and he wonders why he alone seems to realise that everything is now over. Unlike the Trauerspiel dramatists, Barnes considers allegory to be an inescapable condition of knowledge for *Nightwood*. Its arbitrary, incoherent but determined process underlies the doctor's story, and the sheer quantity of fragments that the doctor has collected and shared with his listeners has been in vain. As a modern counterpart of the court intriguer, the doctor has appeared as allegorist, alchemist and conjurer. When Benjamin notes that in the Trauerspiel, 'magical knowledge, which includes alchemy, threatens the adept with isolation and spiritual death', he might have been diagnosing the doctor's final sense of alienation and despair: 'I know it's all over ... and nobody knows it but me' ... 'the end mark my words – now nothing but wrath and weeping', as the soulless materiality of allegory becomes his permanent home.[69]

THE POSSESSED

In the final chapter of *Nightwood*, Robin is drawn to the ancient chapel of Nora's estate, a setting that might itself appear to promise the redemption of allegory's final antithesis. At the moment of apotheosis, baroque allegory abandons the world of material nature and objects, and at the moment of expected transformation in *Nightwood*, Robin places her flowers and toys before a 'contrived altar', in a gesture that seems to promise their sacrifice. As with the fate of the doctor, however, Barnes refuses Robin this final reversal of the allegorical process. Throughout the novel, Barnes has included the image and gesture of going down or bowing down, and in the final scene she appears to intensify its significance through close repetition, as Robin's body lowers itself until her hair drags in the dust. Rather than grant the baroque ascent into spiritual life, Barnes plunges Robin deeper and deeper into the subjective inwardness of melancholy satanic knowledge and its descent towards hell. This repetition of going down is linked to the idea of melancholy by another theory of baroque culture. In their studies of baroque melancholy, both Panofsky and Benjamin note that, as a result of the scientific reflection of Marsilio Ficinus, a new analogy arose between the force of gravity and mental concentration.

The theory of the four humours associated melancholy with black bile, and black bile, in turn, was considered to share an affinity with the centre of the earth. The contemplation associated with the melancholy allegorist, which had for some time been linked to Saturn, now became associated with images of descent into the earth: 'everything saturnine points down into the depths of the earth . . . for the melancholic the inspirations of mother earth dawn from the night of contemplation like treasures from the interior of the earth'.[70] This repeated sense of descent is the momentum of the night-world as both man and animal, thought and body, betray the influence of the melancholy weight of gravity. The circus lions are ponderous and heavy, and the lioness of Robin's encounter goes down before her audience, Nora is described as falling before the image of Robin and her lover, while Jenny and Robin sink down in their carriage, and Felix is habitually doubled over in a bow. Robin's body has the perfume of earth-flesh, while thought and contemplation in the novel, whether waking or dreaming, become a perpetual descent into the earth. In Nora's dreams she talks of 'taking the body of Robin down with her . . . as the ground things take the corpse . . . down into the earth'.[71]

Barnes also locates Robin in the Trauerspiel world of saturnine melancholy through the ruined setting of the chapel and the introduction of Nora's dog. The ruins and monuments of the baroque were the home of the saturnine beasts, and, while the baroque apotheosis signifies the defeat of melancholy, Barnes confirms the power of melancholy in *Nightwood*'s final scene by introducing the figure of the dog, one of the emblems of Dürer's figure 'Melencolia I', and the most saturnine of beasts. Baroque theories of the four humours state that 'the spleen is dominant in the organism of the dog, this he has in common with the melancholic'.[72] Should that organ deteriorate through an excess of spleen, then the human will develop the darker aspect of melancholy, and the dog will become rabid. The latter diagnosis could be applied to the violent and frenzied behaviour of both Robin and the dog in this final scene. While the baroque allegorist betrays the phenomenal, creaturely world, allowing objects and emblems to dissolve in the leap to absolute faith, Robin enacts a strange communion with an animal that is all these things – phenomenal, creaturely and a baroque emblem of melancholy.

Alan Williamson has interpreted Robin's act as 'simultaneously a disintegration into total animality and a masochistic atonement for her guilt towards Nora', and he concludes that Robin 'attempts intercourse with Nora's dog as Nora looks on horror-stricken'.[73] The terms of Monika Kaup's analysis are as abstract as Williamson's are carnal – for her Robin 'disappears at the boundary of the primitive, the mythic, the archaic . . . she is outside the human type'.[74] I would suggest that the significance of Robin's communion with the dog is best explained, not as an apotheosis scene, but as an example of the Trauerspiel scenes that showed the death or decline of the sovereign in his madness, emphasising his creaturely status. Benjamin chooses to illustrate such scenes with a stage direction from the German Trauerspiel *Nebucadnezar* by Christian Hunold. Here, Nebucchadnezzar is introduced in the shape of a beast: 'Nebucchadnezzar is in chains with eagles' feathers and talons he has grown among wild beasts . . . He makes strange gestures . . . He growls and shows his ill-nature'.[75] Robin, in her madness, has also taken on the noises and gestures of the animal: going down on all fours, 'she began to bark also, crawling after him [the dog] . . . Her head turned sideways grinning and whimpering'.[76] As the Trauerspiel sovereign descends further into melancholy and madness, such scenes illustrate that even in the most privileged and refined human, the beast can emerge with alarming power. Robin, as the supreme creature and sovereign in *Nightwood*, the central signifier, at the lowest point in her allegorical descent, is overwhelmed by her creaturely identity. Far from Kaup's definition of Robin as mythical and outside the human type, it is at this point that Robin assumes her strongest and most representative human identity. Benjamin notes that the sovereign falls not only in his own name, 'but as a ruler and in the name of mankind and history . . . his fall has the quality of a judgement, in which the subject too is implicated'.[77] It is not, as Williamson suggests, the guilt of an intimate and particular betrayal that leads Robin to this final act, but the guilt of mankind as a whole in its postlapsarian state.

In *The Arcades Project*, Benjamin notes that: 'the death's head [skull] of Baroque allegory is a half-finished product of the history of salvation, that process interrupted – so far as this is given him to realise – by Satan'.[78] The baroque limits Satan's influence, as the devil interrupts the process of salvation but cannot overwhelm it, while in the modern allegory of *Nightwood*, Satan's power has grown and the process of salvation is not just interrupted, it is defeated once and for all. 'The Possessed' of Barnes's chapter title fall completely within the power of the devil. Benjamin's Trauerspiel study notes that the allegorist is met by the 'scornful laughter of hell', the Satanic laughter 'that overshoots language' and is 'connected with that superfluity of meanings of objects which is a sign of nature's fallen state'.[79] At the point of failed resurrection and despair, Dr O'Connor 'began to scream with sobbing laughter', and in the novel's final paragraph Robin is described 'barking in a fit of laughter, obscene and touching'.[80] Barnes has earlier hinted at this fatal quality in Robin's mirth – in 'La Somnambule' while at prayer in the convent 'she laughed, out of some hidden capacity, some lost subterranean humour; as it ceased she leaned still further forward in a swoon'.[81] This swoon and the sense of some latent quality connected with the infernal regions of the earth both portend the possession of *Nightwood*'s final pages, where that which was previously 'hidden' and 'lost' finally reveals its demonic 'subterranean' form at the point of apotheosis: 'Scorning all emblematic disguise, the undisguised visage of the devil can raise itself up from out of the depths of the earth into the view of the allegorist, in triumphant vitality'.[82] The laughter is touching as it acknowledges and mourns the loss of allegory's moment of redemption. As he edited the novel's manuscript Eliot wanted the word obscene to be replaced by unclean, but Barnes refused this alteration. I would suggest that she did so because this was not the meaning she wished the word obscene to convey. The *Oxford English Dictionary* mentions an alternative meaning that was in use in the seventeenth century, 'ill-omened', an interpretation that can only confirm the presence of Satan at this point in the text.

Laughter would be out of keeping with the melancholy and intensity of these final scenes, were it not the diabolic laughter of allegory's descent towards hell. As allegory has become the inescapable fate of Robin and the doctor, that laughter has become their voice. Baroque allegory cannot be redeemed unless it betrays its own defining qualities. Without redemption, Barnes's modern allegory must therefore retain everything that is peculiar to that aesthetic – the dogged pursuit of knowledge and the bleak and eternal prospect of a world without hope. It points ultimately, not to salvation, but to the Fall itself. For *Nightwood*, the objectless encounter with the God of the apotheosis has become a fate dominated by allegorical objects and emblems. In her loyalty to the allegorical descent, and her denunciation of the baroque flight into abstract spirituality, Barnes can be argued to be more 'baroque' than the Trauerspiel dramatists themselves.

Gesturing Towards the Holocaust

This chapter has argued that *Nightwood*'s 'Bow Down' is connected to the novel's subsequent chapters through the figure of the Jew and a related vulnerable cultural ideal suggested by Barnes's references to Vienna and the year 1880. By using the Trauerspiel as a critical framework for analysing her novel, a sense of this lost liberal and enlightened modernity continues, as parallels emerge between her own characters and those that inhabit the baroque world of courtly intrigue and authoritarian power. Her library contains a particularly controversial analysis of German national and political culture – William L. Shirer's *The Rise and Fall of the Third Reich*. This text was not published until 1960, more than twenty years after *Nightwood* was written, and its sheer popularity among American journalists and the wider public would be enough to explain its place on Barnes's bookshelves. Shirer's work may have been of particular interest to Barnes, however, because it argues, more explicitly than her own allusive connections, that Counter-Reformation and baroque Germany are closely linked to the regime of the modern dictator.

The key German Trauerspiel dramatists of the period were Lutheran Protestants, and Benjamin highlights the preference of Lutheran art and drama for allegory, and the attendant spiritual belief in a restricted life of immanence and dependence on God's grace. All of these details of the Lutheran legacy find their way onto the pages of *Nightwood* through the novel's affinities with the Trauerspiel genre. Shirer's vision of German history argues more dogmatically for a sense of historical continuity between Nazism and baroque Germany. As with Barnes, he focuses on images of the Jew and the absolute monarch, but places them at the heart of Germany's Lutheran identity, stating that the founder of Protestantism was both anti-Semitic and a believer in uncompromising obedience to absolute political authority. He describes Luther's desire to repress Germany's Judaic population and to take away their wealth and possessions. Shirer also discovers in Luther's anti-Semitism a blueprint for German nationalist exclusivity after 1880. He locates the origins of Hitler's anti-Judaic creaturely vocabulary in late sixteenth- and seventeenth-century Germany: 'in his utterances about the Jew Luther employed a coarseness and brutality of language unequalled in history until the Nazi time'.[83] This interpretation of Fascism as the intimate and inevitable successor of Germany's past was scorned in West Germany and widely contested by historians who considered Nazism to be part of a contemporary totalitarian ideal, a phenomenon peculiarly 'of the moment' in 1930s Europe. William O'Shanahan, for example, finds Shirer's text to be 'woefully inadequate' using an 'oversimplified grand design', hovering 'on the surface of events' with little evidence that the author had used relevant microfilm of captured German war records.[84]

While *Nightwood* can be said to present a hostile reading of the Fascist politics of 1930s Europe, Barnes's response to the concept of democracy is also more complex than the liberalism/authoritarianism opposition might suggest. First, the culturally enlightened modernism of Habsburg Vienna is, as the novel's aesthetic suggests, the material of ruin and allegory. When Felix returns to this cosmopolitan city with Robin, he is a mere cultural 'sightseer', whose desperate attempts to resurrect that particular moment in history become a tangled and inaccurate 'flow of fact and fancy'.[85] It is clear that the liberalism of this pre-war democracy has no political currency in 1930's Europe. Barnes's decision to give Robin the surname 'Vote', and this character's affinities with the baroque despot, cannot but recall the ironies and complexities of post-war Germany's electoral process during Hitler's ascent to power. Hitler appeared to consolidate a modern form of sovereignty that involved tyranny with a mass appeal, and a new undemocratic order was quickly accepted by the German people. His success had been achieved, not by revolution, but by constitutional means.

Nightwood's significance as a modern, secular counterpart of the baroque Trauerspiel can therefore be said to evolve from Barnes's awareness of the fate of Jews in Europe, their forfeited state of integration and opportunity, and her sense of the similarities between baroque and contemporary post-war history. Her library's range of reading materials and the aesthetic of the novel itself, suggest these ideas as both a creative resource and a long-term intellectual preoccupation. She conjures up the spectre of seventeenth-century intrigue and tyranny at a time when similar power-structures were being brought to bear on a foundering Weimar Republic and a subsequent Nazi dictatorship. In addition to the information provided by texts in her library, Barnes also enjoyed a particular and intimate insight into the workings of the Nazi party through her involvement with Ernst Hanfstaengl. Their relationship foundered when her lover's passion for all things German led him to choose a German-American bride, and in 1920, having heard Hitler speak at the Kindl Keller, Hanfstaengl became a Fascist, convinced that Germany had found its future leader and a formidable political orator. Barnes turned to her former lover in 1931 when she wanted to interview Hitler for *Cosmopolitan* magazine, but when Hitler demanded the prohibitive sum of $2 per printed word, the idea was abandoned. In *Hitler: The Missing Years*, Hanfstaengl recalls the Nazi leader's early political appearances and some of the techniques behind his appeal as a public speaker, noting that Hitler's addresses differed from those of other public speakers, thanks to a deliberately styled and coordinated physicality. He argues that, while most orators use a stereotyped repertoire of gestures just to find employment for their hands, Hitler's posturing was an 'integral part of his method' and the final visual component within this striking public image was the unusual 'soaring upward movement of the arm'.[86]

In her article 'Fascist Choreography: Riefenstahl's Tableaux', Brigitte Peucker examines the use of staged tableaux in Leni Riefenstahl's film-making. Focusing on 'Triumph of the Will' and the Nuremburg party rally, Peucker's account of the immobile sustained pose of the human actor acknowledges both Benjamin's account of Trauerspiel productions and the re-emergence of this theatrical tradition in Goethe's *Elective Affinities* and the Sturm und Drang movement. Following the tableau vivant from its early use in religious ceremonies through to the pageant of the Nuremburg rally, she argues that the fetishised body-part that was once a relic is first replaced by the statue, and then by the 'living, posed and emblematic body of allegory'.[87] During the rally, workers formed part of these staged tableaux that were designed to celebrate Nazi cultural dominance. Hitler's procession, meanwhile, featured the dictator's body transfixed in the form of a devotional statue, and I would argue that the sudden upward movement of the arm and the frozen quality of the image present him as a modern counterpart to the Trauerpsiel's own tyrant, Herod, and to Robin Vote and her own related gestures. Given Barnes's familiarity with Hanfstaengl's experiences of Hitler, and her interest in this period of German history, such similarities between the physicality of baroque theatre and Fascist political spectacle, provide further hints that Nazi Germany exists as a subtext within *Nightwood*.

Despite these personal connections and insights into the Nazi regime, Barnes's preoccupation in *Nightwood* does not seem to be the identification and blame of individuals. This chapter's opening quotation from Green's *Renaissance and Reformation* suggests that the Thirty Years War and its aftermath in some way evoke contemporary political morality. The Trauerspiel regime combined aesthetic and political expression, while at the same time estranging ethical and political responsibility. Benjamin and Barnes both bring together these two periods in history, using the relationship between allegory and the Fall and stripping history back to the point at which moral judgement first evolved. While sovereignty or dictatorship is exposed as a flawed, vulnerable political practice through the indecision of the prince and the influence of his intriguer, the madness and subsequent death of this tyrant is not presented as morally edifying or instructive. Rather than analysing, commenting upon or accounting for the particular evils of Fascist rule, *Nightwood*'s affinities with the Trauerspiel are part of Barnes's determination to look backwards to the origins of evil itself as Coleman suggests. The novel's characters may suggest strong similarities with the political identities of the Trauerspiel, and their modern Fascist equivalents, but Barnes's use of such details remains subtle and not explicit. As her novel gestures towards the Holocaust and the atrocities of modern dictatorships, she seems to feel that to deal directly with the particular and the immediate is somehow inadequate or even impossible. The guilt of the dictator and the evil of the individual intriguer become secondary to the universal guilt of the created world, in a representation of history as repeated violent episodes of crisis inaugurated by man's Fall into subjective knowledge. As Benjamin concludes, it is this particular neglect of individual agency, the resolving of moral questions into examples of natural history that defines the Trauerspiel genre:

> It is not the moral transgression but the very estate of man as creature which provides the reason for the catastrophe. This typical catastrophe, which is so different from the extraordinary catastrophe of the tragic hero, is what the dramatists had in mind when – with a word . . . they described a work as a Trauerspiel.[88]

NOTES

1. Letter from Emily Coleman to Djuna Barnes, 27 August 1935, *Djuna Barnes Papers*, Special Collections and University Archives, University of Maryland, Series III, Box VII, Folder 3. Henceforth cited as *Djuna Barnes Papers*.
2. Green, *Renaissance and Reformation: A Survey of European History Between 1450 and 1660*, p. 328.
3. Gilbert-Dubois, *Le Baroque en Europe et en France*, p. 288.
4. Ibid. p. 288.
5. Green, *Renaissance and Reformation*, pp. 324–5.
6. Sitwell, *German Baroque Art*, p. 16.
7. Ibid. pp. 26, 18.
8. Green, *Renaissance and Reformation*, p. 328.

9. Letter from Emily Coleman to Djuna Barnes, 1 August 1935, *Djuna Barnes Papers*, Series II, Box III, Folder 6.
10. Letter from Emily Coleman to Djuna Barnes, 27 August 1935, *Djuna Barnes Papers*, Series II, Box III, Folder 6; Emily Coleman, Letter to Djuna Barnes, 5 November 1935, *Djuna Barnes Papers*, Series II, Box III, Folder 7.
11. Marcus, 'Laughing at Leviticus: Nightwood as Circus Epic', *Silence and Power*, p. 228.
12. Ibid. 229.
13. Barnes, Application for a Guggenheim Fellowship, mailed on November 4 1930, *Djuna Barnes Papers*, Series II, Box 8, Folder 26.
14. May, *Vienna in the Age of Franz Josef*, p. 39.
15. Barnes, *Nightwood*, p. 8.
16. May, *The Hapsburg Monarchy 1867–1914*, pp. 175–6.
17. Barnes, *Nighwood*, p. 4.
18. Quoted in Brigitte Hamman, *Hitler's Vienna – A Dictator's Apprenticeship*, p. 328.
19. Judson, *Exclusive Revolutionaries: Liberal Politics, Social Experience and National Identity in the Austrian Empire 1848–1914*, p. 226.
20. Pinnow, *History of German*; Sachar, *A History of the Jews*; Zedlitz-Trützschler, *Twelve Years at the Imperial German Court*; William, Crown Prince of Germany, *Memoirs of the Crown Prince of Germany*; Whitman, *Austria*; Conti, *The Reign of the House of Rothschild*.
21. Benjamin, *Origin*, p. 63.
22. Barnes, *Nightwood*, p. 9.
23. Ibid. p. 9.
24. Ibid. p. 40.
25. Ibid. p. 40.
26. Benjamin, *Origin*, p. 24.
27. Ibid. p. 66.
28. Barnes, *Nightwood*, p. 45.
29. Ibid. p. 61.
30. Benjamin, *Origin*, p. 71.
31. Barnes, *Nightwood*, p. 128.
32. Marcus, 'Laughing at Leviticus: Nightwood as Circus Epic', *Silence and Power*, p. 221.
33. Ibid. pp. 228, 230.
34. Benjamin, *Origin*, p. 69.
35. Barnes, *Nightwood*, p. 122.
36. Benjamin, *Origin*, p. 70.
37. Ibid. p. 85.
38. The German verse is quoted in Gillespie, *Daniel Casper von Lohenstein's Historical Tragedies*, p. 70.
39. Benjamin, *Origin*, p. 129.
40. Ibid. p. 90.
41. Miller, *Late Modernism: Politics, Fiction and the Arts between the World Wars*, p. 124.
42. Barnes, *Nightwood*, p. 48.
43. Ibid. p. 125.
44. Ibid. p. 111.
45. Benjamin, *Origin*, p. 89.
46. Barnes, *Nightwood*, p. 69.
47. Klossowski de Rola, *Alchemy – The Secret Art*, p. 7.

48. Benjamin, *Origin*, p. 98.
49. Barnes, *Nightwood*, pp. 72, 130.
50. Ibid. p. 69.
51. Roberts, *The Mirror of Alchemy: Alchemical Ideas and Images in Manuscripts and Books From Antiquity to the Seventeenth Century*, pp. 56, 110; Klossowski de Rola, *Alchemy – The Secret Art*, p. 108; Watanabe-O'Kelly, *Court Culture in Dresden from Renaissance to Baroque*, pp. 103–4.
52. Barnes, *Nightwood*, pp. 115, 134.
53. Ibid. pp. 85, 128.
54. Klossowski de Rola, *Alchemy*, p. 11.
55. Benjamin, *Origin*, p. 156.
56. Barnes, *Nightwood*, pp. 86–7.
57. Ibid. p. 88.
58. Benjamin, *Origin*, pp. 226–7.
59. Ibid. 229.
60. Barnes, *Nightwood*, p. 74.
61. Letter from Emily Coleman to T. S. Eliot, 25 October 1935, *Emily Holmes Coleman Papers*, Folder 10; and letter from Emily Coleman to T. S. Eliot, 31 October 1935, *Emily Coleman Papers*, Folder 10.
62. Letter from Djuna Barnes to Emily Coleman, 5 May 5 1935, *Emily Holmes Coleman Papers*, Folder 13.
63. Ibid.
64. Barnes, *Nightwood*, pp. 131, 133.
65. Benjamin, *Origin*, p. 232.
66. Buck-Morss, *The Dialectics of Seeing – Walter Benjamin and the Arcades Project*, p. 173.
67. Barnes, *Nightwood*, p. 137.
68. Benjamin, *Origin*, p. 232.
69. Benjamin, *Origin*, p. 229; Barnes, *Nightwood*, p. 136.
70. Benjamin, *Origin*, pp. 152–3.
71. Barnes, *Nightwood*, p. 51.
72. Benjamin, *Origin*, p. 152.
73. Williamson, 'The Divided Image: The Quest for Identity in the Works of Djuna Barnes', *Critique*, p. 74.
74. Kaup, 'The Neobaroque in Djuna Barnes', *Modernism/ Modernity*, p. 98.
75. Benjamin, *Origin*, p. 86.
76. Barnes, *Nightwood*, p. 139.
77. Benjamin, *Origin*, p. 72.
78. Benjamin, *The Arcades Project*, J78, 4, p. 366.
79. Benjamin, *Origin*, p. 227.
80. Barnes, *Nightwood*, pp. 136, 139.
81. Ibid. p. 43.
82. Benjamin, *Origin*, p. 227.
83. Shirer, *The Rise and Fall of the Third Reich*, p. 294.
84. William O'Shanahan, 'The Rise and Fall of the Third Reich: A History of Nazi Germany', *The American Historical Review*, 68.1, October 1962, pp. 126–7. See also Montgomery McGovern, *From Luther to Hitler: the History of Fascist-Nazi Political Philosophy*; Jeffrey Jaynes, 'Review of *The Fabricated Luther: The Rise and Fall of the Shirer Myth*' in *The Sixteenth Century Journal*, 27.2, 1996, pp. 515–17; Uwe Siemon-Netto, *The Fabricated Luther: The Rise and Fall of the Shirer Myth*; Peter F. Wiener, *Martin Luther – Hitler's Spiritual Ancestor*.
85. Barnes, *Nightwood*, p. 41.

86. Hanfstaengl, *Hitler: The Missing Years*, p. 171.
87. Peucker, 'Fascist Choreography: Riefenstahl's Tableaux', *Modernism/Modernity*, pp. 279–97.
88. Benjamin, *Origin*, p. 89.

4

NIGHTWOOD, BAROQUE SOUND AND SCHREI PERFORMANCE

Man may not believe that he is like the animals, he may not believe he resembles the angels. He cannot ignore one and not the other, he must know both.[1]

Critical accounts of *Nightwood* inevitably linger over Dr O'Connor's speeches, their authority, their repertoire of bewildering images, and above all, the sheer volume of text that Barnes devotes to this one voice. Voluble and larger than life, the character of the doctor dominates the novel and clearly exasperates T. S. Eliot and Emily Coleman, as their correspondence with Barnes during the editing process reveals. They urge her to silence and subdue him while moving other characters centre-stage, and I will return to their protests later in this chapter. Early reviewers were certainly preoccupied by this individual's 'stream of prodigious analysis', discovering an authority that structures the text through 'relentless confession counterpointed with oracular pronouncement', and more recent analysis has shared this focus.[2] Sherrill Grace is careful to distinguish between Dr O'Connor's relentless and flamboyant monologues, and passages of similar length attributed to the stream of consciousness technique. She argues that the doctor's outbursts can be compared with the monologues in Expressionist plays through their fragmentation, digressiveness, self-reflexivity and extravagant language.[3] This chapter uses Grace's brief suggestion as its starting point, arguing that many of *Nightwood*'s most distinctive and enigmatic qualities – its presentation of voice and gesture – can

---

be better understood through a study of Expressionist dramas as they appeared on the post-war German stage. These affinities between Barnes's writing and Expressionism can be applied to more than the style and structure of her novel; they shed light on her particular view of human identity and her sense of man's ability to communicate in a postlapsarian world. This style of drama is part of Germany's baroque legacy, and my analysis pays particular attention to seventeenth-century ideas of sound, expression and tableaux.

If Barnes's novel can be argued to engage with the German avant-garde of this period, then why have so few critical accounts explored the similarities between *Nightwood* and Expressionist theatre?[4] One can begin to answer this question by emphasising the distinction between Expressionist dramas as original texts, or translations, and the plays as they were later presented to the theatre-going public. As an American writer with a modest knowledge of the German language, Barnes had access to the English translations, but it is important not to overstate the number and quality of these editions. Few Expressionist plays had been published in English at the time of Barnes's trip to Berlin, with one notable exception being Ashley Dukes' accomplished translation of Georg Kaiser's *Von Morgens bis Mitternachts* (*From Morn to Midnight*). This was published by Henderson's in March 1920 for a performance by the Incorporated Stage Society, and Duke comments in his translator's note that 'it is, I believe, the honour to be a first tribute to contemporary German art'.[5] Both before this date, and once Barnes had arrived in Europe, her familiarity with Expressionist drama owed much to the productions that were staged in her native America and in Germany. In Berlin, in particular, the very distinctive performance styles and techniques that evolved around directors such as Max Reinhardt and Leopold Jessner mean that it is not enough to consider the printed texts alone. As a new breed of actor and director came to dominate theatre reviews, the texts themselves became of secondary importance. Barnes's sense of Expressionist theatre would have been shaped by the individual auteurs and celebrity performers responsible for interpreting these plays, and she heard about these innovations from her Provincetown colleagues before her career in journalism took her to Berlin in 1921.

That such links and similarities have been so little noted can be explained by the short-lived but intense period of ascendency enjoyed by Expressionist avant-garde techniques. As a result of the Nazi campaign against 'Entarte Kunst' (Degenerate Art), no prompt books from any major Expressionist performance remain, and so researchers lack this crucial insight into the world of the director and production ensemble. While German language texts may survive in reprinted editions that post-date Nazi Germany, information relating to the productions themselves is largely restricted to theatre reviews and studies by those who attended Expressionist plays. In this area of research, Günther Rühle's collection of German theatre reviews from the Expressionist period, and contemporary analysis of the movement by Hermann Scheffauer and Kenneth MacGowan are invaluable resources, as is David Kuhn's more recent *German Expressionist Theatre*.[6] Even before Fascism attempted to destroy all traces of Expressionist creativity, the 1920s 'Neue Sachlichkeit' (New Objectivity) movement had turned away from the defining features of Expressionism, its intensity and its distinctive representations of subjectivity. Avant-garde theatre became a sensitive register of Germany's situation after the First World War, and precisely because the art of the Expressionist actor and auteur had proved so responsive to Weimar Germany's sense of post-war crisis, further changes in socio-economic conditions made Expressionism's achievements vulnerable and easily superseded by performance trends that reflected new political and cultural concerns. Renate Benson argues that the movement's demise was so complete, and its native legacy so obscured, that by 1945, young Germans could only learn about Expressionism by turning to the work of Anglo-American writers such as Tennessee Williams and Eugene O'Neill.[7] Here they would find evidence of their cultural heritage as Expressionism's distinctive qualities re-emerged in the work of American writers. This chapter will suggest Barnes's novel *Nightwood* as another such resource for the reader in search of Expressionism's wider influence, and its debt to the baroque.

HALF-MAN, HALF-BEAST – *NIGHTWOOD* AND THE SCHREI PERFORMANCE STYLE

Although Expressionist dramas such as Reinhard Sorge's *Der Bettler* were written as early as 1912, the advent of war delayed their translation from text to stage, and Berlin audiences were among the last to be introduced to the new productions. Expressionism made its formal debut in German theatres between 1917 and 1918, and the Schrei (Scream) performance style that refers to the Expressionist cry or scream appeared first in Munich, Frankfurt and Dresden. Many of the early definitions of Expressionist acting come from Schrei performances, but as David Kuhns suggests, it is unlikely that early productions used the word self-consciously.[8] It has, however, been applied posthumously as a term that captures the vehemence and sense of underlying distress that became characteristic of particular Expressionist stage productions. Initially, this crisis was clearly associated with the anguish of battle – Walter Hasenclever's *Antigone* (1918) censures war from the vantage point of classical antiquity, Ernst Toller's *Die Wandlung (Transfiguration)* (1920) presents a march of limbless war casualties and Reinhard Goering's *Seeschlacht (Seabattle)* (1916) follows the crew of a German battleship as it moves inexorably towards death, through a text punctuated by cries and screams. As Expressionism's focus shifted to the more immediate problems of Weimar Germany's social and economic difficulties, the Schrei was often associated with the central actor and his wider ideological and potentially redemptive significance for society.

Schrei theatre did not reach Berlin until late 1919, so when Barnes arrived in the city, its techniques were still relatively innovative and experimental. While the moment of Schrei defines the acting technique in name, in practice, Schrei performance was a more complex and protracted process incorporating the actor's voice and body in a series of energetic and ecstatic configurations. One of the crucial features of such productions was the fact that movement or stasis and vocalisation were mutually defining components of the actor's repertoire, and I will examine this in more detail in my analysis of staged gesture and tableaux. At this point, it is important to emphasise the layered or interconnected nature of the Schrei. Gesture and vocalisation were not only inseparable, but the distinctive Schrei outburst extended far beyond a simple cry to include long and ecstatic monologues and movements that released intense emotion. Goering's play *Seeschlacht* is a fictional account of the fate of a First World War destroyer, inspired by accounts of the Battle of Skagerrak (Jutland) and its introduction states:

> Die Handelnden sind sieben Matrosen, die im Panzerturm eines Kriegsschiffes in die Sclatt fahren . . . Das Stück beginnt mit einem Schrei (The characters appearing in the play are seven sailors whose battlestation is in the bridge of a battleship on its way to a mission . . . The play begins with a scream.)[9]

So while the scream was often structurally climactic, appearing at the end of scenes or lengthy speeches, this was not always the case.

By examining *Nightwood* in the context of the Expressionist theatre, Barnes can be argued to engage with a long tradition of German drama and performance techniques, and their particular interpretation of man's affinity with the animal world. One of the defining features of Expressionism for writers such as Walter Benjamin and Richard Samuel was the movement's debt to seventeenth-century forms and values. For the baroque writer and artist, the painful conviction that man remained confined to a realm of immanence culminated in the creation of religious images that placed 'even Christ in the realm of the provisional, the everyday, the unreliable'.[10] Sixteenth-century representations had entailed symbolic forms and the promise of transcendence, but the seventeenth century portrayed the least mortal of men trapped within his creaturely identity. I have already argued that one of the defining features of baroque theology is the 'creatureliness' of man who becomes one with the realm of nature and this affinity between man and beast is revived within the Schrei performance style. Kuhns identifies this technique as representing humanity at its most primitively animalistic and its most spiritually sublime.[11] Schrei is an intense, emotional outburst from the subject caught between these two states, and the word translates to mean not only the cry, scream, shriek or shout of a human protagonist, but also the bray of a donkey or the screech of an owl. Bernhard Diebold's study of the various Expressionist performance styles groups them all under this definition, referring to the baroque philosopher Pascal's diagnosis of the human condition: 'man may not believe that he is like the animals, he may not believe he resembles the angels. He cannot ignore one and not the other, he must know both'.[12] It is this tension or split that produces the intensity of Expressionist and baroque vocal performance. The Expressionist writer and theorist Kasimir Edschmid argued that the stage presence of the proto-Expressionist actor and writer Frank Wedekind had restored a forgotten baroque quality to the German stage. With Wedekind's acting 'the fanatic ardour of the greatest German dramatists thrust itself forward with a truly national baroqueness'.[13] This was his legacy for the Schrei performer, who sustained such ardour or intensity because his body and expression were held between points of contrast – beast and angel, stasis and dynamism, speech and movement.

In 1921, the year of Barnes's first visit to Germany, the Munich publishing house Kurt Wolff published Alfred Brust's *Die Wölfe. Ein Winterstück (The Wolves: A Winter Play)*, the controversial drama that gave Expressionism its most literal representation of man's baroque creaturely identity. Set in the forests of East Prussia, the play tells the story of a village clergyman, Tolkening, and his wife Anita. We soon learn that the couple sleep separately, that the clergyman is more than a little wary and fearful of his wife, and that she in turn is preoccupied by two captive wolves that are kept caged outside their home – 'the wolves – She loves them passionately'.[14] Tolkening's focus is explicitly the life of the soul and he is at pains to remind his wife of the spiritual side of her nature: 'There is something deep down inside you striving towards our Great Lord'.[15] Anita keeps the male and female animals separated by a metal grill so that they cannot mate, and, slowly starving the female wolf, she one day allows her to escape knowing that her husband will have to shoot the creature to ensure a swift, merciful end and the safety of the villagers. While she has a clear affinity with the male animal that she keeps, the reader or audience are guided to the possibility that this may be an erotic fascination by dialogue that takes place between the clergyman and his friend Dr Joy. The innocent Tolkening admits to the terrifying power and beauty of this creature and the fact that his wife returns 'glowing' from entering its cage, while his friend's questions establish Anita's lack of interest in the female animal and the fact that the two wolves are kept separately so there can be no cubs, and the male remains frustrated. That evening, with her husband away hunting the she-wolf in the forest, Anita leads the male wolf to her bedroom and her piercing scream is heard off-stage, followed by the sounds of a struggle and then breaking glass. She is found on the bed, naked, her throat ripped out, the wolf having jumped through the closed window.

Robin Vote shares Anita's animal-like movements, the wordless final scream, the desire for communion with an animal that potentially lends itself to sexual interpretation, and the neglect and lack of emotional connection with her child, but Barnes offers more explicit suggestions that her characters are trapped between spiritual and creaturely extremes than these similarities. In the opening pages she describes, 'the very Pope himself shaken down from his hold on heaven with the laughter of a man who forgoes his angels that he may recapture the beast'.[16] Dr O'Connor repeats to Nora the following confession from one of the women of his night-world – 'I am an angel on all fours, with a child's feet behind me, seeking my people that have never been made, going down face foremost'.[17] Their angelic identities can only be represented while they are on all fours, with their faces turned downward, giving them the silhouette of an animal. Dr O'Connor draws parallels between his own knowledge and celestial wisdom, claiming that like the angels and prophets, he has eaten a book, and yet he carries his hands like a dog raised up onto its hind legs. The characters of *Nightwood* may look to the Catholic faith for comfort and inspiration, but simile and metaphor repeatedly remind us of their kinship with the world of beasts.

Having created her characters between these two extremes, Barnes punctuates the text of *Nightwood* with screams and cries that are generally presented as climactic moments at the end of chapters. As the first chapter closes, we hear of an incident in which Dr O'Connor listens to the music of Albeniz's *Córdoba*, a consummate performance, during which the musician looks over his shoulder and urges the doctor to observe some monks in the nearby piazza. The doctor, however, finds an intimate encounter between two king snakes at the window-sill far more engrossing, while the musician screams and puts his hands over his eyes. Here, Barnes contrasts the harmonious sound of music with the non-rational, discordant communication of the scream. During the final section of Chapter 2, Robin gives birth to her son Guido, uttering cries of despair as language fails to adequately express her distress. The third chapter ends with an exclamation of sound without rational meaning, as Nora sees Robin in the arms of another woman. Barnes writes that 'Nora said "Ah!" with the intolerable automatism of the last "Ah!" in a body struck at the moment of its final breath'; the utterance is once again without rational meaning and deliberation, somehow remainimg closer to the body and the trauma of death, rather than the intellect.[18] Chapter 4, 'The Squatter', closes with the cry of the young English girl who has been forced to witness Jenny's violent attack on Robin and, although Barnes uses a concluding exclamation that contains language and readily intelligible meaning, the sound retains an unnatural quality, ill-befitting the speaker. The child is somehow alienated from her own expression – 'In a voice not suitable for a child, because it was controlled with terror: "Let me go! Let me go! Let me go!"'.[19] In 'Watchman, What of the Night', Dr O'Connor reports his own scream as he too cries out when Jenny strikes Robin. As 'Go Down, Matthew' draws to a close, the doctor utters yet another wordless scream, while the final chapter ends with Robin's bark, and these two final outbursts will prove particularly important in analysing Barnes's use of sound and language in *Nightwood*.

BARNES'S AND BENJAMIN'S DISAVOWAL OF LANGUAGE

So if Barnes had become familiar with Expressionist Schrei performances, why did she adopt similar techniques in *Nightwood*, and how do they relate to the text as a whole? Steeped as the novel is in the images and details of a seventeenth-century aesthetic, and as critics such as Diebold and Kuhns have traced Schrei's origins to the baroque concept of man's divided spiritual and creaturely identities, then one can begin to answer these questions by returning to baroque theories of language. How does Schrei as an instant of pure sound unencumbered by rational meaning relate to the image of the beast or creature? Benjamin's study of the Trauerspiel establishes an antithesis between sound and meaning, particularly meaning in its written form. He illustrates this opposition with the example of meaning created under the formal restraint of verse and reason: 'Language which on the one hand seeks, in the fullness of sound, to assert its creaturely right, is on the other hand, in the pattern of the alexandrine, unremittingly bound to a forced logicality.'[20]

For the baroque, sound is a medium that eludes interpretation while the written word seeks to capture truth and meaning. Benjamin writes of the spoken word being afflicted by meaning, it interrupts and thwarts man's full creaturely expressive potential, resulting in melancholy and he cites the work of the seventeenth-century German theologian and mystic Jacob Böhme, so as to distinguish between the human language of intellectual discourse and the language of nature or creatures. The latter manifests 'not as a realm of words . . . but as something resolved into its sounds and noises' – it is predominantly sensuous rather than instrumental.[21]

In *Nightwood*, Robin draws closest to the realm of nature and the creature, and her use of expression keeps close to this evocative, unspoken register that defies meaning. As Barnes herself emphasises in her correspondence, she allows Robin to say very few words during the course of the novel.[22] What remains memorable and distinctive within this character's apparently restricted repertoire of expression are her wordless cries during childbirth, her bark at the novel's conclusion and the songs that Nora fails to understand or imitate. Robin herself sings, 'changing the sound from a reminiscence to an expectation', and 'when the cadence changed, when it was repeated in a lower key, [Nora] knew that Robin was singing of a life that she had no part in'.[23] On each occasion modulation of expression happens at the level of sound, through pitch, rhythm or intonation, and not intellectual meaning. This predominance of harmonious or shrill sound rather than words seems to confirm a sense of alienation between Robin and her lover. Nora observes that when Robin withdraws out of sight to resume her song she 'gave back an echo of her unknown life more nearly tuned to its origin'.[24] Expression without human language and its semiotic conventions appears to allow Robin to separate herself from human intercourse and relations and to draw closer to a distant point of origin. I have argued that, while *Nightwood* contains dates and events that allow the novel a specific historical moment, it also takes as its wider frame of reference history as it originated in the book of Genesis at the time of Creation. It is Barnes's preoccupation with the universal, tainted quality of linguistic expression that leads her to mock Peter Neagoe's (Muffin) calls for the inclusion of cheer and hope in the novel:

> You have to become an accomplice to be any kind of audience. To learn – the apple, paradise etc. Our two Peters eat the fruit and still sit there in paradise inert, beneath the tree of knowledge, or at least Muffin does.[25]

For Barnes, to question the dark vision of *Nightwood* is to deny the fact that one is complicit in its context of fallen knowledge and a flawed use of language.

At this point, Benjamin's 1916 essay 'On Language as Such and on the Language of Man' provides an interesting counterpart for *Nightwood*'s final pages, with its suggestion that language is a possibility for all beings, regardless of the relative naivety or sophistication of their individual consciousness. The essay can be read as an early counterpart of Benjamin's discussion of baroque allegory, sharing its conviction that human language is corrupt as it forfeited its original identity at the moment of the Fall. By examining this critique of fallen discourse, it becomes possible to detect points of similarity with Barnes's fictional representations of human and creaturely communication. In the world of Genesis, language itself was the catalyst for creation – in the beginning was the word – and man shared in this privileged expressive medium through his gift of 'naming'. This human language of naming 'partook most intimately in the divine infinity of the pure word'.[26] With 'name', Benjamin suggests a translation of the mute being of all entities into sound. The premise of the essay is Benjamin's sense of language as communication, a definition that expands to cover the communicative potential of creaturely nature and objects: 'there is no event or thing in either animate or inanimate nature that does not in some way partake of language, for it is in the nature of each one to communicate its mental contents.[27] The original human language of naming preserved the discrete qualities of the thing named, allowing its integrity to remain unaffected. The acknowledged entity was enlivened, or as Benjamin states 'completed', by the act of naming in a way that did not overwhelm or misrepresent its own mental being.

By suggesting that a creature or object has its own 'mental being' or 'mental contents', Benjamin does not seem to argue that it is necessarily cognisant, or capable of thought as we know it, but that it can express itself in language. Such pure language is medial rather than semiotic, allowing a quality of immediacy that dissolves the definition of perception as a process involving a subject, process of knowing and thing known. 'Languages, therefore, have no speaker, if this means someone who communicates through these languages. Mental being communicates itself in, and not through a language'.[28] This emphasises that there is no subject prior to language, no agent witnessing, examining and using that medium. Nor is there an object set apart from language whose meaning must be referred to or conveyed, but 'what is communicable in a mental entity is its linguistic entity' – form and content, object and language are one, and this is the magical quality of language that he refers to.[29]

It is here that Benjamin introduces the idea that languages are of different densities: 'The differences between languages are those of media that are distinguished as it were by their density'.[30] To understand this concept of linguistic density, it is helpful to imagine the mental being of an entity situated within the medium of language as matter exists within space. The density of matter is a measure of its spatial–material ratio, a gauge of how open or diffuse its material arrangement is, or of how intensely this material constituent is compacted or compressed. Creatures and material objects have a greater linguistic density, as their linguistic being is closely bound to their material existence, and therefore not directly communicable in our terms. Human language is more readily communicable, as it is less tightly compacted or dense, but Benjamin insists that it remains only one surface of configuration, and its limits are determined by translation. He associates the acquisition of knowledge in paradise with the initiation of an imperfect practice of translation. Here the gift of naming passed over into a structure of language characterised by exteriority. He distinguishes between the pure sound of naming and the fallen character of language as it descends into concept, abstraction and metaphor with the subsequent evolution of judgement and its attendant distinctions between good and evil. The translation of human language is like metaphor, an act of self-referral, reducing the expressive potential of other creatures and objects to human terms. Against this error, Benjamin advocates an ideal definition of translation in which meaning no longer appears to exist outside language. He states that 'translation is removal from one language into another through a continuum of transformations . . . not abstract areas of identity and similarity'.[31] This is not translation as we understand the term – the passing over of one language into another – but instead, a process in which every individual language is transfigured by, and in turn transfigures, other languages. The momentum of such translation is therefore one of simultaneous exchange between two linguistic registers or identities. 'All higher language is a translation of lower ones, until in ultimate clarity the word of God unfolds, which is the unity of this movement made up of language'.[32] By this, Benjamin seems to indicate that all language is merely a reflected, diminished derivative of the absolute creativity of divine language, but that the latter exists as a shared but distant point of origin, magnet-like, pulling the less sophisticated languages towards it. Judgement in particular, as an instrumental and abstract evolution of human language, defies translation by turning away from that continuum of transformations.

In Chapter 3's discussion of the Trauerspiel characters and *Nightwood*, I show Barnes using details of baroque language to undermine the value of judgement, but in earlier works we also find a sense of the corruption and futility of language as it passes into the realm of morality, justice and legal vocabulary. Her 1917 short story 'The Earth' tells of two Polish sisters, Una and Lena, who work the family land after their father's death. In the hope of promoting collaboration and goodwill, the father has stipulated that each alternate foot of land be left to one sister, so partition and working profitably as an individual becomes impossible. Lena has not studied at school, but her sister Una has learned just enough to allow her to trick her sister into signing over her share of the farm land and becoming an employee rather than a partner. Una draws up an unsophisticated document, claiming that the lawyers require Lena's signature to confirm joint ownership of the land. When Lena realises the deception, she disappears with the two farm horses, the carriage and the Swedish farmhand who had been courting her sister. The letter of the law that initiated this family rift now proves useless, as Una sets her grievances before a neighbour; 'He gave her some legal advice and left her bewildered'.[33] Lena eventually returns married, content, and with a babe-in-arms. She asks her sister to kiss the baby, and in an act of submission far more powerful and compelling than the signature on the legal document, Una complies: '"Thank you", Lena said as she replaced the shawl. "Now you have left your mark, now you have signed"'.[34] The sister whose expression and communication are most closely bound to the realm of matter is ultimately most powerful and effective.

Barnes's sense of the degeneration and vulnerability of human language shares other similarities with Benjamin's critique. In Chapter 3, I examine the many links between *Nightwood*'s Dr O'Connor and the Trauerspiel intriguer – the allegorist responsible for assigning significance to the world around him. Within the world of the Trauerspiel, therefore, this figure must assume a particular burden of guilt in relation to the flawed practice of translation that transforms creaturely sound into human language and Benjamin states that 'the conversion of the pure sound of creaturely language into the richly significant irony which re-echoes from the mouth of the intriguer is highly indicative of the relationship of this character to language. The intriguer is the master of meanings'.[35] This conceited language, that has claimed for itself the task of translating all other entities into its own medium, contains a fatal flaw. Whether referring to Benjamin's theories of baroque language in the Trauerspiel study, or in his 1916 essay, human language appears to function imperfectly, as it is no longer an adequate medium of translation for either creaturely utterance or the spiritually privileged language of prelapsarian 'naming'. Caught between the two, trying in vain to force the linguistic being of other entities into its own linguistic and semantic structures, such language is necessarily erratic. Allegory, as the dominant expressive medium of *Nightwood*, has illustrated this instability through its inherent contradictions, reversals and ambiguities. This language strives to liberate itself from the context of traditional meaning, and Benjamin talks of its being 'constantly convulsed by rebellion on the part of the elements which make it up', as sound and syllable break away from their practised, familiar medium of meaning, or, in Benjamin's terms, their habitual linguistic surface.[36] The word 'convulsion' indicates the violence and tension that precede the moment of freedom or transition between the two languages, and this can be argued to produce the intensity of the scream. If the intriguer transforms creaturely utterance into the meaningful language of man, then Dr O'Connor's final scream can be seen as the point at which he relinquishes his role as the intriguer, the giver of meanings, and falls back into the baroque realm of creaturely sound, unencumbered by the desire for knowledge, definition and intellectual mastery. His desire to verbally explain, excuse and elaborate the secrets of the night-world is finally overwhelmed as, with the Schrei climax, his voice escapes the conventions of language and interpretation.

Barnes's decision to use the wordless sounds and cries of Schrei performance during *Nightwood*'s climactic moments serves to frustrate the reader's expectation that such passages will offer clues, insights and revelations. This apparent suspension of narrative does not, however, represent an absence of communication. While in Benjamin's essay, it is the language of nature that is silenced or distorted by human language, Barnes's decision to set language aside at these key points in the text can be argued to attempt a partial redress of this original sin. We learn that Robin's tendency to communicate through cries and songs of inscrutable meaning takes her closer to a point of origin. This is because Barnes wishes to associate her with a form of expression that precedes the over-determined, conceptual discourse of the Fall. *Nightwood* becomes a text straining at the point of reversal of our corrupt development of language, and Barnes's use of Schrei exposes the arrogance, hollowness and presumption of man's attempt to express everything in his world using his own linguistic terms. In the novel's final scene, as both Robin and Nora's dog appear to communicate wordlessly through a synchronicity of movement, a strained physicality, and finally through crying and barking, that reversal seems complete. The novel closes with an encounter that could be said to offer a configuring of two very different linguistic surfaces, and what seems crucial is the idea of movement or exchange between man and creature. This scene recounts a meeting in which the boundaries or identities of a perceiving, communicating subject and a creaturely object blur and dissolve, as Robin opens herself to transformation and the subsequent expression of something imperfectly apprehended, a form of communication that certainly lies beyond words. Benjamin's ideal remains the God-given gift of naming, but *Nightwood* draws postlapsarian language backwards through the vagaries of allegory, towards an ending that privileges the sensuous, non-rational 'pure sound of creaturely language'.[37]

Long before *Nightwood*, Barnes had experimented with language that gives itself up to the fullness of creaturely sound. In her 1929 short story 'Cassation', the protagonist Katya is introduced to the four-year-old daughter of Gaya. Barnes holds this young child within a creaturely identity by repeating the pronoun 'it': 'Now it was four years old and yet it did not walk, and I never heard it say a thing, or make a sound, except that buzzing cry. It was . . . a sacred beast without a taker'.[38] Gaya urges Katya to regress to a similar state, forsaking instrumental language, reason, logic and scholarship, forgetting argument and philosophy and cultivating instead a state of intellectual oblivion. Katya refuses and leaves the house, returning only once to find the mother 'sitting up in bed with the child, and she and the child were making that buzzing cry, and no human sound between them'.[39] Here the significance of the slide into a creaturely register is ambiguous; while the regression of Gaya allows her to connect with and nurture her own child, there is a definite sense of escape and relief as Katya leaves for the outside world.

Barnes makes a baroque definition of creaturely sound the premise of her final short story 'The Perfect Murder', published in 1942 in the seventy-fifth anniversary issue of *The Harvard Advocate*. The protagonist, Professor Anatol Profax, is a dialectologist and a flâneur of the audible as opposed to the visual cityscape. He wanders the streets of New York recording expressions and figures of speech, so as to classify the speaker for his particular science. For the Professor, speech and language define mankind, but 'what he had yet to lay his hands on was someone who *defied classification*'.[40] Fascinated by the class he names 'the Impulsives', among whom 'there was little labial communication', he hopes to rediscover a quality of human expression that is both primitive and melancholy:

> His Mistress was *Sound*, that great band of sound that had escaped the human throat for over two thousand years. Could it be recaptured (as Marconi thought it might) what might come to the ear? . . . Only a vast, terrible lamentation which would echo like the 'Baum!' of the Malabar Caves.[41]

His ultimate case-study would therefore gesture towards prelapsarian language, focusing on utterance that predates reason and concept. One day, the

Professor encounters a mysterious female circus performer who claims to have let go of the bar of her trapeze and died from the fall. She introduces herself as a strange hybrid – she is at once the Elephant Woman, a trapeze artist, a milliner, hungry, and in her own words, 'a *Trauma*'. As with Robin Vote, her identity combines the creaturely with a terrible quality of innocence and purity: 'I am the purest abomination imaginable'.[42] Barnes's description also emphasises the performer's irrational speech and her lack of engagement with the environment around her, as she neither sits down nor looks at anything. The Professor has finally discovered an aural phenomenon that defies classification, but as Trauma falls onto some musical instruments in his room, he experiences a sensation unknown to him, and feeling at once both cold and gentle, he slits her throat with a penknife. Apparently dismembering her, he places her piece by piece into a trunk. She quickly vanishes, only to reappear in a hansom cab that briefly runs alongside the Professor's own carriage on his journey. In the nonsensical discourse of the Elephant Woman and in the strange composite images of *Nightwood*, the natural and the impossible combine, as Barnes reveals a determination to open out the expressive potential of language and to challenge its power to mediate and capture truth. As she twists language away from the over-precision of its derivate rational forms, she celebrates the enigmatic qualities of sound and expression that hold themselves aloof from judgement and meaning. In 'The Perfect Murder', she goes one step further, as this blend of the real with the magical and outlandish shapes plot and action. Looking back on his terrible deed, the Professor is full of regret at not having at least recorded the circus performer's name, but for the reader the murder is an instinctive and 'perfect' act as Trauma's primitive, irrational expression must be set beyond interrogation, analysis and written classification, all stages of abstraction that corrupted language with the Fall. It is, of course, a perfect murder as the body vanishes of its own accord, but also because the 'great secret' of a more authentic form of expression is preserved.

Defying Eliot and Coleman

Schrei was not simply defined by the creaturely outburst – before this, came the stream of rhetoric known as the ecstatic monologue, and it is here, with the doctor's lengthy, intense bursts of oratory that Barnes engages closely with this particular theatrical convention. As Emily Coleman and T. S. Eliot were helping her to revise the manuscripts for *Nightwood*, both urged her to reduce the volume and number of these eloquent, figurative monologues. In a letter dated 12 August 1936, Eliot tells Barnes that he favours the edited manuscript in which much of Dr O'Connor's conversation has been deleted: 'there is a good deal of the book besides the Doctor, and we don't want him to steal everything'.[43] A year earlier, as Coleman was reading the early manuscripts, she writes 'too much here of the doctor's stories. Still needs cutting! It makes

MODERNISM AND THE THEATRE OF THE BAROQUE

no difference how fascinating they are. It doesn't belong in this book' and later in the same letter she complains that 'it is not life to give a monologue, it is tiring the other person, who would not be listening and the reader feels it'.[44] The inattention of the second party, and the ascendancy of the monologue are integral parts of the Schrei performance style, and the fact that Barnes intended Dr O'Connor's ecstatic speeches to dominate *Nightwood* in this way may in part be explained by the doctor's affinity with Expressionist acting techniques. With the novel's penultimate chapter 'Go Down, Matthew', his speech and gestures bear particularly close resemblance to those of the Schrei performer. Just as the brief, reticent Telegrammstil utterances of the Expressionist actor often culminated in a lyrical and impassioned outburst, so restraint and brevity in movement often erupted into the ecstatic Schrei climax. Such reduction and reserve was designed to produce an enormous emotional pressure that the actor could then channel into subsequent vocal or physical aspects of their performance. In 'Go Down, Matthew', the doctor's movements are subtle, brief and controlled, providing no physical release of tension as his torrent of questions, exclamations and philosophising unfolds. His first action is violent and emphatic as he bangs his fist down on the table, but as his monologues increase in length and intensity, his gestures become more subtle as he lifts his chin and lowers it again, raises the decanter up to the light, holds the stopper to his nose, and then brings his palms together again. On one occasion, the doctor appears to desire a change in his position, but some unnamed constraint means he is unable or unwilling to accomplish this. Barnes keeps the doctor seated at Nora's table throughout this exchange, and while he helps himself to a glass of port on arrival, Barnes makes it clear that Nora brings the decanter to him once he has sat down. Nora, meanwhile, is described pacing about the room, and striking the table, a contrasting physicality that draws attention to the doctor's subdued gesturing. Emotion that can find no expression through these reductive techniques must result in a climax of passion or rage and the doctor's speech contains brief glimpses of this constrained but mounting pressure: '"Stop it! Stop it!" he cried', and 'then in his loudest voice he roared . . . '.[45]

As we move towards his final Schrei outburst, the reader becomes aware of an increasing number of exclamations, and lyrical and figurative sentences that have remained neutral in tone and largely unqualified by adverbs, are suddenly delivered 'sarcastically' and 'angrily', anger that Barnes describes three times.[46] In terms of movement, once the doctor rises from his seat after some twenty-six pages of desk-bound discourse, he resumes the awkward, non-mimetic physicality of the Expressionist actor, staggering as he reaches for his coat and standing in melancholy silence. Here, Barnes maintains the balance that was a hallmark of 'baroque contrast' in Schrei performance styles. This contrast sustained the actor's body at a point of tension between extremes of movement and speech, physical paralysis was accompanied by eloquence and dynamism in terms of thought and speech; and vice versa, as the gesturing, active body coincided with silence and bewilderment. Just before the novel reaches its close and the doctor gives his final discourse, Barnes also emphasises his divided baroque angelic/creaturely identity. He boasts to Nora that he is one of the uninhabited angels, and yet a few pages later, an unidentified voice pulls the doctor's identity in the opposite direction: 'Funny little man . . . the Squatting Beast, coming out at night'.[47] The tension that traditionally underlies the Schrei outburst has been established at the level of movement, and through the figurative devices used to describe the doctor. After pages of abstract and protracted discourse on the night, the Schrei reaches its ecstatic climax with the following passage, as Dr O'Connor makes his exit: 'Get out! Get out! he said. What a damnable year, what a bloody time. How did it happen? Where did it come from? He began to scream with sobbing laughter'.[48]

In a letter dated 27 August 1935, Coleman urges Barnes to revise the novel's manuscript by giving more narrative space to the lovers and less to the doctor – 'you have not concentrated on the tragedy of Robin and Nora . . . the effect of the novel ought to be the effect of Othello, a woman's Othello'.[49] Barnes had other ideas. She creates the doctor as *Nightwood*'s Schrei persona, because traditionally the central character's performance must distinguish him from the rest of the Expressionist ensemble, all of whom will lack his insight and understanding. Patterson offers an example of this dramatic technique from Kaiser's *From Morn to Midnight*, a play in which the cashier leaves behind his dull, repetitive job, and is transformed through a series of encounters with other citizens.[50] With each transformation, the actor needed to alter his performance to include the ecstatic techniques of Schrei stagecraft; alterations in speech and movement that traditionally suggested the acquisition of knowledge and set the central actor apart from the less complex abstract figures around him. By identifying the doctor with these methods, Barnes can be argued to subtly highlight his importance as the central consciousness of the novel, giving a certain authority to his discourses on the night-world and its characters, despite Eliot and Coleman's extensive editing and their determination to diminish his central role. His final Schrei outburst can therefore be heard as an accurate diagnosis of the collective fate of the novel's characters as well as explaining his claims to exclusive knowledge:

> 'I know it's all over, everything's over and nobody knows it but me
> – drunk as a fiddler's bitch' . . . He tried to get to his feet, gave it up.
> 'Now', he said, 'the end – mark my words – now nothing but wrath and weeping!'[51]

Schrei Gesture and Tableaux

Schrei performance techniques were not limited to distortions of speech. Gestures took the actor's body beyond its mimetic or naturalistic identity, as the figure of the protagonist took on the jagged, stylised angularity first seen in Expressionist paintings and woodcuts. Movement became more difficult to identify with action, intention and effect, becoming an art of posturing and mime. This sculptural use of the actor's body had again defined the Trauerspiel dramas of the German baroque, where the section of the performance that we would recognise as the interlude, presented displays of expressive statuary. Examples and ideas from previous scenes were reinforced through visual representation, as a tableau vivant with up to six or seven such examples of frozen movement arranged on stage at one time. The Expressionist will to abstraction and distortion meant that these baroque displays were continued, but without their mimetic or illustrative function, and they became incorporated into the main body of the production. The Expressionist director Leopold Jessner was well known for keeping actors transfixed on stage during episodes when they were silent. Kenneth MacGowan's 1922 review of this director's work recalls that:

> Jessner's actors, if they are not speaking and if their emotions are not being very markedly played upon, are held motionless. They do not move a limb, I have heard that, in a ballroom scene, Jessner kept dozens of players absolutely immobile in the poses of the dance, while the two principals talked.[52]

This particular use of the actor's body was not always initiated by the director, as Expressionist playwrights demanded sculptured forms within their stage directions. Reinhard Sorge's play *Der Bettler* (*The Beggar*), for example, calls for a group of prostitutes and lovers to posture as a monument. Mel Gordon's analysis of a particular subdivision of the Schrei drama, the Ich (I or ego) drama, describes the central ecstatic actor surrounded by secondary figures who arrange themselves in an unusual tableau – 'dozens of choral performers who created grotesque but picturesque poses'.[53] New techniques in stage lighting could create a sharpness of line, emphasising the rigidity of the posed body, and removing any unintentional shading and blurring of form caused by footlights. Gösta Bergman suggests that the precision of the statuesque Expressionist figure was not the result of disciplined physicality alone: 'actors are sculptured forth by a simultaneous illumination by means of two or more light sources'.[54]

In *Nightwood*, the reader also has a strong sense of the human form transfixed and sculpted by the author. During the opening chapter at Count Altamonte's party, we hear twice of the living statues, entertainers who are remarkable for their ability to hold a pose without movement for long periods of time. This is the Count's favourite form of entertainment, a preference that, significantly, leads Felix to assume that the Italian aristocrat is German. Barnes also describes Robin and one of her lovers as if they are extensions of a garden statue, as the two women are held motionless in their intimacy:

> Looking down into the garden in the faint light of dawn, [Nora] saw a double shadow falling from the statue, as if it were multiplying . . . she saw the body of another woman swim up into the statue's obscurity, with head hung down . . . her arms about Robin's neck, her body pressed to Robin's, her legs slackened in the hang of the embrace'.[55]

This sculptural quality of Expressionist stagecraft referred to the human form carefully arranged and frozen in time, but also to gestures that the actor had begun and was not allowed to complete. The unfinished gesture, and the movement broken off half-way, seemed particularly important in Expressionist performance and, again, Barnes includes this detail in her own character's heavily stylised postures, continuing to stress the affinity with sculpted form. She offers an elaborate description of the lovers Jenny and Robin sitting at a table:

> Jenny leaning far over the table, Robin far back, her legs thrust under her, to balance the whole backward incline of the body, and Jenny so far forward that she had to catch the small of her legs in the back rung of the chair [. . .] thus they presented the two halves of a movement that had, as in sculpture, the beauty of a desire that is in flower, but that can have no burgeoning, unable to execute its destiny.[56]

Some Expressionist poses or interrupted movements, such as the crucifix pose, were repeated so often they became the hallmarks of the era. The final scene of Georg Kaiser's *From Morn to Midnight* takes place in a Salvation Army hall, where 'the background is formed by a yellow curtain embroidered with a black Cross'.[57] As the cashier shoots himself, Kaiser's stage directions state that he 'has fallen back with arms outstretched against the Cross on the back wall.'[58] Another popular pose transfixed the actor with his arms raised high in the air. Barnes introduces a similar gesture to *Nightwood*, when we are given the image of Robin, clasping her baby son, her arms high in the air. The narrative makes it clear that Robin is caught as if suspended in this pose, and she is later described by Nora repeating this gesture with the doll they share. These passages seem to belong to a theatrical production rather than a novel, with Robin prompted by a stage direction – each time she performs this incomplete gesture, whether she is holding young Guido or the doll, she moves centre-stage into the middle of the room.

Barnes underlines the suspended or abridged quality of movement in these passages by repeating a similar scene at a later stage, but this time allowing the gesture to proceed to its completed position. As mentioned earlier, on one occasion, Robin does hurl the doll to the floor and crushes it with her heel, its china head covered with dust. The stylised arrangement of Robin and Jenny's bodies, frozen in their broken arc of movement, is likewise repeated later in the text, at the end of the carriage tour of the Paris woods. This time the proximity of the two bodies results in a fully realised gesture of violence:

> Jenny struck Robin, scratching and tearing in hysteria [. . .] and as Jenny struck repeatedly Robin began to go forward as if bought to the movement by the very blows themselves, as if she had no will, sinking down in the small carriage, her knees on the floor, her head forward as her arms moved up in a gesture of defense; and as she sank, Jenny also as if compelled to conclude the movement of the first blow, almost as something seen in retarded action, leaned forward and over, so that then the whole of the gesture was completed'.[59]

As with her earlier description of the two lovers seated either side of a table, Barnes uses painstaking detail to document each vector of movement, in a slow-motion tableau of execution and physical response that seems to defy the intention and control of the protagonists. The fact that Robin's maternal bond with her son, and her relationship with Jenny, have been presented to the reader through images of sculpted movement that have remained incomplete for many pages, increases our sense of the tension behind this abridgement. As Kuhns' study of the original dramas concludes, 'this pattern of compressive reduction and explosive expansion, in fact, was the essential rhythm of Schrei ecstatic acting'.[60] According to the laws of Expressionist stagecraft, the destructive intensity behind each finally accomplished action is inevitable. As readers considering *Nightwood* in the context of these performance techniques, we have a heightened sense of the violence and power inherent in these movements, as the tension of physical restraint is released.

BARNES'S EMBLEMATIC MODERNISM

While Schrei expression may have suggested to Barnes certain details that correspond with her own critique of language, how does this use of non-linguistic sound, so powerful in the context of a theatre production, translate into the world of *Nightwood*? One particular quality of Expressionist ecstatic performance, seemingly present from the time of the movement's earliest works, may have led Barnes to consider it for the very different register of a novel. Herbert Blau's analysis of Oskar Kokoschka's early Expressionist drama *Mörder Hoffnung der Frauen* (*Murderer Hope of Womankind*) suggests that an entire performance could be carried out at the level of Schrei intensity, and that the scream could thereby assume a visual or material quality. This play's ritualistic and brutal confrontation between man and woman and their companions ends in the death of every character except the central male protagonist. The drama, with its many cries and screams, leads Blau to write:

> What seems palpable about the play, even visceral on the page, is that it requires a staging . . . pitched visually at the summit of a scream, not the *Ich* or *Geist*, but a *Schrei*, with every decibel soaked in blood.[61]

The idea that Schrei could become visibly manifest, or somehow assume a material stage presence, may have led Barnes to consider similar images for the pages of her novel. In short, Schrei performance was never simply a single cry, an absence of language or a scream – as a climactic moment, it was both visible and audible, and therefore completely sensually engrossing. This method of acting is described as the 'absorption of sound into sight' and is epitomised in the performances of Werner Krauss:

> Apparently it would have been impossible to separate the vocal element from the physical element of his acting as it is to distinguish between the sensation of a wild predator's shriek from that of its physical leap-to-the-kill. We don't hear as much as see the animal scream so absorbed is the aural into the more dominant visual image.[62]

This blend of abstract, irrational sound and exaggerated physicality allowed Schrei a peculiarly graphic quality that can be applied to two of *Nightwood*'s most startling scenes. Dr O'Connor's final appearance in the novel places him in the classic Expressionist crucifix position as he falls forward on to the table making the shape of a cross, and in the same passage he makes his final scream: 'he came down upon the table with all his weight, his arms spread, his head between them'.[63] Robin's last moments find her animal-like, on all fours, crying and barking, and on both occasions it is difficult to say which component of the Schrei outburst is most powerful. As with their counterparts on the German stage, movement or stasis and vocalisation have become mutually defining. Barnes also adapts this technique of complementary sound and movement, sharing the scream and posture between two separate characters – Robin's sculptural pose as she embraces another woman is paired with Nora's 'Ah!' and her fall to her knees. Barnes uses a scene that effectively alienates Robin and Nora to suggest their intimacy – the Schrei moment usually attributed to one individual is here inextricably the work of two protagonists.

So in *Nightwood*, Barnes has produced a novel that is both striking and unusual in its stylised gestures and movement and its extravagant rhetoric, both qualities which find strong parallels on the Expressionist stage. At the same time, the theories behind Schrei and Trauerspiel performance echo her own conviction that man is trapped between a spiritual and animal identity. The novel does, however, represent a turning point in Barnes's work – it is the first significant text to be submitted for publication without illustrations. Her interviews and early journalism often included portrait sketches of the subject, such as her drawings of James Joyce and the journalist Irvin Cobb.[64] *The Book of Repulsive Women* has its Beardsleyesque figures, while *Ladies Almanack* and *Ryder* contain images that imitate or reproduce the style of French folk art publications, notably the 1926 *L'Imagerie Populaire*. In the case of *The Book of Repulsive Women*, some controversy remains over the pairing of individual rhythms and images, but the illustrations of *Ladies Almanack* and *Ryder* have an explicit connection with their text. As Douglas Messerli concludes in his 1994 introduction to *The Book of Repulsive Women*, one might go so far as to say 'that Barnes's literary method is, in fact, an 'emblematic' one, in that her writing generally relies on visual elements that supplement, intensify and clarify aspects of the language'.[65]

The Expressionist Schrei performance style had suggested to Barnes a repertoire of heavily stylised techniques that allow her to continue this illustrative or emblematic form of writing, but without the inclusion of separate illustrations. The poses and gestures of the Schrei performer with their attendant vocal outbursts, adapted to the world of *Nightwood*, create images of graphic fixity and extensive detail like those of an illustration. The visual image is, however, suggested and not set before the reader in printed form. While sculpting the human body into strong and distinctive lines, Barnes can also select and withhold elements of the image, so that we are at times left with little more than a sharply executed silhouette. *Nightwood* translates established images from Barnes's work into more avant-garde, abstract representations, as becomes clear when comparing Robin with the female who is beloved of the Beast Thingumbob in *Ryder*. In Barnes's earlier novel, the character Wendell goes fishing with Julie and Timothy and is asked to tell them a story. He obliges with the tale of the Beast Thingumbob, a creature that slays lions, has wings and paws and yet is able to feel compassion and anger. Thingumbob's beloved is a daughter of the underworld, who accepts the Beasts' love, but who must die as she gives birth to its ten sons, returning to the gods at the point of her death. Her strange female form combines animal and human features:

> of large limbs, and of a beauty outside of the imagination . . . She was terrible in her ways, which simply means that her ways were not our ways . . . Her feet were thinly hoofed . . . and her face was not yet.[66]

The accompanying illustration depicts the beloved with a Junoesque body and a blank, featureless face, with the exception of two eyebrows. *Nightwood*'s Robin Vote is similarly heavy in build, and one of the few facial details we are given is, likewise, her finely arched eyebrows. Both Robin and 'the beloved' are described as beautiful, in 'the beloved' that beauty is anonymous and elusive – 'outside of the imagination' and 'her face was not yet', while Dr O'Connor says that recalling Robin after she has left 'was as easy as the recollection of a sensation of beauty without its details', and admits that at no time did he ever have a clear image of her.[67] The difference lies in the fact that 'the beloved' is literally a hybrid of woman and beast, she can only materialise as a mythical figure in Wendell's folk tales, fixed by the illustration. While her hooves remain real, replacing feet, Robin's image is developed through many lines to become an eland with 'a hoof raised in the economy of fear', a metaphor that is so layered and complex that the reader is never quite sure how the eland relates to Robin.[68] She remains a woman. The fact that the characters of the night-world speak and move according to Schrei technique, becomes an even more subtle way of linking them to animal counterparts, as the technique is itself the result of tension between human and creaturely identities.

Identifying these similarities does not help us to finally categorise *Nightwood*; Barnes did not set out to write her own Anglo-American Expressionist novel, adapting the love story of Nora and Robin to the ideas and conventions established by German stage performances. The Schrei and its related physicality do, however, offer Barnes a pre-existing model of expression that allows her to write within her favoured 'emblematic' mode, while engaging with the avant-garde tendency towards representational ambiguity and instability. These devices of abstraction, excess, anonymity, obscurity and autotelia join narrative techniques such as the complex, layered metaphor, all of which ensure that the night-world and its inhabitants remain inscrutable. In the same way, the theories behind Schrei and Trauerspiel performance are not exclusively responsible for the novel's preoccupation with man's spiritual identity and his affinity with the animal world. Barnes had been exposed to the innovations in German avant-garde theatre, art and writing for many years, and *Nightwood* can be seen as the product of her responses and interest in certain formal and thematic aspects of this movement. The close connection between the distinctive physical form of the Expressionist actor and the language and voice of their performances, allows Barnes to continue the strong bond between word and image that Messerli considers central to her aesthetic, while offering an expressive medium that is developed from the very themes and identities that preoccupy her own writing.

Benjamin's analysis of Charles Baudelaire suggests that the poet parried the shocks of modernity with his body. The distinctive physicality of Expressionist stagecraft did not just attempt to deflect those shocks but sought to refashion them into a creative, expressive medium. As Kuhns writes: 'an allegorical face and body . . . a typifying rhythmic pattern of movement, and evocative voice – to name the historical moment in this way, to embody its chaotic spirit, was hopefully to acquire some control over it'.[69] Chapter 2 has described the exchange of qualities between the modern subject and object within the practice of allegory, and the way in which the decay, petrifaction and death associated with allegory enter the inner life of that subject. The Expressionist performance techniques that I have examined in relation to *Nightwood* provide the ultimate experience of this internalising of allegory's destructive momentum. By making graphic presentations of subjective and usually intense inner states, the Expressionists turned the human subject into an object. At the extreme of subjectivity that is Schrei Expressionist performance, man himself becomes an abstract and empty signifier, without developed characterisation, psychological complexity and mimetic detail – he becomes the frozen, sculptural emblem of his own allegorical intention. More importantly, these details from German avant-garde theatre suggest that allegory is not only the underlying creative medium in *Nightwood*'s figurative language and characterisation, but also in the physicality and vocalisation of its protagonists.

NOTES

1. Kuhns, *German Expressionist Theatre – The Actor and the Stage*, p. 103.
2. Desmond A. Hawkins, 'Views and Reviews', *The New English Weekly*, 29 April 1937, p. 51, quoted in Marcus, 'Mousemeat: Contemporary Reviews of Nightwood', *Silence and Power – A Reevaluation of Djuna Barnes*, pp. 201–2. Louis F. Kannestine finds Dr O'Connor's speeches lengthy and 'overwhelming', while for Judith Lee, this voice is prolific because of the sheer number of tasks its undertakes: Louis Kannestine, *The Art of Djuna Barnes: Duality and Damnation*, p. 93; Lee, 'Nightwood – The Sweetest Lie', *Silence and Power – A Reevaluation of Djuna Barnes*, p. 216.
3. Grace, *Regression and Apocalypse – Studies in North American Literary Expressionism*, p. 154.
4. Grace's chapter 'The Dark Night of the Soul – Djuna Barnes's Nightwood', in Part Three of *Regression and Apocalypse*, is the only existing study of any length to examine Barnes as an Expressionist writer.
5. Kaiser, *From Morn To Midnight – A Play in Seven Scenes*, p. v.
6. Rühle, *Theater für die Republik, 1917–1933*, a wide-ranging collection of theatre reviews from the Expressionist period; Scheffauer, *The New Vision in the German Arts*; MacGowan *Continental Stagecraft*.
7. Renate Benson, *German Expressionist Drama: Ernst Toller and Georg Kaiser*, p. 9.
8. Kuhns, *German Expressionist Theatre*, p. 101.
9. Goering, *Seeschlatt (Seabattle) – The German Text with an English Translation*, p. 1.
10. Benjamin, *The Origin of German Tragic Drama*, p. 183.
11. Kuhns, *German Expressionist Theatre*, p. 103.
12. Diebold, cited Ibid. p. 103.
13. Edschmid, cited Ibid. p. 103.
14. Brust, *Die Wölfe. Ein Winterstück*; Brust, *The Wolves: A Winter Play*, in *Seven Expressionist Plays: Kokoschka to Barlach*, p. 128.
15. Ibid. p. 117.
16. Barnes, *Nightwood*, p. 4.
17. Ibid. p. 81.
18. Ibid. p. 57.
19. Ibid. p. 67.
20. Benjamin, *Origins*, p. 210.

21. Ibid. p. 204.
22. Letter from Djuna Barnes to Emily Coleman, November 8 1935, *Emily Holmes Coleman Papers*, University of Delaware Library, Newark, Delaware, Folder 12.
23. Barnes, *Nightwood*, p. 51.
24. Ibid. p. 51.
25. Letter from Djuna Barnes to Emily Coleman, November 8 1935, *Emily Holmes Coleman Papers*, Folder 12.
26. Benjamin, 'On Language as Such and on the Language of Man' *Selected Works, Volume I, 1913–1926*, p. 69.
27. Ibid. p. 62.
28. Ibid. p. 63.
29. Ibid. p. 63.
30. Ibid. p. 66.
31. Ibid. p. 70.
32. Ibid. p. 74.
33. Barnes, 'The Earth' in *Smoke and Other Early Stories*, p. 107.
34. Ibid. p. 108.
35. Benjamin, *Origin*, pp. 209–10.
36. Ibid. p. 207.
37. Ibid. p. 209.
38. Djuna Barnes, 'Cassation' in *Spillway and Other Stories*, p. 26.
39. Ibid. p. 30.
40. Djuna Barnes, 'The Perfect Murder' in *The Harvard Advocate, 75 Anniversary Edition*, 1942, p. 6.
41. Ibid. p. 7.
42. Ibid. p. 9.
43. Letter from T. S. Eliot to Djuna Barnes, 12 August 1936, *Djuna Barnes Papers*, Special Collections and University Libraries, University of Maryland Libraries. Series II, Box 4, Folder 60.
44. Letter from Emily Coleman to Djuna Barnes. 27 August 1935. *Djuna Barnes Papers*, Series II, Box 3, Folder 6.
45. Barnes, *Nightwood*, pp. 121, 124.
46. Ibid. p. 131.
47. Ibid. p. 134.
48. Ibid. p. 136.
49. Letter from Emily Coleman to Djuna Barnes, 27 August 1935, *Djuna Barnes Papers*, Series II, Box 3, Folder 6.
50. Michael Patterson, *The Revolution in the German Theatre, 1900–1933*, p. 78.
51. Barnes, *Nightwood*, p. 136.
52. MacGowan, *Continental Stagecraft*, p. 139.
53. Gordon, 'German Expressionist Acting', p. 46.
54. Bergman, *Lighting in the Theatre*, p. 371.
55. Barnes, *Nightwood*, p. 56.
56. Ibid. p. 61.
57. Kaiser, *From Morn to Midnight: A Play in Seven Scenes*, p. 47.
58. Ibid. p. 58.
59. Barnes, *Nightwood*, p. 66.
60. Kuhns, *German Expressionist Theatre: The Actor and the Stage*, p. 108.
61. Blau, 'From the Dreamwork of Secession to Orgies Mysteries Theatre', p. 272.
62. Kuhns, *German Expressionist Theatre: The Actor and the Stage*, p. 108.
63. Barnes, *Nightwood*, p. 136.
64. Barnes, *Interviews*, pp. 291, 131.

65. Messerli in Barnes, *The Book of Repulsive Women: 8 Rhythms and 5 Drawings*, p. 8.
66. Barnes, *Ryder*, p. 119.
67. Barnes, *Ryder*, p. 119, Barnes *Nightwood*, p. 39.
68. Barnes, *Nightwood*, p. 36.
69. Kuhns, *German Expressionist Theatre: The Actor and the Stage*, pp. 226–7.

5

BAROQUE BODIES: AGENCY, EXPRESSION AND MOVEMENT

Strike up, my boy, – no fear – no hesitation/ Til you begin no chance of inspiration.[1]

Allegory, Trauerspiel and Schrei performance have sculpted a body that is rigid, tense, lifeless or fractured, a body in which vitality and intention are frustrated and subdued, and whose rhythms follow the futile repetitions of allegory or the destructive violence of absolute sovereignty. This chapter will examine two baroque sources, the philosophy of Baruch Spinoza and the Italian commedia dell'arte, both of which reverse the above aesthetic while remaining centred within the human body. The trance-like paralysis of the Trauerspiel prince and the empty, forlorn practice of collecting objects so as to assign new meaning to them are replaced by the disciplined physicality of a body that is sensitive and subtle, and, above all, susceptible to the movements and gestures of bodies placed around it. An overwhelming sense of isolation and alienation disappears, making way for a performance imperative to connect with, and respond to, the world around the individual, generating graceful and elegant lines, and easy, fluid gestures. As Isadora Duncan, Edward Gordon Craig and Wyndham Lewis respond to these sources with varying degrees of optimism, enthusiasm, and in Lewis's case, no small amount of scepticism, I will examine their understanding of a baroque body's unscripted action.

ISADORA DUNCAN: SEVENTEENTH-CENTURY PHILOSOPHY AND MODERN
DANCE

Isadora Duncan was very aware of her vision's debt to the seventeenth century
and as she returned to Berlin in early 1905, she wrote to her lover Edward
Gordon Craig, including a quotation from an unreferenced text that had
clearly bought her pleasure. Having acknowledged Baruch Spinoza's work as
'Divine Philosophy', she draws Craig's attention to the following tribute to
Spinoza and his fellow pantheist, Giordano Bruno:

> Their miserable existence and death in this western world is like that of
> a Tropical plant in Europe. The banks of the *Sacred Ganges* were their
> spiritual home. There they would have led a peaceful and honoured life
> among men of their own mind.[2]

Haeckel himself repeats again and again in *The Riddle of the Universe* that
'we adhere firmly to the pure, unequivocal monism of Spinoza', claiming to
have discovered in *Ethics*, and in Goethe's more recent championing of this
philosophy, the most profound and authentic philosophy available to the
modern world, an authority to which science, philosophy and religion must
return after a lapse of some 200 years.[3] The confidence and consistency of
Spinoza's argument provided 'the purest and most rational *monism*' and he is
credited with being the first thinker to understand the profound importance
of monist principles and to introduce them to the discipline of science. For
Haeckel, his work is all the more extraordinary as it evolved without the
empirical data and proofs available to scholarship in the late nineteenth and
early twentieth centuries.[4]

Duncan's recognition of *Ethics* as Divine Philosophy was not an ironic reference to the text's apparent dissidence and heresy, an interpretation that alienated scholars and theologians during the seventeenth and eighteenth centuries.
Spinoza did undermine orthodox Christianity by conflating God and Nature
at the expense of revelation and a personalised deity, but God nevertheless
remains at the centre of his monist cosmology as the immanent cause of all
phenomena. Rather than creating the universe by stages or as one unique
undertaking, God becomes the eternal cause of everything that happens in the
natural world. This is not the pantheism of mystical experience, but one of
precise, monist logic, whereby 'God or a substance consisting of infinite attributes, each of which expresses eternal and infinite essence, necessarily exists'.[5]
For both Spinoza and Descartes, to define substance is to establish the structure of the universe and the phenomena included and understood within that
structure. While *Ethics* evolves as a critique of Descartes' theory of knowledge,
the text also represents an affirmation of the latter's metaphysical dualism in
many of its propositions. The first and most significant definition shared by

the two is that of substance itself. Descartes proposed three different categories of substance, including descriptions of essence and individual bodies, and these Spinoza rejects. It is Descartes' third category of substance as *causa sui* (*cause of itself*) that becomes the one exclusive concept within *Ethics*, and all of its attributes must be explained in terms of the nature of that one universal substrate: 'Except God, no substance can be or consequently, be conceived'.[6] Within both dualist and monist theories substance as *causa sui* is therefore synonymous with God.

The remaining two categories that Spinoza adopts from Cartesian philosophy are those of *attribute* and *mode*. He writes that 'an attribute is what the intellect perceives concerning a substance, as constituting its essence'.[7] Despite the infinite number of attributes that constitute *Deus sive Natura* (*God or Nature*) man can only discern two infinite *attributes* – thought and extension – and these are not simply mind and body respectively. Extension is the system of physical bodies or objects occupying a position in space and determined by laws of motion, while its counterpart is the system of ideas existing within the *attribute* of thought. So we can arrive at a limited but satisfactory understanding of God through both *attributes*, but they do not qualitatively reflect substance, suggesting instead the range or diversity of substance itself. Spinoza's concept of the *mode* refers to transient, finite modifications of substance, dependent properties or individuals defined by God that remain partial, imperfect differentiations or reflections of *Deus sive Nature*.

An understanding of Duncan's engagement with this philosophy requires first a familiarity with the shifts in terminology introduced by Haeckel's appropriation of the laws of substance for evolutionary science. In texts such as *The Riddle of the Universe*, the *attribute* of extension becomes matter or infinitely extended substance, and *motion and rest* becomes energy or force. Haeckel concurs with Spinoza's definitions in that 'all individual forms of existence, are but special transitory forms – accidents or modes – of substance', and soul or spirit are described as 'sensitive and thinking substance'.[8] Although Spinoza identifies two *attributes*, claiming equivalent significance for both, his focus seems to be the realm of extension and the fundamental laws of *motion and rest* that underlie the existence of all phenomena within his monist system. This bias of exposition in *Ethics*, and the inevitable emphasis on laws of movement, transformation and form that preoccupied Haeckel while interpreting Spinoza's work, make this philosophical approach of particular interest to a performer intent on developing a discourse of dance that is both the inspiration for choreography and a means of connecting human beings with the wider universe. Before Duncan's period of study in Germany, she had travelled to Paris, taking a studio in the Rue de la Gaieté. Her copybooks dating from this period contain sections from Rousseau's philosophy of education, but more significantly with respect to her later engagement with Spinoza's monism, quotations from Descartes' theory of mind in relation to body, theories that she went on to contradict.[9]

CHOREOGRAPHY AND *CONATUS*

In *The Touchstone* of October 1917, Duncan's commentary 'The Dance and its Inspiration' was published in the form of a Greek philosophical dialogue. Here, she responds to the question 'how is woman to learn the correct form of her body?' by acknowledging the merits of exercise in the gymnasium and the quiet contemplation of sculptured beauty in museums.[10] Duncan's ultimate suggestion, however, is that 'her own body must become the living exponent' of that form through the art of dance.[11] Her writing repeatedly defines this particular art-form in opposition to ballet with its rigid movements, restrictive costumes and defiance of gravity, and is equally dismissive of most other dance forms favoured by modernism – the rhythms of jazz behind the modern fox-trot and the ungainly routines of the Charleston. She goes so far as to claim that 'I am not a dancer ... What I am interested in is finding and expressing a new form of life', and it is here, with this fundamental rediscovery of the connection between movement and form in the individual body, and the equivalent characteristics in all matter, that her debt to Spinoza begins.[12] The dialogue continues by asking where the dancer is to search for this great fountainhead of movement and the answer is one of reproach for the questioner:

> You ask this ... as if woman were a thing apart and separate from all other life, organic and inorganic, but she really is just a link in the chain and her movement must be one with the great movement which runs through the universe.[13]

These claims of kinetic identity between man and universe are certainly unconventional; in particular, the continuity suggested between lithe dancer and inorganic life, but both ideas can be explained by returning to individual passages of *Ethics*, where the concept of *conatus* and the differences between living and non-living matter are set out. For Spinoza, the difference between inorganic and organic entities is simply one of structural complexity, with sensation, energy and a degree of consciousness or subjectivity possible even in inorganic molecules. Haeckel developed this definition by stating that all matter contained soul, by which he meant a level of psychic activity, and this in turn allowed him to explain evolutionary science in hylozoistic terms. In *Die Lebenswunder* (*The Wonder of Life*) he controversially replaced the Christian Trinity with the eternal Trinity of Substance – motion, matter and inner subjectivity or feeling – with the latter quality unifying all matter.[14]

Having established this fundamental unity, Spinoza goes on to outline his sense of identity, but this theory is set out in terms of velocity and movement and not substance: 'Bodies are distinguished from one another by reason of motion and rest, speed and slowness, and not by reason of substance'.[15] Rather than each individual body establishing itself as discrete and apart from other bodies, Spinoza's theory of *conatus* allows the body to be constantly modified and influenced by those bodies around it as well as being defined by its own apparent nature. Monist individuality is, therefore, essentially relative and not exclusive. *Conatus* refers to the individual body's power of self-maintenance or integrity, and identity is preserved if the proportion of *motion and rest* or energy among the ultimate particles that make up the body remains uniform. All bodies manifest *conatus*, a striving towards self-preservation, and provided the overall balance of *motion and rest* is sustained, then their identity is stable and their power is potentially enhanced by interaction with external bodies: 'The human body, to be preserved, requires a great many other bodies, by which it is, as it were, continually regenerated.[16] So each person or entity exists at the centre of an elaborate network of connections with their environment, a context that Spinoza understood to include the air pressure around a body, social and cultural organisations, collectives and inanimate objects as well as other organic life-forms. The cosmos as a whole becomes an eternally restless, reciprocating, striving system of energy, and this rhythm, or as Duncan puts it 'the great movement which runs through the universe', underlies her sense of the dancer as a mere link in that chain of exchange.[17]

Looking inside the human body, Spinoza also acknowledges that to be an individual is to be made up of other bodies and that 'the human body is composed of a great many individuals of different natures, each of which is highly composite'.[18] Change in any individual is attributed to the speed of its elementary particles and their ability to harmonise and coalesce. For Duncan, form and movement in the natural world are always broken down into these elementary particles that underlie Spinoza's theories, and their characteristic manifestation or patterning as waves. She claims that 'the waters, the winds, the plants, living creatures, the particles of matter itself obey this controlling rhythm of which the characteristic line is the wave'.[19] It is the task of enlightened dancers, through observation and study, to attune themselves to these natural movements and to make them the inspiration for their performance. In her discussion of the pursuit of ideal form and movement, Duncan insists that the dancer 'shall be painter, but as part of a great picture she shall mingle in many groups of new changing light and color'.[20] Stuart Hampshire says of Spinoza's monism that 'the changing colours and sounds to which we refer in the language of common-sense are properly described in terms of light-rays and vibrations and these in turn are ultimately explained (by Spinoza) as exchanges of energy among elementary particles'.[21] In *The Touchstone*, Duncan confirms that this is also her perspective, and having already broken her own analysis down into rhythms of elementary particles, she asks the rhetorical question: 'does not sound travel in waves, and light also'.[22] The rhythmic unity of these waves of light, colour and sound, and the susceptibility to exchange and affect suggested by *conatus*, allow her to claim a sublimation of the dancer's body into rays or waves of particles. In her 1920 'The Philosopher's Stone of Dancing', she begins by acknowledging dancers who discipline the body into movement, and others who lead the body into dance by concentrating the mind and recalling feelings or experiences. Her ideal, however, is a third category of dancer who can convert the human body into a luminous fluidity, 'the flesh becomes light and transparent, as shown through the X-ray – but with the difference that the human soul is lighter than these rays'.[23] In another description, it is not only waves of light but waves of sound that effect the desired sublimation. Here, she discovers the solar plexus as the central spring of all movement and cultivates the ideal state for her dance by focusing attention and strength in this one centre: 'I found that thereafter when I listened to music the rays and vibrations of the music streamed to this one fount of light within me – there they reflected themselves in Spiritual Vision, not the brain's mirror, but the soul's'.[24] The latter distinction between brain and soul was to become a crucial one for her monist discourse.

When discussing the bounding movement of animals and birds that have their liberty, Duncan also refers to the undulating waves that characterise the ocean, and time and time again she refers to an eternal quality for all movement. In her lecture to the Berlin Presse Vereine, 'The Dance of the Future' ('Der Tanz der Zukunft'), she claims 'each movement reaches in long undulations to the heavens and becomes a part of the eternal rhythm of the spheres' and this is a description that derives from Spinoza's contradiction of Cartesian motion.[25] Descartes had argued that motion was added to the universe during creation as the result of the will of a transcendent divinity, and that change perceived through the *attribute* of extension arose from this single intervention or event. Spinoza's metaphysics contradicts this doctrine by arguing that movement is innate within matter and that the quantity of motion in the universe has always been constant while manifesting or arranging itself differently across time. When Duncan talks of the eternal movement of particular phenomena within nature, she does not mean that they have existed as a constant ratio of *motion and rest* from a distant point in time until the present, but rather that the movement which defines *conatus* in monist philosophy has no intellectually identifiable beginning at all; it has always been present. Nor has there at any point in time been stasis or torpor in this baroque world-picture, the 'rest' delineated in Spinoza's description of *motion and rest* is simply an equilibrium achieved between the forces or energies countering one another in the particular body or bodies analysed. As Spinoza writes in Section Two of *Ethics:* 'A body which moves or is at rest must be determined to motion or rest by another body . . . and that again by another, and so on, to infinity'.[26] In 'The Dance of the Future' Duncan claims that the self-expression of the accomplished female dancer will illustrate this eternal chain of movement within nature, revealing how each part is transformed into the next, and descriptions of her dancing certainly stress the fluid interconnectedness of gesture and posture. Developing the principle of *conatus* within her choreography, she argues that each movement contains within it both previous movements and the movements that were to succeed those of the present moment:

> the primary or fundamental movements of the new school of dance must have within them the seeds from which will evolve all other movements, each in turn to give birth to others in an unending sequence of still higher and greater expression.[27]

The dancer thereby produces sustained motion capable of eternal renewal.

When Lillian Loewenthal described Duncan's philosophy, she stressed the desirability of smooth continuity in movement and an absence of abrupt, abbreviated or incomplete gesture.[28] The movements themselves were shared by all active human beings, unlike the painstakingly executed postures and the interrupted movements of the ballerina. Isadora and her pupils performed fluid sequences of jumps, elevations, skipping, walking, reclining and spinning, but these were refined and intensified beyond the everyday, befitting the strong, disciplined and supple body of the dancer. It is the monist quality of sustained movement in the dancer's body, and its exchange of *motion and rest* with the surrounding world, that the American modernist painter Abraham Walkowitz seems to capture in his sketches and drawings of Duncan. Walkowitz was first introduced to his muse in the studio of August Rodin, and his fascination with Duncan's form and choreography led him to produce some 5,000 pictures of her, always portraying her engaged in dance. Her heavy body and strong classical lines lent themselves well to his bold, simplified sweeps of graphite and colour, and Walkowitz continued to produce these images long after Duncan's death in 1927. Some of these pictures, such as the 1916 crayon and graphite *Isadora Duncan*, do not illustrate the dancer's body in isolation, but go on to include strokes and swirls framing Duncan's outline. Unlike the sculptural bodies of baroque tableaux and Schrei performance, whose abridged movement suggests tension, stasis and jagged, isolated form, Walkowitz's images capture both a single gesture or pose and the continuing exchange between dancer and her environment. In the *Sunday Call* of May 1941, he offers an explanation for this aura of lines around her body: 'See, I draw a circle in the air, you cannot see it, but it is there just the same . . . The swirls represent the forces of Isadora's dance', and the analysis goes on to acknowledge that the parallel lines indicate the impact of her movement on the space that surrounds the dancer.[29]

Duncan envisaged movement as the way in which an individual soul expresses itself, but the ideal dance that she celebrates in her theory expresses both the dancer's soul and a world of correspondences between man and cosmos that have *conatus* and *motion and rest* as their organic basis. Descartes' metaphysical dualism had argued that mind and body represented two distinct systems, with mind constituting a separate substance and the faculty of reason and intellect protected from the changes and modifications manifest in nature. Spinoza's deductive monism no longer associated mind with reason and consciousness in this way, but rather his insistence on the shared continuity of matter, energy and sensation throughout nature established an organic definition of mind that resolved the problematic duality. This rejection of Cartesian intellect and the subsequent ascendancy of body are behind Duncan's description of intellect as a subsidiary or derivate process in our interaction with the environment. In her autobiography, *My Life*, she writes: 'The brain after all is but the superfluous energy of the body. The body, like an octopus, will absorb everything it meets, and only give to the brain what it finds unnecessary for itself'.[30] This analysis follows closely the definitions of *Ethics* that describe the susceptibility of the human body and its potential to be enhanced in a greater variety of ways by the *motion and rest* of its environment when compared with plants, animals and objects. By 'absorb', Duncan means the body's ability to be regenerated by other bodies according to the principle of *conatus*.

The ultimate goal of her dance in both theory and performance is to transcend the Cartesian split between mind and body and she hopes to achieve this by cultivating form and movement that will somehow realise the simultaneity of the two: 'the dancer of the future will be one whose body and soul have grown so harmoniously together that the natural language of that soul will have become the movement of the body'.[31] Time and time again, she acknowledges a distinction between 'brain' and 'soul', with the former interpreted according to the limited Cartesian sense of intellect and the latter a correlate of mind in the full sense of Spinoza's definitions, linking man to the cosmos through the monist assertion that all matter possesses soul, subjectivity and sentience. As motion is the fundamental principle structuring causality, change, stasis and identity in the monist universe, and soul is a material entity, it seems a natural progression for Duncan to believe that soul can be best expressed through movement in the human body, a movement that is in complete harmony with *motion and rest* as exhibited by the wider universe. She believed that the dancer's movements and gestures were not simply interpretations or reproductions of thought or emotion, or *modes* experienced under the *attribute* of thought, but were instead the thoughts and emotions themselves. In this, she followed Spinoza's assertion that the mind is the expression in idea or thought of the successive states of the body, or that human perception experienced under the *attribute* of thought is essentially the counterpart of changes in the human body. It is a theory of choreography that repeats the monist conviction that mind and body may be experienced or conceptualised independently because they occur under different, incommensurable *attributes*, but are, in fact, ultimately identical and without the sense of intellect-led causality and reaction suggested by Cartesian dualism.

Duncan's style of dance and its primary influence are often cited as specifically Greek, and given the time that she and her brother Raymond spent studying Hellenic sculpture, vases and bas-reliefs in the British museum and the Musée du Louvre, the pilgrimage to Athens and the Temple built at Kopanos as the family home, this connection is perhaps inevitable. Despite this undeniable fascination with Greek culture and civilisation, her choreographic art owed little to crude imitation and as the artist Eugène Carrière suggests: 'she thinks of the Greeks, and only obeys her own self'.[32] Nor does this particular aspect of her research and devotion represent a distraction from monist philosophy. As Haeckel's chapter 'God and the World' emphasises, all the great Hellenic thinkers before Plato were convinced of the essential unity of the universe, *apeiron*, nature and God, body and spirit. He names Anaximander of Miletus, Empedocles, Thales and Heraclitus as examples of scholars who promoted pantheistic or monist beliefs. The hours that Duncan spent studying Greek artworks represent, instead, an attempt to recover the inspiration and the state of consciousness from which these recorded movements evolved. As Duncan sees the body itself as a mere instrument for the expression of soul, to focus on the Greek pose or gesture as an end in itself would serve no purpose. She sought instead to work backwards from these physical ciphers or hieroglyphs and towards the impulses from which they originated. They represent a merging of classical civilisation, baroque philosophy and contemporary art that lends her dance a timeless quality.

So analysis of Duncan's theory reveals that the body is the substance through which soul or spirit manifests in the world. Haeckel had focused on matter and forces of nature that could be applied to morphology, but Duncan returned to a philosophy that is more akin to the doctrines of *Ethics* in its focus on the human body and soul. While many religions had granted human beings an exclusive subjectivity grounded in the conviction that they possess an immortal soul, Duncan shares the monist interpretation of human subjectivity as inherently flawed and dependent, and by following the baroque concept of *conatus*, she defines that subjectivity for her reader and audience as a phenomenon that extends far beyond the visible, physical outline or presence of the body, and is constantly modified and revitalised by surrounding bodies. That subjectivity is not focused in the mind and, as with its counterpart in the realm of baroque allegory, it exists in a realm of immanence where reason has been displaced by more humbling interpretations of human knowledge that emphasise qualities shared with other aspects of the natural world. As with allegory and the Trauerspeil's Tragedy of Fate, the object assumes a certain power over the vulnerable and unstable subject as rigid distinctions between the two disappear. In terms of theory, at least, the spontaneity of her technique, and the fact that choreography evolves from impulses peculiar to the *conatus* of each individual, acted as checks to imitators of Duncan's success, because the dancer could no longer rigidly adhere to the details of scripted performance. Dance itself was not seen as a taught repertoire of pose and gesture, but as a means for the mortal finite *mode* that is the individual performer to access and participate in the eternal dynamism of nature. This in turn connected the audience to the harmonising waves of energy that flowed through the body of the dancer, allowing Duncan to assert the redemptive potential of her particular discipline and expression of life.

EDWARD GORDON CRAIG AND *THE MASK'S* COMMEDIA DELL'ARTE

In his beautifully illustrated *Scene* of 1923, Craig detailed the four decisive phases that he believed to define the evolution of theatre. The commedia dell'arte dominates the entire third stage, preceding modern perspective scenery while the first scene in his history is the stone edifice that formed a backdrop to the Greek dramas, and then performance drifts to the austere medieval church, where both audience and actor unite in worship, observing the spectacle of suffering and martyrdom. The medieval onlooker soon tires of the tableaux and the maimed body of Christ set against the suffocating gloom of the church. Craig's spectators then walk out into the sunshine, finding themselves transported to the late sixteenth century, where they are soon intrigued by three strange figures moving against the yellow-grey of an urban wall. The body, once transfixed with pain, has been replaced by laughter and great freedom of movement: 'The same three strange figures leaping and gesticulating . . . not *really* at all like those images with the torn faces . . . they are laughing all the time'.[33] This is the birth of the commedia dell'arte, and the audience is a little unsettled at first by so much energy and irreverence, but they are always delighted, and the theatre itself has become a simple street or a mound of earth.

Craig's essay 'The Actor and the Ubermarionette' first appeared in *The Mask* in April 1908, many months before he and Dorothy Nevile Lees discovered, translated and published the many sources that would allow them their detailed account of the commedia. So, given that the Italian comedy was to become one of the most significant subjects of Craig's research into the history of theatre, how does it follow on from the ideas set out in the 1908 essay and how could it enhance the Art of Theatre? The Ubermarionette is something of an enigma in Craig scholarship thanks to the fact that, however many times he returns to this term, his definition of the model actor remains strategically inexact. He may suggest the many theatrical flaws that he wishes to leave behind, the original inspiration for his ideal, and the qualities of movement he aspires to, but precisely who or what the Ubermarionette should be has prompted much disagreement. Olga Taxidou and Patrick LeBoeuf have explored the possibilities of string puppets, giant marionettes, actors hidden within padded costumes and behind masks, Craig's emphasis on theatrical technique, and the apparent contradictions between the commedia player and the ideal of the Ubermarionette.[34] This figure is clearly designed to replace the actors of the Victorian theatrical tradition, as they appear on the realist stage. The Ubermarionette is not, Craig insists, a legacy of the doll, but rather a descendant of the stone images of ancient temples at a time when the human body was not used as material in the Art of Theatre. He locates the kingdom of the original divine puppet or marionette in Asia, where the figure was used to represent man in ceremonies that celebrated Creation or the realm of Death. Unlike the actor or the modern puppet, these early theatrical forms embody a certain grace, reserve and subtlety, qualities that were lost as the public began to seek self-reflective, mimetic representations. Craig tells of the arrival of two women who try unsuccessfully to imitate the appearance and gestures of the temple puppet; the resulting excess of emotion, self-consciousness and personality of this wretched caricature 'is the first record in the East of the actor'.[35] The body of this theatrical personality is unpredictable and weak: 'the actions of the actor's body, the expression of his face, the sounds of his voice, are all at the mercy of the winds, of the emotions.[36] The Ubermarionette was to overcome these physical, emotional and psychological limitations, their mimetic representations and the arrogant personality of the actor.

So if the actor's role is to diminish, then what can the commedia dell'arte, as a performance style that owes so much to the skill of the actor, offer Craig's ideal? Perhaps the most charming and politic practice for his theories was that of improvisation, an art that led performance towards drama and creativity and away from tightly scripted plays and literary texts. Craig argues that the commedia's neglect of literary tradition augurs the success of modern directors who are likewise impatient with the ascendancy of the playwright. In the January 1911 edition of *The Mask*, Craig's article 'The Commedia dell'Arte or Professional Comedy' dismisses those who view improvisation as 'a poor or affected kind of thing', the fabric of children's play rather than adult theatre.[37] As late as 1924, *The Mask* was still championing extemporised performance, this time in the article 'LONDON AND COTTON WOOL', where Craig writes as the fictitious theatre critic Henry Phips.[38] The latter has recently returned from the capital, where he has relished his creature comforts and the city's dizzying array of cigarettes and tobacconists. He is a traveller for whom exercise is a matter of shuffling indolently across the soft, thick Axminster of hotel carpets, before finally coming to rest in the luxurious upholstery of a theatre stall. London cossets him, its entertainments celebrate the twin spirits of 'Lull and loll', and its streets and walls are paved with cotton wool.[39] Phips's subject is his recent purchase of some rare books on improvisation, a practice that he dismisses as it requires a regrettable degree of intuition from the actor, and a yet more distressing measure of wit and discernment on the part of the spectator. He also alludes dismissively to *The Mask*'s 1923 translation of the scenario from the baroque commedia *La Schiava*, thereby focusing his hostility towards improvised drama on the commedia dell'arte.[40] Through Phips's enervated, satirised perspective, Craig is able to suggest that the actor of the non-extempore tradition is complacent, content for his work to remain a profession rather than an art. The actors of improvised theatre, meanwhile, require an athletic intuition to create their own dialogue, while their audience are deemed intelligent, attentive and prepared to pay for the 'ordeal' of imaginative engagement with the actors as well as for their seats.

In his desire to transcend the playwright entirely, Craig's commedia archive provides him with exceptional documents and texts. Perhaps his most striking discovery is the rare Italian book mentioned by Phips, *La Schiava Comedia Nuova E Ridiculosa*. A scenario from the first act is published in the 1923 edition of *The Mask*, alongside an English translation and Craig's editorial commentary. The book in its entirety is a mere eight pages long, containing the canovaccio for a three-act play and the Prologue. The commentary stresses that the contents of each act fit onto a single page approximately six inches by four inches, and that each scenario offers 'telegraphic' information and a few modest stage properties – a purse and two particular costumes.[41] Craig is anxious to restore dignity to masks such as Magnifico (Pantalone) and Gratiano (Il Dottore), rescuing them from the absurd pantomime caricatures of the late nineteenth century. The scenario details establish a debt of 200 scudi between Gratiano and Magnifico, so Gratiano sends his Zanni to the bank for the money while Burratino decides to sell a young lady, who in turn happens to be beloved of Magnifico's son Fulvio. All this is a matter of simple, abbreviated description rather than literary genius, and the freedom to elaborate, digress and invent in the moment is clear given the incredibly concise framework offered to the actors.

The commedia actor, however, did not have complete freedom to extemporise on stage. Improvisation was always offset by a basic framework of scenarios and lazzi that were discussed before the performance and formed part of a stock repertoire of conventions passed down from earlier commedia actors. *The Mask* contains brief mention of Riccoboni's definition of lazzi as a derivative of 'lacci', the Italian word for ribbons, threads with which the actor joins together parts of the action that might appear disconnected.[42] They involve making jokes, expressing fear or performing tricks and physical actions. The vocabulary of weaving or embroidery continues with the presentation of the scenario or plot as *canovaccio*, a term that translates to mean a canvas on which to embroider. The scenario is like a stencil on cloth and the actors are then at liberty to add to and embellish the initial design which is presented to them by the Corago, or manager, before they perform. Craig uses

Andrea Perucci's 1699 'Arte Rappresentativa Ed All'Improviso' to describe this meeting, where characters are introduced, lazzi chosen and entrances and exits decided.[43] Perucci cautions that the actors should not trust to having played particular scenarios before, as the Corago often changed the details with each performance

The Mask devotes articles to the seventeenth-century diarist and writer John Evelyn, an Englishman whose travels offer lively, anecdotal accounts of Italian baroque theatre and do much to enhance Craig's celebration of commedia improvisation. Evelyn tells of an invitation to an Italian Academy in early 1645 where he is privileged to witness 'ingenious exercises' in speech and language alongside the more customary disciplines of debate, poetry recital and general scholarship.[44] Craig concludes that the Italian actors who practised such ingenious exercises in their attempt to meet the expectations of an exacting commedia audience 'must have been rather fine speakers and rather exceptional in other ways'.[45] He explains that the details from Evelyn's diary help him to understand how spontaneity kept the Italian language vital and continually evolving, and how distinguished commedia actors such as Isabella Andreini, herself a member of the Academie dei Intenti, went on to become poets, linguists and epistolary writers. Accomplished improvisation was the sign of an intelligent, resourceful and versatile mind. In his essay on the pre-Shakespearian stage, Craig adds more talented commedia actors to his list, the first being Isabella Andreini's husband Francesco, who mastered six languages, then Andrea Calmo, the actor, singer, writer and friend to Michael Angelo (Michelangelo).[46] Angelo Beolco finds mention as a commedia improviser and actor, whose speeches blend historical and mythological allusion with contemporary detail, displaying both wit and learning. Craig's list goes on to mention the actor and Corago Flaminio Scala and the famous Arlecchino, and darling of the courts Tristano Martinelli. A clue to the curious appeal of the actor at this point in Craig's research comes in the form of Drusiano Martinelli, brother to Tristano. Although Drusiano became an actor in his own right, following in his sibling's footsteps and playing the mask of Arlecchino himself, he achieved far greater distinction as a director and manager, conducting the first company of commedia players to venture to France in 1600.[47] So Craig's respect for this particular incarnation of the actor was perhaps less a matter of compromising his dislike of the theatrical 'personality' and more a matter of focusing on the fact that this particular baroque actor was often evolving towards a different role entirely. These celebrated men and women became scholars, linguists, writers, researchers and directors, and even when such exceptional talent paused to put pen to paper and to record scenarios, their literary endeavours were limited to a concise and pardonable amount of text, so they were never in danger of alienating Craig by becoming playwrights. In his account of the commedia dell'arte, Craig does not go so far as to deny the more humble performance tradition, the actors who rubbed shoulders with charlatans, beggars and saltimbanchi on street corners, while their peers enjoyed royal patronage. His argument is rather that it matters little which tradition the dramas evolved from, the theatrical conventions were the same. Craig is, however, guilty of lingering over the talents and privileges of the Andreinis and Martinellis, because he clearly sees them as worthy predecessors of his Theatre of the Future.

However sparkling and ingenious the commedia soliloquies or dialogues became, Craig believed that dramatic authors had focused on language as a form of expression for too long: 'intensity of passion can only be suggested by an act . . . an act which dominates the silence not which sinks under it'.[48] Commedia dell'arte appealed to Craig's theatre of the future because its expressive potential had long been focused in physical gesture, movement and mime, and the actor's body in turn had assumed a new significance. The performers did not translate precise instructions from the author's page, but experienced the role directly through their bodies in a way that, for Craig, was far more immediate and compelling. As with Duncan and her dancers, athleticism and physical discipline were the prerequisites of accomplished improvisation and spontaneity in performance, and the mask of Arlecchino in particular skilfully combined strength, cat-like agility and a certain awkward grace that allowed this figure to walk on stilts, fall head over heels, topple safely from buildings and turn somersaults with the best of the saltimbanchi. Just as Duncan urged her dancers to observe the rhythms and cadences in nature all around them, so Craig purchased birds and animals for his school in Florence so that the students could observe both forms and movements that might enhance their physical performance. Such theatrical menageries were accepted in earnest in Italy as a catalyst for dramatic expression, and in the commedia this practice informs the action in great detail. The 1622 'Lazzi of the Cat', for example, reveals Arlecchino imitating this animal's rituals of cleaning, scratching and hunting, while the 'Lazzo of the Crane' involves a magician transforming Arlecchino into this bird complete with a gradually extending neck.[49]

The baroque commedia, in general, created a far more dynamic and crude material world than its counterparts on the English and French stage. Alongside the saturnalia and scatological performing bodies, the displays of naked flesh, the endless chamber-pots and enemas, and examples of lecherous behaviour in both young and old, these dramas also promoted a more refined use of the human body. Luigi Riccoboni's 'Advice for Actors' might seem an unusual choice for inclusion in *The Mask*, as his work coincides with the twilight years of the baroque commedia and as he attempted to regulate performance with censored, literary dramas that defied the popular oral tradition. Some of his imperatives for the actor, however, do echo Craig's concerns in the Ubermarionette essay, as he cautions actors against following nature too closely and reproducing the mundane in their performance techniques. He also shares Craig's contempt for the actor's 'personality' or intrusive ego, warning against having too good a conceit of oneself. The second Canto of Riccoboni's tract suggests that the actor should be strong, well proportioned and not too profligate of action, avoiding the 'the marking of every comma with a gesture'.[50] The actor must forget his body: if he feels the emotions correctly, then they will produce the appropriate physical expression.

Another more subtle technique that offset the commedia's breathtakingly robust, violent and acrobatic physicality brought the actor's body into a strange and studied equilibrium with the facial mask. The commedia mask generally covered the top half of the face, some extended further to include chin pieces and mouths, and they were moulded from leather or papier-mâché. The features were clearly recognisable and did not change from one performance or company to another. Arlecchino, for example, always had a half-mask with playfully arched eyebrows and a wart, while Brighella's mask was olive-tinted, with a full mouth that betrayed his sensuality and a sardonic expression. This readily identifiable, stylised shape allowed for the abstraction of the actor's individuality, and the uncomplicated, standardised characterisation meant that the masks enjoyed none of the intricate complexities and contradictions favoured by the playwright. Brighella was always manipulative, cunning and ruthless, Il Dottore was always grave and prolific in his scholarly discourse, and the Captain was fierce and heated in his appearance but cowardly in his nature. As early as 1910, Craig's article 'Chantecler and the Return of the Mask' had drawn attention to a performance of Röstand's play as an event that allowed the mask and facial expression to triumph on stage for the first time since the baroque period. The drama is 'of animal life, played by actors in animal masks' and its warm reception with Parisian audiences confirms Craig's belief that masks are central to his plans for revolutionising modern theatre.[51] Pierre Duchartre gives his own account of the highly disciplined physicality demanded by the commedia mask: 'if the body was lacking in plastic eloquence the mask was meaningless', the two complemented one another and produced the restrained grace and refinement in movement that Craig sought in the Ubermarionette.[52] Duchartre goes on to suggest that the mask presupposes 'a constant perfected play of the body which is an art in itself', and once the art has been mastered then 'if the body was subtle in its play the mask became a far more effective means of expression than the muscles'.[53] Duchartre seems to suggest a displacement of expressive potential from one part of the actor's form to another, and a sublimation of emotional response that precludes the flawed, exaggerated interpretations of the realist stage.

The final redress delivered to Craig's bête-noire by commedia performance comes with the repeated stress on reciprocity and unity with one's fellow actor. In his Preface to Le Théâtre Italien, Evaristo Gherardi honours the commedia actor:

He fits his words and actions so perfectly to those of his colleague that he enters instantly into whatever acting and movements are required of him in such a manner as to give everyone to believe that all they do has been prearranged.[54]

This susceptibility to the gesture, physicality and verbal cues of the other players again allowed commedia improvisation to counteract the conceit and personality of the actor that Craig objected to, while promoting collaboration and a mutual sensitivity that set them apart from other baroque performers. A gesture, mime or glance from one could solicit an action or riposte from his fellow actor, ensuring that no one actor could excel in isolation and that accomplished improvisation depended on responsive and talented individuals behind each mask. This reciprocity was not limited to the stage, but defined the relationship between the players and the audience as well. The commedia players would address the spectators and their performance was intended to be deliberately provocative, to charm and involve and to encourage the audience to share approbation or censure as the performance progressed.

So while the quality of movement desired by Craig during the writing of 'The Actor and the Ubermarionette' and *The Art of Theatre* might have been closely associated with the puppet, his research and his study of the commedia represented a further modification of the ideal and the possibility that the model actor might at last overcome the weaknesses of the realist stage. The commedia remained an infinitely flexible model for reinterpretation and appropriation during the modernist period, but that adaptation was often reduced to key motifs and allusions drawn from the more polite, elegant French masks recreated within Romanticism and Symbolism. Craig's intervention in this commedia legacy cannot be overstated, as he refocused the narrative on original sources, archival treasures and detailed academic scholarship, the result of a unique combination of passion, knowledge, dedication and location. For Craig's interpretation of the commedia and for Duncan's assimilation of Spinoza's philosophy, movement and agency became metaphors for thought, improvisation, spontaneity, responsiveness, reciprocity, pace, the unexpected, and the individual's connection with others and with the natural order around them. Their baroque sources represented a corrective for exclusivity, personality and for the contingencies of an untrained human body plagued by emotions, distracting thoughts and by clumsy, involuntary physical tics and imperfections.

WYNDHAM LEWIS: FICTION, CRITIQUE AND THE COMMEDIA

Between 1908 and 1910, as Craig worked on early editions of *The Mask* and refined his research into the Italian commedia, Wyndham Lewis was celebrating this form of baroque theatre as the blueprint for his first novel, *Mrs*

Dukes' Million. Here the obstinate, dishevelled and somewhat eccentric Mrs Dukes presides over lodgings in Marbury Street, London, and is left a fortune by an absent husband who has abandoned her some thirty years before the story begins. The Oriental Corago, Sarandur Khan, gathers together an Actor-Gang to play the masks of real and imagined individuals, and these roles will promote the intrigues, robberies and impostures that the company specialise in. The canovaccio set before the players requires them to abduct the real Mrs Dukes and replace her with the young actor Evan Royal, while filling the landlady's house with a cast who can support him in the deception and help to secure the inheritance. The company's Arlecchino is undoubtedly Royal, an accomplished improviser who takes up residence as one of Mrs Duke's lodgers under the name of Mr Nichols. He wastes no time in asking his landlady to sit for him so that he can paint her portrait, thereby making an accurate study of her person, voice and mannerisms. Other members of the company join him – Mr Hillington as Mrs Dukes' business adviser, Mrs Beechamp, a slatternly charlady played by the beautiful Lucy, who is undoubtedly the player's Columbine, a mysterious Belgian gentleman, a selection of bogus policemen, and finally, Hercules Fane, who must perfect his own mask as understudy to Royal's Mrs Dukes and replace Royal when necessary. The landlady herself is spirited away to spend most of the novel languishing in a drugged stupor, tended by players disguised as doctors and nurses, until the farcical scene where she collapses, having glimpsed Royal disguised as herself on a train bound for Liverpool.

The novel's scenarios are fantastic in their audacity and exhilarating in terms of the skill and dangers involved, and there is only the sordid reality that Khan must make their performances pay financially to detract from Lewis's interpretation of life lived as commedia improvisation. By translating the performance from the stage to the wider world, Lewis makes an uncharacteristic link between art and life:

> We improvise. No pieces are written for us. The actors act the part as they go along . . . I wanted to see actors no longer bound by the 'piece' they had to play, but to *act* and *live* at the same time'.[55]

However well the players may research and rehearse their masks, they cannot predict what will happen as the intrigue develops. As the commedia shapes and controls the lives not only of the players but of those who unwittingly become their audience, Lewis is able to work the reciprocity that characterises the original baroque dramas to tense and hilarious extremes. Perhaps Royal's most challenging scenario comes after the officious and interfering curate Mr Higgenbotham overhears Mrs Beechamp and the Belgian lodger discussing the difficulty of securing the landlady's inheritance and takes his concerns to the police. Fane returns to Marbury Street to find the curate, an Inspector of

Police, a detective, Mrs Beechamp, the Belgian, and Royal's incarnation of Mrs Dukes all disputing the possibility of a plot to defraud the heiress. Lewis acknowledges that Royal, 'wonderful actor as he was, and a nerve that could be wrenched about in all directions and not give, needed all his resourcefulness in this moment'.[56] He is instantly alert to the possibility that Higgenbotham might mention a previous visit from the police (disguised members of the Actor-Gang) and quickly resolves to dismiss this as part of the suspected plot. He then uses the great deference paid to the wealthy heiress to make the most of her authority, outmanoeuvring the curate, convincing the police that only the Belgian could be part of such a plot, while the Belgian supports Royal's performance, confounds the investigation with this compelling but impenetrable accent, and suspicions are allayed. Royal's passion for extemporised performance means that even as he, Fane and Lucy make their final plans to leave the Liverpool house, the lovers are not aware of this modern Arlecchino's plans, as he is 'an improviser by choice' and determined to defer everything until the last minute.[57] When Royal is abducted by the Passion brothers, Mr Hillington and Mrs Dukes (played on this occasion by Fane) are forced to improvise their way through the farce of the exploding cough and the suspicious doctor in true commedia style until their fellow actor can escape and resume his rightful mask.

Lewis also gives full reign to the reciprocity between commedia actor and audience in terms of the novel's plot and characterisation. Even Cole, Mrs Dukes' son, becomes complicit in the canovaccio, sensing the deceit, yet preferring Royal's version of pipe-sharing motherhood to the company of the original landlady. As part of their final escape, Fane and Royal hire a German marching band for the day, and Lewis elaborates the role of the baroque audience from dialogue and response to full participation. Just as some baroque performances gave the audience their own masks, so 'the Germans played up to Royal and Fane wonderfully ... they enjoyed themselves. They gave reign to their fancy'. When the kidnapped Royal escapes back to his lodgings, convinces the doctor and the clerk from Truman and Hatchett that all is well, and his bewildered audience disperses, he is so exhilarated by the success of his improvisation that he decides to make the mask his own. He became 'trenchant, more sarcastic than ever, overbearing, and recklessly energetic', in fact more like the subversive and physically boisterous zanni of the baroque commedia.[59] Nor does Lewis overlook the physical comedy of the loud and grotesque commedia body, as Royal makes his escape inside a safe, only to be discovered when his snores are heard by the law firm handling the inheritance. With this conceit, Lewis offers his reader a modern adaptation of the traditional commedia Lazzi of the Sack, but this time the audience and not the hidden body are the deceived party.[60] The frantic donning of masks and disguises, Royal's buffooneries, his Arlecchino-like agility, and his increasingly indignant and uninhibited version of the heiress, all follow the baroque tradition. As to the violence, the sadistic floggings and punishments, the endless teasing and tormenting of masks who are all too easily duped – these became stock commedia transgressions that were formalised through routines such as 'The Lazzi of the Killing' and the 'Lazzi of the Bastonate'.[61] Then as the cruel humpbacked mask Pulcinella left Italian shores in the late seventeenth century and settled in English theatre, this violence intensified as he set about splitting his wife's head in two, killing her parents and tossing babies from windows. There is enough brutality and bloodshed in Royal's stabbing of the policeman, his murder of the butler, and the mysterious dispatch of the Passion brothers by Khan's assassins and his giant sphynx-like consort, for the novel's debt to commedia to feel authentic and balanced.

So Lewis's first use of the commedia did not serve critique or instruction, but delighted in the defining qualities and narrative potential of commedia performance as a melting of art into life that explores just how far a consummate improvisation might take a company of actors and those who unwittingly become their spectators. Some sixteen years later, however, in *The Art of Being Ruled*, the commedia dell'arte serves a different purpose entirely, questioning and then undermining the value of precisely this synthesis of art and life. Lewis's chapter 'The Disappearance of the Spectator' opens by questioning whether art and life should be one and the same thing. Turning his attention to the subject of modern theatre Lewis discovers innovation and promise on the Russian and German stage, while regretting an intellectual deadness that presides elsewhere in Europe. Tchekov's tales of introverted individuality are now obsolete; the vogue is for collectivising representations of a class or profession, or of the masses rather than individual men, and attendant upon this standardising or abridgement of characterisation is an attempt to do away with the barrier between the audience and the actor. On the side of art, we find the actor, the author and the artist, while on the side of life, we find the audience, spectator or public, and he views attempts to overcome detachment and distance between the two with grave suspicion.

Lewis was clearly familiar with Craig's research into the commedia tradition and *The Mask*, and he mentions the Gordon Craig School and the director's passion for using masks as an attempt to negate the personality of the actor. With a turn of the page, we are then back in the world of commedia again, and this time Lewis attributes the growth of improvisation in the theatre to a lack of 'sympathetic', character-led dramas. He notes that modern extemporised performances in this baroque tradition displace the written text, and the result is 'an amusing reversion to the "Commedia delle Arte"', whereby actor and audience disappear and the public take to the stage inventing and prattling as if they were infants beguiled by the joys of nursery role-play.[62] For Lewis, all of this constitutes art that is 'wilfully created chaos' while for Craig the same qualities – improvisation, the liberties taken with the literary text, the privileg-ing of action over dialogue, and a lack of developed characterisation – promise the regeneration of modern performance.[63] It is clear that for Lewis, modern theatre and art in general are vulnerable to a coalescing of art and life, artist and spectator, and he sighs over the fact that such conditions threaten a 'stage at which *everybody* is capering about, smudging pieces of paper . . . bellowing in every room, and scribbling couplets on every wall'.[64] The representative of so much random, enthusiastic but ill-considered endeavour is the amateur, and at this point in time, Lewis simply urges the would-be improviser to remember the dignity and pleasure to be found in the quiet, passive contemplation of the spectator. Improvisation, a sinister merging of audience and artist, a mania for action and participation, and the figure of the amateur, are clearly inseparable, but having identified commedia practices with the dilettante, Lewis is content to alert his reader to a more developed consideration of these ideas elsewhere.

The elsewhere in question is Lewis's essay *The Dithyrambic Spectator* (1931), and here he begins by acknowledging that in an age of industry, art has been superseded in every practical realm of life by the machine, and the Fine Arts 'if they survive at all, survive as a sport, as a privilege of the wealthy, negligently indulged in'.[65] While art had originally promoted human survival, Lewis laments that it now promotes only pleasure and vanity, constituting a 'sort of grown-up nursery, where the rich can be kept young', amusing them-selves in their studios as the fox-hunter does among his hounds and trophies.[66] The amateur now seems to rank alongside Gertrude Stein, the Sitwells and the Tyros as a practitioner of the inane, impish art of the child cult. In the final section of the essay, the links between improvisation, the decline of art, the rise of the amateur and the disappearance of both spectator and artist are developed through a discussion of Jane Harrison's text *Ancient Art and Ritual* (1913). As a classical scholar and anthropologist, Harrison's focus is the devel-opment of Greek theatre, and she details the transition between choric perfor-mance and Attic drama. She and James Frazer are clearly of the same mind in maintaining that art evolved from early ritual. Harrison argues that the theatre of the Greeks was originally an orchestra, allowing no separation between actor and spectator. All rituals enacted there were centred in the gesture, mime and vitality of the human body and not in detached contemplation and the calm play of intellect and inspiration that Lewis values in both audience and artist. So Lewis is clearly at odds with Harrison's celebration of a return to these conditions in modern theatre, and art in general.

Harrison's ideas and discoveries influenced both avant-garde theory and practice in early twentieth-century theatre, and she turns to Artistotle's *Poetics* to identify improvisation as an archetypal practice in performance history: 'Tragedy – as also Comedy – Aristotle says, was at first mere improvisation – the one (tragedy) originated with the leaders of the Dithyramb'.[67] For Lewis, the significance of the Dithyrambic Spectator was that he or she was in fact a participant and not a spectator at all. The Dithyramb was an impassioned dance or physical performance carried out in honour of Dionysus, and, in Harrison's analysis, the emphasis is placed on the rhythm and intensity of movement and voice, and on collective involvement. During these festivals and celebrations, and long before the heroic individualism of Homeric narratives, there was no distinction between the audience and the actor or performer, and no self-conscious aesthetic identity; all were worshippers, all performed. Harrison draws her reader's attention to the etymology of the Greek word 'dromenon' as 'a thing done', and these cultural practices focused on the actions of the body, and physical creation and completion with a view to promoting desired events: 'The ritual dance was a dromenon, a thing to be done, not a thing to be looked at', actions performed so as to anticipate or recapture a particular coveted aspect of life, and 'Dithyrambos' means the Divine Leaper, Dancer and Lifegiver.[68] With the ascendency of Greek drama, it is as if so much physical exertion must somehow be stilled, silenced and hidden. Even fateful killings must take place off-stage and the differentiation between spectator and artist increases as action is eclipsed by contemplation. The Dithyrambic Spectator finds fault with Harrison as she commends a return to the practices of ritual within modern theatre and the Fine Arts. Lewis acknowledges that performers are being recruited from the audience and this 'return of Everyman into the arena or choral acting-place is, true enough, occurring universally', with spectators becoming amateurs and performance approaching the 'full blind collective ecstasy' of Greek ritual once more.[69]

So to read The Dithyrambic Spectator alongside 'The Disappearance of the Spectator', and indeed The Art of Being Ruled as a whole, is to see the commedia dell'arte as at once primitive, baroque and modern. Its celebration of improvisation and of the vigour of the human body, its challenge to the literary text, the collective identity of its performances and the blurring of boundaries between stage and stalls, the primacy of fixed forms and stereotypical actions such as lazzi and the commedia masks, all suggest the baroque performance as a tradition that gestures both backwards and forwards in time to the earliest practices of ritual and to the twentieth-century stage. In fact, Harrison might well have been describing a commedia troupe and their audience when she writes of early Greek ceremonies where the individual dancers sink and merge their personalities through the wearing of masks and disguises, and action follows a common rhythm until the group become one.[70] It is a performative bias that defined commedia improvisation during the baroque period, and during the modernist revival that so troubled Lewis and delighted Craig. When Dr Sztrakoniczky reviewed the 1912 performance of Riccoboni's Le Defiant at the National Theatre in Budapest, he praised a performance that 'brought the public and actors close together . . . I never before saw men of such different orders and ranks . . . understand each other so well, or feel so closely related and so essentially one as last night', and it is easy to imagine Lewis shifting uncomfortably in his seat at the thought of so much collective engagement and unashamed lack of differentiation re-emerging in the modernist period.[71]

'The Disappearance of the Spectator', however, appears in a text with a panoramic socio-political gaze rather than a single-minded fascination with theatre, and Lewis's references to commedia and improvisation are both historical details and metaphors that situate themselves at key contested points in his discussion of subjectivity in modern capitalist society. In *The Art of Being Ruled*, Lewis has an equivalent for the stereotyped commedia masks with their rigidly defined qualities and their equivalents on the contemporary stage: 'people ask nothing better than to be *types* – occupational types, social types, functional types'.[72] So the citizen of liberal democracies slides with some satisfaction and relief into the limited range of masks presented to him, conventions that offset genuine individuality. Lewis also seems undecided as to the degree of liberty that modern subjectivity should enjoy and the desirability of social control. Improvisation as practice in socio-political terms suggests a degree of freedom and spontaneity that is quite at odds with Lewis's argument that uniformity of personality and opinion is subtly prescribed for the modern subject by education, film and the popular press. So while that subject believes himself to be inventing and responding with originality, he is, in fact, tightly scripted in rather slick and insidious ways. Improvisation is, therefore, flawed because it is an illusion, but also because it is perhaps not desired after all. If the stereotyping of commedia masks and lazzi give a predictable quality to performance, then this is quite in keeping with Lewis's interpretation of a public pricked only by custom and routine, ease and indolence, and not by extemporised wit and ingenuity.

It is odd that Lewis should on the one hand present this dull, resigned state of obedience as something sought after, readily accepted and even necessary, while criticising the democratic system and liberal values that fostered its many comforts. In fact, he appears to favour the blatant authoritarian rule of Fascism and Communism rather than the covert control of post-war liberalism. Improvisation and the freedom afforded by democracy would work only if the public had recourse to the insights, introspection and self-determining thought processes of the genuine, professional artist and could therefore transcend their scripted performances. His essay 'Creatures of Habit and Creatures of Change' is at pains to introduce 'The Dithyrambic Spectator' as an overview of the arts created by the rise of Communism, and, once again, Lewis's gaze is split between the theatre proper and the arts and government in general. Here, the defining qualities of commedia and ritual are also applied to democracy's alternatives. Lewis was clearly familiar with Haeckel's evolutionary science and his monist philosophy and in 'Creatures of Habit and Creatures of Change', he laments the collapse of biological definitions between species, and between man and the lower animals, while expressing trepidation that the time may be fast approaching when divisions between organic and inorganic forms, and subsequently mind and matter, will also disappear. While Haeckel and his *Riddle of the Universe* are not explicitly referenced, this ultimate collapse of boundaries is precisely the scientific and philosophical reality that his adaptation of Darwinian science proposes. Lewis then goes on to argue that Communism has promoted a similar toppling of barriers and definitions: 'with the évontai intoxicated with dogmas of action, swarming onto the stage, snatching the masks and robes from the actors and returning to the primitive conditions of the dithyrambic ecstasy'.[73] The wealthy privileged classes become bohemian iconoclasts in a sham display of fellowship with the multitude, and Lewis returns us neatly to democracy once again: 'Oppression by a democratic "equal", it is understood, is not oppression'.[74]

As with so many of his recurring images and ideas, the commedia dell'arte is a provocative and contradictory reference within Lewis's fiction and critique. It clearly represents the ascendancy of action and the human body over careful scrutiny and reflection, and of collective identity over individual talent. With *Mrs Dukes' Million*, he embraces commedia's metatheatricality, that animated consciousness of illusion and reciprocity on the part of actor and audience that Lewis pushes to the extreme, allowing the delighted viewer to cross over and play his own mask, thereby realising the disappearance of the spectator that later seemed to cause him so much dismay. The novel delights in commedia physicality, beautiful and profane, comic and violent. In his essays, a far more ambiguous commedia identity emerges, combining ritual and modernity with the baroque stereotypes to produce images that complicate key points in Lewis's aesthetic and political arguments. Commedia connects to a democratic ideal and yet, in Lewis's eyes, few subjects seem well placed to take advantage of that idea, thanks to the strategies and blandishments of the state. This particular form of baroque theatre represents a coalescing of art and life that repels him, and yet he realises that art must engage with life at an emotional level, and the artist must guard against assuming a remote and unsympathetic identity. By identifying the possibility of mock improvisation, he also plays on the fact that baroque commedia was not without its rehearsals, its stock action and its heavily stereotyped practices. Commedia dell'arte becomes a metaphor that leads us to question whether performance and democracy are simply about reproducing the ideas of the author or the authorities, and to ask just how much of that performance is created spontaneously and collaboratively by the newly empowered audience. To view Lewis's engagement with the commedia in the context of his work as whole is to understand that what unsettles him most are the links backwards to that collective, unstructured experience of life that had its roots in ritual, links that Harrison would draw forwards into modernist creativity. The coming together of participants in a way that allows life to overwhelm and distort art, driven by the impulse to action, and indulging a gross physicality, all of this defines ritual and is for Lewis clearly more powerful, subversive and enduring than any practice or representation that he might cherish within fine art or literature, or any that he might scorn as part of a popular consumer culture premised on talentless amateurs, imitation and reproduction, and an undiscerning public taste. It is precisely this unease and sense of restless, layered signification that leads Lewis to return to the commedia once more and to fashion from it the aesthetic of an entire novel, adding satire to critique with *The Apes of God*.

NOTES

1. Quoted in *The Mask*, 9, 1923, p. 13.
2. Letter from Isadora Duncan to Edward Gordon Craig, in Duncan, *Your Isadora: The Love Story of Isadora Duncan & Gordon Craig Told Through Letters and Diaries*, p. 68.
3. Haeckel, *The Riddle of the Universe*, p. 17.
4. Ibid. p. 237.
5. Spinoza, *Ethics*, I, P11, p. 7.
6. Ibid. I, P14, p. 9.
7. Ibid. I, D4, p. 1.
8. Haeckel, *The Riddle of the Universe*, p. 177.
9. Duncan, Irma, *Isadora Duncan – Pioneer in the Art of Dance*, p. 5.
10. Duncan, Isadora, 'The Dance and its Inspiration', first published in the periodical *The Touchstone*, in *Isadora Speaks: Writings and Speeches of Isadora Duncan*, p. 42.
11. Ibid. p. 42.
12. Duncan, 'Love and Ideals', first published in the popular periodical *The Mentor*, in *Isadora Speaks: Writings and Speeches of Isadora Duncan*, p. 118.
13. Duncan, 'The Dance and its Inspiration', pp. 43–4.
14. Haeckel, *Die Lebenswunder*.
15. Spinoza, *Ethics*, II, L1, p. 41.
16. Ibid. II, IV, p. 44.
17. Duncan, 'The Dance and its Inspiration', p. 44.
18. Spinoza, *Ethics*, II, 1, p. 44.
19. Duncan, 'The Great Source', in *The Art of Dance*, p. 102.
20. Duncan, 'The Dance and its Inspiration', p. 43.
21. Hampshire, *Spinoza: An Introduction to his Philosophical Thought*, p. 65.
22. Duncan, 'The Dance and its Inspiration', p. 45.
23. Duncan, 'The Philosopher's Stone of Dancing', in *The Art of Dance*, p. 51.
24. Duncan, *My Life*, p. 84.
25. Duncan, 'The Dance of the Future', in *The Art of Dance*, pp. 56–7.
26. Spinoza, *Ethics*, II, L3, p. 41.
27. Duncan, 'The Dance of the Future', pp. 55–6.
28. Loewenthal, *The Search for Isadora: The Legend and Legacy of Isadora Duncan*, p. 11.
29. Walkowitz, *Line Dance: Abraham Walkowitz's Drawings of Isadora Duncan*, p. 3.
30. Duncan, *My Life*, pp. 163–4.

31. Duncan, 'The Dance of the Future', p. 62.
32. Duncan, *My Life*, p. 91.
33. Craig, *Scene*, p. 7.
34. Taxidou, *The Mask: A Periodical Performance by Edward Gordon Craig*, pp. 124–32; LeBoeuf, 'On the Nature of Edward Gordon Craig's Ubermarionette', *Theatre Quarterly*, 2.6, May 2010, pp. 102–14.
35. *The Mask*, 1.2, April 1908, p. 14.
36. Ibid. p. 3.
37. *The Mask*, 3.7–9, January 1911, p. 99.
38. *The Mask*, 10.1, January 1924, pp. 29–30.
39. Ibid. p. 30.
40. *The Mask*, 9.1, 1923, pp. 12–13.
41. Ibid.
42. *The Mask*, 4.2, October 1911, p. 115.
43. Ibid. p. 113.
44. *The Mask*, 10.3, July 1924, 10.3, p. 107.
45. Ibid.
46. *The Mask*, 6.2, October 1913. pp. 151–6.
47. Ibid.
48. *The Mask*, 5, October 1912, p. 108.
49. Gordon, *Lazzi: The Comic Routines of the Commedia Dell'Arte*, p. 11.
50. *The Mask*, 3.10–12, April 1911, p. 178.
51. *The Mask*, 2.10–12, April 1910, p. 171.
52. Duchartre, *The Italian Comedy*, p. 42.
53. Ibid.
54. Evaristo Gherardi, quoted in *The Mask*, 3.10–12, April 1911, p. 169.
55. Lewis, *Mrs Dukes' Million*, p. 66.
56. Ibid. p. 101.
57. Ibid. p. 295.
58. Ibid. p. 359.
59. Ibid. p. 235.
60. Gordon, *Lazzi: The Comic Routines of the Commedia Dell'Arte*, p. 14.
61. Ibid. p. 17.
62. Lewis, *The Art of Being Ruled*, p. 176.
63. Ibid.
64. Ibid.
65. Lewis, *The Diabolical Principle and the Dithyrambic Spectator*, p. 163.
66. Ibid. p. 167.
67. Ibid. p. 208.
68. Ibid. p. 224; Harrison, *Ancient Art and Ritual*, pp. 35–6, 104.
69. Ibid. p. 235, 238.
70. Harrison, *Ancient Art and Ritual*, pp. 9–49.
71. Sztrakoniczky, in *Alkotmany*, reproduced in *The Mask*, 5.1, July 1912, p. 86.
72. Lewis, *The Art of Being Ruled*, p. 167.
73. Lewis, 'Creatures of Habit and Creatures of Change', in *Creatures of Habit and Creatures of Change: Essays on Art, Literature and Society 1914–56*, p. 149.
74. Ibid. p. 149.

6

THE APES OF GOD AND THE WORLD OF THE COMMEDIA

In fact in a sort of ill-acted Commedia dell'Arte, with its Panatalones and Arlechinos (the family of the Finnian Shaws monopolising the Harlequin role, however unsuited for it), this family circle passed its time.[1]

Arlecchino would find as much to satirise, as much to raise a laugh from in the life of today as ever he found three centuries ago.[2]

When *The Apes of God* first came into print in 1924, it piqued readers' curiosity by appearing as select passages in Eliot's literary review *The Criterion*, and by 1927 Lewis had submitted individual sections, including 'Mr Zagreus and the Split-Man' and 'Chez Lionel Kein, Esq', to an unnamed American publishing house. The American reader's report appears in Lewis's *Enemy Pamphlet 1 – Satire and Fiction* (1930), and notes that the novel seems to have no strict plot and a pleasingly discursive narrative.[3] Other positive reviews appear alongside it, with Frank Swinerton of *The Evening News* calling for more explicit clues when trying to pair particular modernists with the novel's assortment of Apes, while Richard Aldington discovers the novel and its devastating roman à clef subtext to be 'the most tremendous knock-out ever made'.[4] S. Mais of *The Daily Telegraph* commends the text's masterly analysis of modern art and its splendid measure of farce, and Lewis's prose and dialogue are commended as without equal.[5] In 1930, the private edition of the text finally appeared, with trade copies following in the spring of 1931, and the scandal and outrage that greeted the first publication quickly obscured other critical responses. Despite

Swinerton's apparent doubt and confusion, the majority of readers found it all too easy to pair individual modernists with their simian counterparts. The Apes themselves are artists, writers and cultural celebrities who aspire to the avant-garde artworks and bohemian identities of their Parisian counterparts, but who ultimately fall far short of their achievements. As the hapless Dan Boleyn is sent forth into modernism's world of salons and coteries to make a study of this unfortunate species, the identities of Lewis's victims become clear. Julius Ratner is a sly dabbler in many professions, blending the distinguishing traits of James Joyce with those of the modernist poet John Rodker, while the novel's Proust aficionado, a rather foolish, indignant Lionel Kein, is identifiable as the novelist and translator Sidney Schiff. Horace Zagreus is the alter ego of poet and prankster William Horace de Vere Cole, while Lady Fredigonde's nephew Richard Whittingdon is the painter Richard Wyndham. Once the Sitwell siblings are cast as the Finnian Shaw family, however, all the other Apes are eclipsed, and Lord Osmund, Lord Phoebus and Lady Harriet preoccupy Lewis for the entire final section of the novel. Lewis felt obliged to defend himself from charges of libel in *Satire and Fiction*, and perhaps a little intoxicated by the commedia aesthetic of masks, disguise and improvisation that he had created, he assumed the identity of editor of the Arthur Press, when neither employee nor publishing house existed.

This chapter's opening quotation forms part of our introduction to the Finnian Shaw family who are preparing to host a Lenten party that will dominate the second half of the *The Apes of God*, and Lewis seems to distance himself in this paragraph from the commedia tradition in its domestic Finnian Shaw adaptation. Theirs is clearly a travesty of the original genre, poorly cast, clumsily delivered, serving vanity and artistic self-conceit rather than authentic forms, and it is here that critics have been content to leave the commedia element of this satire. As Alan Munton turns his attention from *The Wild Body* to Lewis's post-war fiction and *The Apes of God*, he suggests a relinquishing of any sustained engagement with the commedia, its masks and its unashamed, boisterous physicality in favour of occasional figurative allusions:

> By 1914 Lewis' concern with cultural matters had displaced the early comic figures from his work. His interest in Nietzschean tragedy, in Vorticism, and the position of the creative artist in a bourgeois society mean that his Carnival themes are diminished to metaphor and image . . . The travelling players have been left far behind.[6]

He goes on to argue that by filtering much of the magic and theatre of the fêted commedia through the thoughts of Dan Boleyn, Lewis exposes the Lenten celebrations as tawdry artifice. The hospitality, spectacle and abundance that define the period of carnival are reversed by the mock celebrations at the Finnian Shaws' Norman grange, with its meagre fare, cheap costumes and grudging welcome. Likewise Peter Caracciolo's reading of the Bailiff in *The Childermass* as a descendent of the Italian commedia's Pulcinello does not extend to other texts.[7] At first glance, Lewis does indeed seem to forsake the larger-than-life mountebanks and other masks in favour of references to the commedia dell'arte that are little more than affectations and flourishes. The cubed, brightly coloured Harlequin's motley that decorates the Lenten party invitations, the ancient truculent giantess Sib, a deaf and wheezing society matron who is described 'pirouetting amid the Fêtes Galantes of the Naughty Nineties', the 'rice-powdered face out of a Victorian harlequinade' belonging to one of the light-fingered houseguests hoping to plunder the Finnian Shaw silverware, self-conscious references to the melancholy, isolated artist figure in his commedia dell'arte guise as 'poor Pierrot Phoebus' – all of these images represent an inauthentic commedia legacy put to absurd use and far removed from the baroque original.[8] The Harlequins and Pierrots of Osmund's world appear in their symbolist or Victorian incarnation, hybrids that flatter the Sitwells' aesthetic aspirations by suggesting a certain sensitivity or vivacity for the artist's role, while pandering to the Finnian Shaw youth cult with its vibrant images from the world of myth and pantomime. The vocabulary and trappings of the commedia stage may appear in faithful reproduction, as 'concetti, soggetto, repertorio', 'cloaks of the Dottore', and airbladders and rice-powder, but Lewis makes it clear that these are simply faded conventions through which the family can act out their countless feuds and intrigues.[9]

Casting His Company

This is certainly one interpretation of the fate of the baroque commedia in *The Apes of God* but further study of its seventeenth-century masks and scenarios makes possible a very different analysis. This present chapter will argue that the hosts and principal guests of Lord Osmund's Party combine for Lewis to form an almost complete troupe of players, and the commedia performance that Lewis creates for his Apes is as subtle and thoroughly researched as the Finnian Shaws' is explicit and perfunctory. It is a performance that, like all good productions, owes everything to the casting of characters, and as a family so well versed in the minutiae of commedia history, the Sitwells must surely have felt the sting of Lewis's own preferences in the allocation of masks. While the opening quotation stresses that the Finnian Shaws are keen to monopolise the role of Harlequin for themselves, Lewis offers the part to Zagreus, the character whose preoccupations and views seem at times closest to the author's own. Mel Gordon notes the agility and athletic physicality of the original Harlequins: 'tumbling, stilt-walking ... balancing were associated with Arlecchino's normal means of locomotion'.[10] It is Lionel Kein who draws the reader's attention to this quality in Zagreus, smiling 'at the large sea-rover handsomeness of his guest – with long gracefully-stamped lines, the healthy skin . . . all the magnificent physical balance'.[11] Although in his sixties, Zagreus appears intense, restless and excitable, his face coloured with a tanned, hectic flush. Pamela Farnham notes that he seems always to be in a tearing hurry, while Ratner diagnoses the hyperactivity of thyroid dysfuntion: 'Zagreus is a clear case of surplus thyroid stimulation . . . It gives people . . . that feeling of the great *importance* of everything'.[12] This too is the role of Harlequin, a mask defined by the commedia actor Luigi Riccoboni as a 'series of extravagant capers, of violent movements and of outrageous blackguard-isms.'[13] Arlecchino was at once rude, provocative, clownish and obscene. Zagreus is not shy to oblige with the required blackguardisms and obscenity, insulting Lord Osmund's kitchen staff, addressing Ratner as 'you sewer-rat . . . Cloaca' and giving offence to the Keins wherever possible.[14] The early com-media dell'arte Arlecchinos were played by the Gelosi company's Simone of Bologna and then the Accesi troupe's Tristano Martinelli, but it was Giuseppe-Domenico Biancolelli, a particularly witty and erudite actor of The Fiorelli-Locatelli players, who was responsible for offsetting Harlequin's energy and buffoonery with a certain insight, gravitas and lively repartee. Through his interpretation 'Harlequin became witty, astute, an utterer of quips and some-thing of a philosopher'.[15] Zagreus's critique of the Apes' cultural world and aesthetic values, and his display of occult knowledge as he dresses for the role of conjuror, are therefore not out of place for Arlecchino. It is this particular role that confirms both Zagreus and Arlecchino as part of the legacy of the early mountebank performers, and the chief charlatan in particular, with one of Pamela Farnham's guests referring to Horace as a charlatan during the tea-party. Although several zanni in the commedia dressed up as magicians, it was Arlecchino who, as principal zanni and orator, took on the defining qualities of this quack-doctor as the troupes left the marketplace and consolidated their appeal. Besides peddling potions and cures of dubious origin, the charlatan was a magician and illusionist practising sleights of hand: 'half astrologer, half magician, nimbused by a certain mysterious terror, he traded on the superstitions of his audience'.[16] This Shaman-like figure with his catalogue of esoteric emblems and occult amulets is recreated by Zagreus in his disguise as conjurer for the Lenten party performance, and there is a touch of the coarse charlatan manner in these ritual preparations – 'Mr Zagreus had been licking his improper digit and sticking it up his nose'.[17] At this point, Lewis is explicit in drawing together the strands of his composite clown as costume, props and identity now all point towards Zagreus's commedia mask – his costume fea-tures a phallus hanging from his belt, and 'a Harlequin's pouch of red leather', and his half-mask 'gave him a personality of the commedia dell'arte'.[18]

Zagreus's role as Arlecchino is behind the player's descent into Lord Osmund's kitchen, a place of sub-demons, under-devils, smoke, hell heat and spitting flames. It is left to Ratner to clarify the division of their commedia world into two distinct realms: the kitchen with its zanni as 'the domestic inferno . . . under the upper world which for sun had Osmund and for moon Phoebus'.[19] The connection between Zagreus and the underworld is included because commedia dell'arte often performed a descent into hell, as is only fitting given Arlecchino's origins from fire and brimstone. In his discussion of this mask's demonic ancestry, Robert Lima looks back to the *Historiae ecclesiasticae libri XIII*, a Norman manuscript that records a French monk confronted one night by the family of Herlichin: 'a spectral host of relentless demons who marauded the countryside on certain winter nights at the same time of year as the carnival celebrations'.[20] Arlecchino is said to charm his way through the underworld rescuing those held prisoner by Pluto or Hades. Robert Henke details the death of a Venetian buffoni, Zuan Polo Liompardi, assigned to hell in a similar way and accompanied by the devil Farfarel.[21] He entertains the buffoni, or devils, and they bare their buttocks, dance, make merry and improvise. Lewis is not shy of similar improvisations for his own buffoni in hell, as Dan, whose clothes have caught fire in the kitchen, finds his own buttocks bared much to the amusement of Ratner and Zagreus. While lingering in the kitchen, Zagreus himself is described as 'the cursed devil' and 'ill-bred old brawler', as he becomes peculiarly animated and uncouth in his mask's native environment.[22]

Lewis seems to suggest the hopelessly naive, love-struck Dan for the role of Pierrot in his Commedia of the Apes. The genealogy of Pierrot is generally traced to the Italian commedia character Pedrolino, a minor role given to the youngest son in the troupe, a defining youth that Lewis is at pains to stress when Dan is interrogated at Pamela Farnham's tea-party: 'Why you are a CHILD! You are younger than Jimmie'.[23] In *Pierrot: A History of a Mask*, Robert Storey identifies the catalyst of transformation from Pedrolino the Italian peasant to the more familiar French Pierrot as a 1665 performance of Molière's play *Don Juan ou le Festin de Pierre*, in which a short scene between a country girl and her slow-witted swain Pierrot charmed audiences.[24] Inspired by this success. the Italian players performed their own version of the play, *Il Convitato di Pietra*, reclaiming the mask that was initially their own. For many scholars of the commedia, Pierrot and Pedrolino became one and the same. Lewis's guileless Pedrolino retains the honesty of the original, his frustrations in love as he is constantly wrong-footed by Zagreus, and his gluttony and fondness for alcohol. In fact, the young Irishman's thirst for champagne produces some of the novel's most memorable commedia buffoonery, as he repeatedly falls over, toppling Starr-Smith at the same time and reproducing the stock 'Lazzo of Tripping Up'.[25] Dan's isolation, his wide-eyed misinterpretation of virtually all aspects of London life, and the story of the farmer's son and the black cow that is offered as an explanation of genius, are all in keeping with the bucolic innocence of the commedia Pierrot. Zagreus's giddy, sentimental acolyte may proudly accept his quest as ape-hunter, but he is unmanned at every turn of the page. The whip-brandishing virago who demands that Dan strip to become an artist's model, the arsenal of whips admired by Jenny and Dick Whittingdon, the ageing Lothario Caldicott who professes ardent admiration for Dan while believing him to be a lady, the fierce bluster and fisticuffs meted out by Starr-Smith – all of these episodes reduce Zagreus's prodigy to an almost permanent state of anxiety, shame or terror, confirming that, like the original Pedrolino, he is 'utterly the slave of fear'.[26] To identify Zagreus and Dan according to these commedia masks is to illustrate Constant Mic's rule that the first zanni introduces confusion and mischief quite voluntarily, while the second creates disturbance through his blunderings. Zagreus with his practical jokes, goading repartee and general air of hyperactivity follows Mic's definition of the first zanni as the performance's dynamic, comic force, while Dan's heavy physicality and thwarted genius confirm him as the second zanni and a changeless, stationary counterforce.[27]

Maurice Sand provides an account of a particular Pedrolino adventure in which a drinking bout with Captain Spavento leaves the zanni drunk, and he falls to the ground later remembering and understanding nothing of his master's complaints and accusations.[28] This scenario may well have provided the blueprint for Dan's champagne oblivion at the party and Zagreus's subsequent criticism of this drunken behaviour in a letter that leaves the young man bewildered by visions of himself as a belligerent, bone-breaking giant. Here, as Dan is held to account for the mischief of Starr-Smith's lazzo of violence, he joins Pedrolino as the one zanni who is repeatedly punished for tricks and misdemeanours carried out by other members of the troupe, and who responds with bewildered self-reproach.[29] Following commedia scenarios such as Flaminio Scala's *Flavio the Fake Magician*, Dan also mirrors Pedrolino when he is ordered by the magician (in this case, Zagreus in costume) to dress as a woman and remain that way for the course of the evening.[30] One of Dan's most puzzling and remarked-upon idiosyncrasies is his almost wordless presence at even the most animated and provoking conversations. At Lionel Kein's house, for example, Zagreus interprets this for his host as the mark of genius in his young disciple: 'He will probably remain tongue-tied now for the rest of the visit . . . He's positively too shy to speak! It is the shyness of genius'.[31] It is also, however, the mark of Pierrot, described by Charles Baudelaire as 'mystérieux comme le silence, souple et muet comme le serpent' (mysterious as silence, supple and mute as the serpent).[32]

So if the prized commedia alter egos of Harlequin and Pierrot have fallen to Zagreus and Dan, what masks remain for Osmund and Phoebus? For the eldest Finnian Shaw sibling, Lewis reserves the vecchi mask of Pantalone, the ageing Venetian bachelor who dominated the financial world of the baroque performances, just as Osbert Sitwell did within his own domestic circle, thanks to a generous allowance from his father, Sir George Sitwell. Pantalone's irrec-oncilable passions add much to the Italian comedy, and Lewis does not scruple to use the less polished and unflattering Italian mask in his satire. Pantalone is mean and covetous, and yet adores luxury and ostentation, much as Osmund is anxious to display the Finnian Shaw repertoire of baroque splendour, artistic scholarship and aristocratic patronage, while serving his guests tinned sardines, Heinz tomatoes and flagons of Kia-Ora orange squash. Pantalone is peculiarly sensitive to both genuine offences and imagined grievances, and yet is slanderous and argumentative, a prey to emotional extremes and cursing, with Rudlin noting that 'he has a long memory, never forgets or forgives the slightest past transgression'.[33] Lewis no doubt saw Osbert Sitwell's volatile temperament and catalogue of feuds and vendettas with Noel Coward, John Collings Squire, Aldous Huxley, Wyndham Lewis himself, and the Golden Horde (the name that the Sitwell siblings gave to their mother's relations with their upstart aristocratic pretensions) as evidence enough to secure the part. Lord Osmund, Osbert Sitwell and Pantalone all have a heavy hooked nose, while Lord Osmund and Pantalone both attempt to disguise their ageing, over-indulged form in tight-fitting clothes, and Magnifico's scarlet cloak or jacket is reproduced in the vivid pink of Lord Osmund's dressing gown. The baroque Pantalone or Magnifico routinely performed routines from the 'social-class rebellion lazzi', interactions where the master asks a servant to carry out a task and the servant does this in such a way as to defy orders, thereby inverting power and exasperating their employer.[34] Lord Osmund is introduced to the reader through a similar lazzo, in which he asks the servant Peters to remove some logs from the fire as it is too warm, and Peters responds by removing them all, then, when reprimanded, returns two to the grate and pours water on them to make them smoke, hitting them to create more fumes and ignoring Lord Osmund's protests.

The etymology of Pantalone's name can also be playfully translated to fit Lord Osmund's aspirations, as the term, 'Pianta-leone', refers to the custom whereby Venetian merchants 'planted the lion' of the flag of St Mark wher-ever new lands were conquered and territories acquired. Osmund, whose real desire was to be a society lion himself, one of those coveted literary and artistic talents hunted by society hostesses for their poetry readings and parties, finds himself overlooked in Lewis's novel. The hostesses for their part dismiss him as a 'lion-skin stuffed with pedigrees and Bradburys . . . an Ape in "lion's" clothing not worth powder and shot of a "Leo"-Diana'.[35] Instead Lord Osmund is commissioned to seek out genuine leonine talent and grudg-ingly 'plant the lion' in drawing rooms across Chelsea so as to secure his own invitation. Il Dottore, as a friend and sometimes rival of Pantalone, could only be Lord Phoebus, Lewis's fictional incarnation of Sacheverell Sitwell, and as the latter was a private, gentle-natured, placatory man when compared with his siblings, Lewis's satire here is light and suggestive. There are, however, too many similarities between the learned Dottore and the youngest Finnian Shaw to be ignored. Sacheverell's ability to talk at length, combining encyclopaedic scholarship with esoteric fragments of history and art, anecdote and details from his adventures in Europe, must invite comparison with the commedia academic from Bologna whose pedantry and lengthy monologues boasting of his travels and reading lead Rudlin to define him as 'an anthologist of scraps of seeming significance'.[36] The Bonassus that old Cockeye (Sir George Sitwell) gives to Phoebus suggests the donkey or ass that Il Dottore often rode onto the stage during the baroque performances, providing Lewis's modern Gratiano with his commedia steed.

The ageing military figures introduced to the Lenten party by Lord Osmund's footman are Lewis's 1920s equivalent of the commedia Il Capitano mask. The sheer number of heroic military veterans in the novel – Colonel Ponto, Major Updick, Captain Alphonso Teach and Commander Perse – is in no way out of keeping with the Italian baroque. During the late sixteenth and early seventeenth centuries, the character of Il Capitano came in many guises and nationalities: the Spanish Matamoros, the Milanese Captain Spavento, and the French Fracasse to name but a few. Lord Osmund's own colonels and captains have all the sham swagger and bravado of their commedia counterparts and the unmasking of this pretence is just as important to both performances. The downfall of the baroque Captain and the revelation of a more humbling social and military identity is the stock fate of this commedia character, while in Lewis's version, Admiral Benbow's revelation that Commander Perse is an imposter show Lewis to again copy commedia scenarios, embellishing them with lazzi as Starr-Smith delivers an irreverent kick to the rear of old Colonel Ponto. The pugnacious Starr-Smith, or Blackshirt as Dan calls him, has his commedia double in the mask of Scaramuccia, which translates to mean 'skirmish'. Like Pierpoint's truculent political secretary, Scaramuccia dressed all in black and was keen to dual with whoever fell in his path, proving adept at avoiding blame and retaliation for his violent acts. Just as Dan is held responsible for the injuries that Blackshirt has inflicted on Ratner during the Vanish, so in the original commedia performances, innocent onlookers were accused of Scaramuccia's villainy.

The last mask to mention in any detail here is Julius Ratner, a Jewish publicist, writer, poet, pornographer and sometimes money-lender and he bears a striking resemblance to the zanni Brighella as a jack of all trades and a cynical observer of his fellow men. Ratner too has a pitiless eye 'framed principally for the functions of measuring and watching . . . always fishily *watchful*', and he has Brighella's promiscuous charm in his encounters with the fairer sex, flirting with his charwoman and seducing nurses in quick succession.[37] Lewis also offers us Ratner's seduction of the Fakir's wife by way of revenge on the Fakir himself, again following Brighella as an individual 'sure to take his revenge eventually, either upon his aggressor or upon the nearest substitute'.[38] This zanni 'insinuates suspicions, flatters vanity' and Ratner combines blandishments and provocation with revenge on the nearest subject when he vents his hatred of Zagreus on the far more vulnerable and credulous Dan.[39] While flattering the young protégé, Ratner tries to plant seeds of doubt by alleging that Zagreus is a homosexual, and highlighting his penchant for morons and for plundering the wit of others. Duchartre writes that 'Brighella's spine is so flexible that he can insinuate himself into any sort of nook or cranny, and disappear completely like his competitor the rat', and Ratner is many times labelled in these terms – 'spy-rat' or 'sewer rat'.[40] Even the pornographer's unusually sallow, yellow-tinged complexion repeats the dull yellow or olive-tinted mask peculiar to Brighella.

SATIRE AND FICTION

So while Lewis offers detailed and precise correspondences between the original commedia masks and their 1920s counterparts, how does the baroque performance relate to the novel's intentions, its methods and overall design? In 1930, Lewis published *Satire and Fiction*, a defence of *The Apes of God* that later reappeared in modified form in *Men Without Art* (1934). These two publications established his own definitions of satire, while justifying his choice of subject and technique in the wake of the novel's disappointing reception. My analysis will consider both the pamphlet and the much longer *Men Without Art*, beginning with Lewis's decision to pit narrative satire's strong visual bias against the 'stream of thought' prose favoured by Woolf, Proust and their disciples. The latter's attention to psychological detail and representations of flux and contingency is for Lewis the work of the 'time eye', a shadowy and unreliable orb that peeps out intermittently at the world around it, rather than subjecting it to steady scrutiny. The satiric eye, meanwhile, fixes victims with an unforgiving stare, lingering over 'their shells or pelts, or the language of their bodily movements'.[41] Lewis does on occasion look out at the world of Apes with the time eye, but it is reserved for peculiarly unworthy and uninteresting specimens such as the Victorian relic Lady Fredigonde, whose obvious decay and imminent demise lend themselves well to dull introspection and a flickering, squinting attention to the world around her. Even here, Lewis does not neglect the frail, superannuated shell that houses the vain thoughts and foibles, and once we move away from the Prologue and the curtain rises on the Apes, we are back in a world of unyielding surfaces and reassuringly defined forms. In fact, Lewis makes this a defining focus, insisting in both *Satire and Fiction* and *Men Without Art* that 'no book has ever been written that has paid so much attention to the *outside* of people'.[42] Laughter is the result of the satirist's representations of a dense, lumpish, indelicate, sensual, obscene human body, and Lewis stresses that we should never lose sight of our mortality and the extent to which we are grounded in our five senses.

The commedia mask and its related physicality offered Lewis just such a coveted shell and language of bodily movements. Each mask involved the crystallising of traits and distinctive physical identities, stereotypical awkwardness or agility, and coarse bodily functions. When Lewis draws attention to the significance of hunger, thirst, metabolism, gestation, courtship and reproduction as the building blocks of satire, he is simply listing the core material of all comic lazzi.[43] So, first, The Apes of God provides the description of the character's rigid, clumsy or exuberant movement, and then the more subtle associations of commedia physicality further qualify that image, with the effect of layering a precise identity and appearance. As the commedia actor often used stock actions and routines, the Apes are further humiliated, and Lewis emphasises this with repetitions of their customary, hackneyed responses, set-pieces for salon life such as the 'full scandal lazzi' with which they repeatedly greet shocking news.[44]

Rather unusually, given his distaste for movement and action in The Art of Being Ruled and The Dithyrambic Spectator, Lewis's theory of satire urges the reader not to forget just how significant physical action is, and to remember that The Apes of God 'is also a book of action'.[45] There may appear to be a contradiction here between Lewis's claims and apparent priorities and Hugh Kenner's sense that the text is static and lacks plot.[46] There is, however, no inconsistency, simply a misunderstanding as to what Lewis means by action in the context of his novel. Action comes first with the minutiae of description as individuals struggle with the material realm in which they are anchored – bodies flounder and fall, they are scorched, punished, dressed inappropriately, manhandled, and fail to move as required, while the inanimate objects that surround them enjoy a certain slick superiority, an effectiveness that recalls the stage properties of the baroque Tragedy of Fate. As an Ape kindergarten gathers in Grotian Walk for a fractious discussion of art and to view a collection of whips, Dan, who has by this time warmed to the task of Ape-watching, tries to hide himself away on an empty settee. The plump, opinionated Jenny, wife of Bloggie, a 'rich mountebank marine-painter', decides to join him but as she sits down, the settee begins 'to oscillate with a billowy movement that flung Dan from side to side. He was compelled to steady himself against the massive walls, which backed this too elastic, distinctly choppy, surface', and was moved uncomfortably close to his pursuer.[47] When he tries again to make his escape, the settee flings him back against its sides. Even without the malicious agency of objects being present in the same room as the Apes, they still manage to dictate characters' identities and actions in the most insidious and unexpected ways. The boats that Jenny's husband paints prevail over her significance and her agency throughout the chapter. Dick believes Jenny should 'trim her sails', and she is steadily overwhelmed by one nautical image after another.[48] As she tries to move towards Dan 'rolling heavily, and with a considerable list', guided only by a 'roving, half-blind old piratic eye', she is 'so stricken with involuntary momentum, so inclined to sag to starboard' that her progress is clumsy and doubly alarming for the seated Ape-watcher.[49] Boats in full sail seem to possess her physical body, so that each vigorous but wayward action is uncomfortable, clearly not of her own volition, and frustrating to the subject.

So the object in the world of Apes assumes the upper hand, and Lewis's commedia players shrink to the level of commodities or bundles of refractory impulses. While the whips in Grotian Walk come alive with a 'sleek and sinuous waggle' of their own, Mrs Farnham is moved to ask the staggeringly passive Dan 'Is it true, Mr Boleyn, that somebody has *made you* – that you have been manufactured like the – Hoffmann doll?'[50] Lewis writes of the shell collector Matthew Plunkett that 'a muscular spasm was set up about a group of ribs', and when he sinks down beside a table 'a manner of expectant vigour a little electrified the limp trunk'.[51] As the disciples of Proust entertain their guests, Isabel Kein sits at one end of the table and her husband at the other, when suddenly 'a loud clap of laughter burst from Kein's mouth, it rattled and tossed for some moments along the table' like an object spilling from a pocket to the embarrassment of the owner and the amazement of the onlookers seated around him.[52] The abstract sound takes on a tangible and obtrusive reality and a momentum all its own. Time and time again, Lewis's Apes seem to perform movements that they have neither countenanced nor approved, and the parts of the body involved seem to act with a rather furtive rival agency. This is not a new technique in Lewis's presentation of the absurd, as, in 1918, the bohemian artist Frederick Tarr suffered from the same separation of mind and body but with a clear difference – Tarr develops sly, elaborate strategies for reclaiming the initiative:

> If ever taken off his guard, he made clever use immediately afterwards of his naieveté. He beamed on his slip. He swallowed it tranquilly, assimilating it with ostentation to himself. When some personal weakness slipped out he would pick it up unabashed, look at it smilingly, and put it back in his pockets.[53]

Formidable, secret and objectified, these expressions of the physical body, the instinct and the senses require vigilance on the part of the subject. The body betrays the individual into foolish or uncomfortable action, while the intellect, lagging a little behind, must claim the power of intent and the ease of familiarity, thereby retrieving at least the appearance of self-determination. As Tarr arrives at Bertha's apartment, he is cautious, and has hardened himself against feelings of tenderness and interest, so that he can break off their engagement without relenting. He is, however, soon unmanned and disconcerted by his own immoderate laughter, and he fears that it will undermine the strength and sincerity of his protests, and his resolve as he attempts to extricate himself from his attachment:

> He sat down squarely in front of her, hardly breathed from his paroxysm, getting launched without transition. He hoped, by rapid plunging from one state to another, to take the wind out of the laugh's sails. It should be left towering, spectral, but becalmed behind.[54]

Trying to ignore the unintentional explosion of mirth, Tarr responds in the same breath by blaming Bertha for the outburst, and his counter-attack, for one so accustomed to these impulses of insubordination, is as a reflex in itself. There is nothing that can be done to diminish the lingering presence and impact of the laugh, but by affecting poise and a lack of concern, Tarr hopes to diminish its power to distract Bertha from the solemn matter in hand. The Apes, however, seem quite unable respond to these tensions with Tarr's ingenuity and insight, and they remain resigned, baffled and humiliated. Here, Lewis's commedia theme allows yet another unflattering contrast with the original baroque players. The latter certainly performed slips, tumbles and apparently unsolicited movements and expressions, but this was the work of a highly disciplined, coordinated body, and the clowning was quite intentional. In the 'Lazzo of the Knock', for example, Pedrolino wakes from a sleep, only to inadvertently bump, crush and then strike all the masks around him.[55] Arlecchino too performs ridiculous falling fits, attempts not to topple from ladders, pratfalls into baths, and in the 1688 'Lazzo of Getting Inside', he stands at the top of a ladder and then falls through the window and returns straight back through the door all in one movement.[56]

Objects also intervene to transfer activity away from the subject and into the realm of language. As Dick greets Lady Fredigonde, hiding his distaste for this decaying Victorian relative, Lewis writes:

> His hands knotted, presented symmetrically like buffers in the pockets of the soiled mauve bags – face inclined to the ground – the bright essence, regardless-of-cost, left burning in his staring head-lights – the spacious involuntary tonsure now visible as he slightly rolled forward his head, the good Dick paced away from her, faced unstably about and returned with the action of that refractory child being dragged along by something like its umbilical cord, while mischievously but indolently it kicks objects in its path, to obstruct high-handed Nanny's dragging.[57]

There are objects in the path of the reader too, obstructing our progress to easy comprehension. The movements and gestures performed here are obscured: we are offered one clause and then another, but the connection is unclear. The objects responsible for distracting our gaze include buffers, pockets, bags, a bright essence and head-lights, all in confusing succession, before Dick is finally allowed to move his head. Images or items that relate to Dick's new Bugatti, like the boats in Bloggie's paintings, seem to intervene to make the associated subject falter and become absurd. Any movement that follows this momentary focus on the nephew's tonsure is again confusing. His head is somehow 'involuntary' – an adjective that is surely more attuned to his clumsy, frustrated motion. Then, as his head rolls forward, his body moves away from Lady Fredigonde, wobbles in its retreat and then returns grudgingly. His frame is dragged by an invisible cord and Dick's approach to his aunt is petulant and resistant. The words and images leap and exchange connections, while the character flounders, and the result is a bright, detailed, confusing and visually distracting pictorial aesthetic. Action here sees Lewis relishing the intellectual exercise of shaping the rather obdurate world of matter that has vexed and hindered the victim of satire: 'The intellect athletically enjoys itself in the midst of matter, and is not afraid of objective things because it has the power to model them and compose a world of its own out of objective substance'.[58]

So the satirist can relish the material world simply because it can be mediated, stylised and mastered through language and image, while it may defy all three interventions at the level of lived experience, confounding the subjects of Lewis's mockery at every step. Satire details a world where an objective material perspective and a heightened awareness of the absurd predominate and are inseparable. Lewis refers to a crucial sense of detachment, the 'transcendental viewpoint which is explicit in laughter', but which we must use sparingly: it 'must just tip and gild as it were the wings of all our philosophies', illuminating without overwhelming or destroying.[59] With 'transcendence', he is not suggesting an otherworldly perspective, but is thinking in terms of judgement and understanding, aspiring to a vantage point from where he can approach self-knowledge, and from where he can execute a deliberate and almost complete intellectual separation between himself and the material and individuals he critiques. The ascendancy of inanimate things in *The Apes of God* is not the dreamy coalescing of subject and object found within the stream-of-consciousness technique. Lewis has a clear sense of the distinct object and its interference in the life of the Apes, and the ability of these objects to overwhelm and even to inhabit Lewis's selection of dilettantes is one of the many ways in which he suggests an enervated, hollow quality within modern subjectivity. While in the commedia performance, physical action was often swift, incisive and even athletic, Lewis displaces that energy, and it is not human bodies but the words on the written page that surprise and impress, performing feats of skill, changes of pace, unexpected flights, tumbles and tricks.

Following responses to *The Apes of God* as a roman à clef, Lewis also stood accused of selecting rather mediocre prey. His response was to claim that the satirist chooses those of middle standing, because individuals who are revered and promoted in a way that already far exceeds their merits could hardly be made to look more ridiculous. The accusation that he uses rather nondescript characters is perhaps inevitable, as satire concerns itself with individuals of gossip-column calibre, but shies away from emphasising their importance. For Lewis, it is, in fact, realism that has a taste for the genuinely inconsequential. Perhaps the most striking claim that Lewis makes for satire in general, and certainly for that particular category practised in *The Apes of God*, is that it represents a non-ethical treatment of characters and situations. He sees moral-ity as a shifting and relative standard, with good and evil denoting different qualities and eliciting different responses according to time and place: 'the moralist today is installed upon a veritable quicksand, as well as the "irre-sponsible" laughing figure he would denounce'.[60] The satirist may often prove to be a complex of orthodox moral and amoral values. His ethical purpose might also suffer from the intricacy of his ideas and their highly intellectu-alised expression, both of which could overwhelm a more modest, essential understanding of good and evil. Lewis also feels that the life promoted by a conscientious and principled mind, as its thoughts become more sophisticated and abstract, may actually prove detrimental to the majority and untenable once those values come to be applied at a practical level.

So, for Lewis, there are no absolute standards of virtue or vice and perhaps for satire's particular aesthetic purpose, the terms 'real' and 'unreal' are more serviceable tools of analysis. By way of example, he highlights the word 'vulgar', an important card in matters of moral judgement, but one that the satirist must now play with caution, as it is no longer the prerogative of the educated elite. Vulgarity is an accusation that can be directed by the coal-bearer at his master, 'accompanied by the sneer of an aristocrat', suggesting the employer to be wealthy but without manners and a sense of social responsibil-ity, 'a mere money-man'.[61] So the term has lost its particular association with those of a lower status. The matter is further complicated as the artist cannot satirise those who are clearly not vulgar and stupid, but must inevitably be criticised for aiming his barbs at individuals who have precisely those qualities in abundance and may subsequently be seen as unworthy targets. Lewis states that, like Dryden, he has chosen his victims not because they are naughty, but because they are dull. To remove moral censure is to prevent the subject turning villainy to account. So Lewis's argument seems to suggest that the victim must first endure the implied criticism and ridicule, and then a disconcerting lack of notoriety. If that subject's crime has simply been to be uninspired, common-place, and to fail of genius but not to prove dishonourable, then there need be no guilt in the laughter – the victim is absurd rather than reprehensible. The satirist who has presented their subject without brilliance, but also without the frisson of iniquity, is therefore twice as culpable in the eyes of audience and victim, as the glamour of the genuinely vicious is felt as a loss by both.

PATRONAGE AND COURT PERFORMANCE

The original Italian commedia dell'arte serves Lewis's purpose well in matters of satire and social critique. Official censorship of performances was not introduced until the eighteenth century, while during the seventeenth century it was left to the sovereign to license or prohibit as they saw fit.[62] Civil and ecclesiastical authorities, meanwhile, objected to the commedia's profanity, its associations with charlatans and their counterfeit remedies and with itinerant beggars and vagabonds. Companies were persecuted and excluded from towns wherever possible, but it was not the naked flesh and mountebanks alone that caused concern. Commedia improvisation allowed the players to engage with all manner of contemporary social, political and economic situations, and with personalities who had cultivated celebrity or come to public attention. While censorship in the eighteenth century was designed to establish an essentially didactic theatre and safeguard moral standards by outlawing extemporised performance, the brevity of scenarios and the sheer spontaneity and freedom enjoyed by companies during the 1600s were very difficult to police. Often the exact social or political significance of an individual improvisation would be decided by the interaction between spectator and actor, and would remain unique to that performance. Winifred Smith notes that 'the Gherardi ... satirised corruption of public officials, the charlatanry of the so-called learned classes, pedantry of the Academy, the hollowness of professions of honour'.[63] The commedia endured for more than two centuries precisely because the stock lazzi and fixed qualities of each mask were infinitely adaptable in presenting different personalities or social and political situations. Edward Gordon Craig notes that the commedia performance was always attuned to the time and events that surrounded it: 'it was topical, and its satiric thrusts could be cruel and instantaneous and unpredictable'.[64] Just how bold and quick-witted such impromptu responses became is clear from Count Carlo Gozzi's account of his performance as Pantalone's wife Luce. Gozzi explains that in the absence of her long-delayed Pantalone she (he) improvises by trying to suckle her baby with a man's chest to amuse the audience. Noticing a beautiful and self-assured young woman called Tonina in the theatre's front box, a siren of dubious career with a catalogue of catastrophes to her name, the actor begins to address the baby as if it were an infant Tonina. The mother warns the child that she would rather that God cut short her young life than that she should fall into immoral ways. The knowing audience are delighted, the victim of the satire leaves the theatre angry and indignant, while Gozzi acknowledges that 'personal allusions were allowed perhaps a little too liberally' on the com-media stage.[65] So when Lewis casts the precociously learned Sacheverell as Il

Dottore or the self-publicising Osbert with his youth cult as Pantalone (the Venetian merchant was always in pursuit of a much younger wife or lover), he was simply elaborating an age-old tradition of irreverent humour and mortification, and capturing it for the page and posterity. The commedia actors often escaped prosecution as the improvisations were lost as soon as they had been performed, but Lewis had to face accusations of libel as every barb was immortalised in print.

If commedia performance originated in Italy's streets and piazzas on portable trestles and benches in front of lower-class spectators, then how could Lewis's description of the Finnian Shaws' celebration lend itself to comparison with the baroque originals and serve his satiric purpose? Ingenuity and talent established the reputations of many commedia companies and this popularity, in turn, secured royal patronage and patrician audiences in Italy and France alike. Some players enjoyed favouritism and many indulgences at court – Prince Vicenzo of Mantua agreed to become godfather to Isabella Andreini's daughter Lavinia, while Tristano Martinelli was summoned to perform at the marriage of Henry IV to Marie dei Medici in 1600, and the queen later became godmother to his son.[66] Lewis would have been keen to mock the Sitwells as artistic patrons as they were venturing to produce their own art, but also because they had disappointed him in their role as sponsors of his work. He wastes no time in suggesting Lord Osmund's courtly pretensions, introducing him as 'the head as it were of the procession', entering the dining hall for the banquet, where 'he sweeps majestically forward' followed by his court retinue of family, guests and attendants.[67] In the baroque period, artworks and literature were the prerogative of the upper classes, with spectacles and performances designed to display and consolidate power over the masses. Lewis allows the Finnian Shaws 'a suggestion of the sumptuous', with a painting of Scaramuccia by Severini and Malayan masks, but these touches of taste and finery are soon overwhelmed by 'tactless table ornaments' and ugly 'pseudo-Etruscan' vases.[68] The Lenten celebration is referred to as 'their private theatre, this is Lord Osmund's dramatic troupe and household-cast at full strength'.[69] Kristiaan Aercke notes that during the late sixteenth century, more festive performances began to be staged in the private setting of the court itself.[70] These were for a select audience and were designed for the purpose of self-affirmation, promoting respect and admiration. The monarch as sponsor-ruler had always led public processions, and they continued to participate once performances moved to a private hall or theatre inside the court, with a banquet always complementing the play. So it is easy to read Lord Osmund and his siblings as patrons of both modernist and baroque art-worlds in the early 1920s, into the role of sponsor-ruler, and also to find a parallel for their strange retreat to the family library. Baroque engravings and paintings reveal that the sponsor-ruler did not communicate directly with guests, but sat in the centre of the theatre with his back to the spectators and facing the players.[71] Baroque festive performance therefore established a sequence of invitation and ostentation, followed by rituals that were designed to reinforce a sense of exclusivity and detachment, strengthening awareness of hierarchy and the distance between host and guests. Having carefully invited their not-so-select array of media figures and fashionable Chelsea herds to the celebrations with a view to securing a place in gossip columns and forthcoming poetry anthologies, the Finnian Shaws 'barricaded themselves in upstairs as though all these people had got in against their will'.[72] The library, one of the most defining symbols of the baroque period and 'the soul of our host', becomes a sanctuary that betrays Lord Osmund's desire to remain aloof, while highlighting the family's sham hospitality and general disdain for the public they seek to impress.[73] Their display and the particular choice of guests represent an attempt to consolidate publicity, celebrity and a power that can no longer be enjoyed simply by being a lord and a patron of the arts. Lewis plays on the traditional rapport between commedia audience and the masks, as the guests and spectators at the Lenten party are invited to participate, their curiosity piqued by the celebrity players and their backdrop of paintings and artefacts, and then they are snubbed and excluded. The Finnian Shaws form part of a commedia troupe, so that the reader can identify similarities, but also recognise their failure to fulfil defining conventions, such as the reciprocity of performance.

The General Strike

Lewis's satire is not simply a matter of the Apes' spurious social and aesthetic practices. The playful arrogance and elitism of the Sitwell commedia is in stark contrast to the original baroque performances, with their clear focus on current economic and political issues. In the final section of the novel, 'The General Strike', we follow a despondent Dan across London, realising that he is quite oblivious to the strike action. Lewis was not in the habit of introducing events from contemporary history into his works of fiction, so the strike itself, and its relationship to the novel's overall design, were clearly significant. Paul Edwards draws attention to a particularly sensitive passage written by Lewis for *Paleface* in 1929, while he was still working on *The Apes of God*. The subject is the General Strike and its subsequent economic hardships, and Edwards acknowledges that this, for Lewis, is an 'unusually concrete picture of signs of political failure since 1926':

> There are hundreds of thousands of miners and their families in England today who are out of work and without the proper requirements for animal life. Against the London parks at night penniless people lie huddled in their hundreds. Our streets both day and night swarm with every variety of beggar.[74]

So the industrial action of 1926, with its economic and political repercussions, appears to be a rather singular preoccupation. The strike itself lasted a mere ten days, and had been long anticipated by all sides, with the police doubling recruitment in areas near to the coalfields. The mine-owners had responded to Britain's economic difficulties defensively, wanting to cut wages by 13 per cent and to add an hour to the collier's working day. On 6 March that year, the government's Samuel Commission published a report acknowledging that the pay-cuts were unavoidable, but the colliers rejected the findings, beginning their strike at midnight on 3 May. They found a broad base of support as the building, iron and steel industries and workers at British docks and railways joined the strike action, with 2½ million employees downing tools on the first day. In *The Apes of God*, as Dan leaves the Apes and ventures out into the deserted streets of the capital, Lewis mentions the violent clashes between police and strikers that took place in the capital on 6 May. The conflicts spread to Edinburgh, Glasgow, Hull and Liverpool, while the government retaliated by arresting communists and confiscating supplies of paper, preventing publication of the TUC's *The British Worker*. As the strike continued, Baldwin's Conservative government presented the unrest as a challenge to the state and a catalyst for civil war, and relations between the TUC and miners deteriorated. James Thomas, the Chairman of the General Council of the Trades Union Congress, became increasingly nervous, and he and the other political leaders betrayed the miners by accepting a compromise that did not safeguard pay. Although the initial public response was an increase in the numbers of those striking, many drifted back to work and the miners soon found themselves isolated.

Having noted Lewis's concern for the country's miners and beggars in *Paleface*, Edwards goes on to note that the itinerant band who stand suspended in time outside Lord and Lady Follet's house at both the beginning and the end of the novel are just such a group of 'unemployed mendicants', and they also have turned to performance to earn money.[75] Their introduction is yet another way for Lewis to bring together the worlds of authentic baroque commedia and the Sitwell forgery for satiric effect. The Prologue to *The Apes of God* serves the commedia theme well, as it is quite distinct from the rest of the text in its focus on Lady Fredigonde, its internalised narrative, and even Lewis's choice of italicised typography. The commedia Prologues were also quite unconnected with the performance that followed. Lewis's Prologue opens the novel with a drum roll and itinerant beggars, just as drum rolls introduced the arrival of the travelling commedia players and their vagrant counterparts to Italian towns in the late sixteenth and seventeenth centuries. So Lewis is inviting us to examine the economic depression and the travelling beggars whose drum-beats so unnerve Lady Fredigonde, alongside the dispossessed of sixteenth- and seventeenth-century Italy, who were also forced to become itinerant beggars and to perform for donations, blending the roles of actor and vagabond. As Henke observes, in Italy, the medieval legacy of travelling mendicants was thoroughly assimilated in the language of the commedia performance. Ever-present hunger, destitution and constant travel are reasons why 'both documentary and performance commedia texts convey a much more palpable sense of the material body and its needs than English analogues', and baroque Venice, as the heart of professional commedia performance, was particularly affected by poverty and epidemics.[76] Before the stereotyped masks were established, early zanni adopted names such as Zan Fritatta (omelette) and Zan Farina (flour) emphasising the buffoons' constant daydreams and attempts to secure a meal. Arlecchino often had a spoon tied to his belt or wandered onto the stage with his hand inside a pot of macaroni, while his little family of Arlecchini were depicted begging for food. The 'Lazzi of Hunger' involved characters chewing on their shoes or other stage properties, while the 'Lazzi of the Royal Taster' placed Arlecchino before a lavish banquet, accompanied by a Royal physician who repeatedly snatched dishes from him, with the excuse that they cause apoplexy.[77]

Before further comparing the modern and the baroque, it is helpful to pause and detail the events of the General Strike of 1926 as they unfolded in political history rather than across the pages of Lewis's fiction, and to examine Osbert Sitwell's role in proceedings, as presented in the fourth volume of his autobiography. Here, Sitwell insinuates himself into the strike narrative somewhat obliquely, admitting that he relies on second-hand information, but alleging that the matter is of some importance as he has been closely involved in negotiations to end the strike action, and because he sees the style of arbitration as representative of both the period and of the country's political discourse in general. The Sitwell siblings emerge aloof and slightly dazed from events that precede the strike, because performances of *Façade* had engrossed them until the last week in April and the industrial action began on the night of 3 May. Osbert claims that the dispute is of particular significance to him, as coal smoke is his native air at Renishaw, and he goes on to profess friendship with the miners as well as a clear understanding of their harsh living conditions. The deadlock clearly presented him with an opportunity to resurrect keen political interests that had been thwarted by a failed campaign to enter Parliament in 1918. Scarborough was the location of the Sitwell family home, Wood End, and the constituency of Scarborough and Whitby elected a Member of Parliament for the first time during the 1918 General Election. Lord Osbert stood as the Liberal candidate, but lost to the Unionist William Gervaise Beckett by 11,764 votes to 7,994.

Sitwell's autobiography is keen to stress the innate political abilities of the company that he keeps during the strike. He is summoned by Lady Wimborne, a glamorous hostess whose political intelligence and consummate hospitality lead her to preside over strike negotiations, and Sitwell interprets her role as 'all pervasive'.[78] Her husband, Lord Wimborne, has strong democratic sympathies, and his secretary, Mr Selwyn Davies, is also presented as an important intermediary in the process of arbitration. The highlight of their collective endeavours appears to be several luncheon parties and informal meetings that brought together James Thomas of the TUC, John Alfred Spender, editor of the *Westminster Gazette*, Ethel Snowdon, wife of the former Labour Chancellor of the Exchequer, the Marquess of Londonderry who was present as a moderate coal owner, and the Chairman of the BBC, Lord Gainford. Stanley Baldwin rejected the proposals put forward by Lord Wimborne and Thomas, and, significantly, the possibility of lifting the miners' lockout was never discussed by Sitwell's coterie.[79]

It is easy to understand Lewis's decision to introduce the General Strike as an event that frames the novel and his distaste for Osbert's particular intervention in proceedings. By bringing images of itinerant beggars from both baroque and modern periods together through the commedia theme, Lewis can be said to invite comparison of the treatment and presentation of that distress. While the most famous and privileged commedia actors continued to perform hunger and misfortune in front of their royal patrons, so as to elicit compassion and financial relief for the poor, Lord Osbert's boasts of fellow-feeling and concern for British colliers lasted no longer than the term of hostility and drama that ended on 12 May 1926. The celebrated baroque Arlecchino, Tristano Martinelli, once a piazza charlatan himself, never forgot to acknowledge or to remind his public of the poverty and famine that itinerant groups faced. As the miners' strike dragged on into the November of 1926, however, with the colliers locked out of the pits and dependent on charitable donations, soup kitchens and the pitiful provision of Poor Law relief, Osbert's consideration and sympathy seemed to vanish with the opportunity for self-promotion and political involvement.[80] He had boasted of familiarity and respect for the colliers and their love of gardening, fishing, whippets, and the great outdoors, but it was a familiarity that had been expedient in justifying his ability to engage sympathetically with the political situation, and a respect that had resulted in no practical measures of support. In the summer of 1926, this self-styled Harlequin turned his attention back to the world of literary endeavour, working with Sacheverell on *All At Sea: A Social Tragedy in Three Acts for First Class Passengers Only*, an unsuccessful joint venture that was published in 1927. The treachery and a link between the intractable coal magnates and the Sitwells is quite explicit in *The Apes of God*, when Blackshirt tells Dan that the Finnian Shaw museum, with its talentless guests, undrinkable wine and gimcrack ornaments, is 'still supported [. . .] upon the plundering of a tenantry, upon money taken from miners', a reference, no doubt, to the fact that the discovery of coal in Renishaw park had once been responsible for a restoration of the Sitwell family fortunes, and to the mining villages of Renishaw and Eckhart that nestled behind the park trees.[81]

Osbert's strike narrative contains much of the theatrical self-publicising that Lewis and Huxley disliked so intensely in the Sitwell family. In *Laughter in the Next Room*, Osbert presents himself as a hero in one of Gabriele D'Annuzio's novels, awaiting the call to political action from his palace, and he offers the reader a rather melodramatic image of himself walking 'footsore, heartsore' across the empty streets of London, without transport as the taxi drivers are striking.[82] The reader can only marvel at such impolitic self-pity, given Sitwell's cosseted view of strike proceedings from plush drawing rooms and lavish dinner parties at the vast, Palladian Wimborne house, a venue coveted by the neighbouring Ritz Hotel for expansion. His account of the negotiations emphasises tension, danger and ennui with every anecdote and recollection. Even once the strike has ended, Osbert seems reluctant to relinquish the turmoil and unrest that might have placed him centre-stage, dwelling on 'the immense evils the country had so narrowly escaped' long after the event, as if he felt that his own unique contribution must be an elaboration of the worst possible eventualities for both sides.[83]

In *The Dithyrambic Spectator* and *The Art of Being Ruled*, Lewis was clearly suspicious of the realms of action and performance with their multitude of spectators anxious to trespass in the realm of art. In *The Apes of God*, Lewis appears far more comfortable and poised when grappling with these troubling interlopers, and they are captured and subdued by their many satiric commedia dell'arte parallels. This treatment extends the theatrical metaphor that Lewis introduced with the earlier critical texts, reducing the Apes to stereotypes, where there are clear similarities between the modern and the baroque, and humiliating them as clumsy, narcissistic and unaccomplished, where there are marked differences and even inversions of the original genre. The baroque commedia players took on many of the traits of their mask rather than imposing their own personalities in performance, and, in the same way, the Apes are defined by their allotted masks, forfeiting the unique talent, originality and marks of distinction that were central to the Sitwells' carefully crafted public image, and Lewis implies that they succumb to these stereotypes with some enthusiasm. The many inversions practised within carnival and commedia conventions, as the lower orders usurped the roles, professional identities and social status of those of higher rank, can only highlight the real imitation at work in the novel, as Apes commandeer the roles of genuine artists so as to better display their personalities and provoke gossip. The most telling of these inversions plays with the defining commedia talent for improvisation. In *Mrs Dukes' Million*, Lewis allows Royal and his fellow actors an ever-increasing liberty to depart from Sarundar Khan's canovaccio, until each new difficulty and its solution becomes pure improvisation. In *The Apes of God*, Lewis translates extemporised performance back in the opposite direction, with Zagreus purchasing or plundering Pierpoint's scripted speeches, while drawing attention to his own minimal inventions and adaptations. Isabel Kein suggests that Zagreus would make an excellent actor, thanks to his formidable memory and ability to recite Pierpoint's writings to the letter: 'there is our great and dear friend Pierpoint's text – orally preserved'.[84] Zagreus's own tentative additions, and his fear that they may spoil the original communication as a whole, show just how far from confident commedia extemporisation this particular Arlecchino has strayed. He follows Pierpoint's sentences and strategies of critique to the extent that Lewis seems to be replacing the role of corago with that of literary playwright: 'every word, like everything else about him, *borrowed*'.[85]

With so much precise commedia detail woven into the world of the Apes, why did Lewis not draw attention to the commedia archetypes in his defence of the satire or to exonerate himself from the charges of libel attendant upon a roman à clef? Part of the answer may lie with the fact that the Sitwells themselves would be painfully aware of the traits that the Finnian Shaws share with the baroque commedia masks, and at the same time unwilling to acknowledge having recognised any similarities, thereby adding further ridicule to the more explicit biographical satire. Lewis could craft a series of scenarios that might escape the notice and condemnation of those who talked in terms of libel and yet deliver a telling blow to the Sitwell siblings, who knew the minutiae of commedia tradition all too well. The family's reputation as arbiters of cultural taste owed more to the baroque art-world than to any other period or style, so Lewis would have taken particular pleasure in using it to unravel that celebrity. The novel is certainly embellished with carnival detail – the Bonassus, for example, suggests the donkey or King of Asses that was often substituted for King Carnival during the celebrations. The illustrations that introduce each of the eight sections of the novel have often confounded readers, and the strange seated human figure at the beginning of 'Lord Osmund's Lenten Party' is no exception. The bird-like head with its sharp, downward curving hooked beak is, however, reminiscent of the very early commedia masks that were made from papier-mâché and had an eagle-beaked nose, before the masks became more clearly defined and the anonymous carnivalesque masks were replaced. The image is therefore a fitting introduction to Lewis own commedia performance. Carnival and commedia do occupy the same public spaces, using the same conventions of inversion, disguise, and mockery of the grotesque human body, but in terms of the definitions and ideas that preoccupy Lewis in his critique of modernist culture, commedia and carnival are in many ways quite distinct. In fact, some of the contradictions inherent in Lewis's many references to the commedia stem from its liminal identity as an experience neither shared as unmediated folk culture nor assimilated and tamed within the written text or scripted performance. Carnival is part of the collective ritualised participation that Jane Harrison celebrates in classical culture, while commedia is poised between this and the clearly defined conventions of viewer and artist or performer that, for Lewis, defined high art. Commedia is an art-form that has at least consented to accept a division of sorts between spectator and masks but one that cannot completely break with carnival's instinct to participate, and this reciprocity between commedia audience and players threatens the neat divide that Lewis demands in art.

It is clear from Lewis's account of the 'time eye' that modernism has moved too far from the public, collective experience of carnival, with its externalised aesthetic of sensuous forms, eccentric physicality and profane bodies. Modernist art has come to rest in an intimate, internalised world of psychological detail and flux, a world in which Lewis himself cannot settle, and the commedia represents a pause in this regrettable telescoping inwards, a compromise that still embodies his preferred medium of surfaces and exterior shells. While carnival transgression was always a tacit acknowledgement of the vulnerability of the ruling classes and state authority, representing a power that predates all systems of government, in *The Apes of God*, that collective will and energy, the revolutionary potential of the lower orders, has been neatly contained by the ruthless counter-measures of Baldwin's cabinet, the Trades Union Congress, and a timid middle class who were all too ready to associate popular unrest with the worst excesses of the Russian Revolution. The commedia provides Lewis with images and conventions that allow social, political and aesthetic critique, but ultimately not transformation. Lady Fredigonde may die in the arms of Zagreus and the Sitwells' pretensions may be held up to ridicule, but those who deliver the indictment, for all their censure and playful transgression, are ultimately complicit in the sins of the Apes. Mischief in the form of Zagreus may contend with the churlish Lenten sobriety of Lord Osmund, but Zagreus turns out to be an Ape in Arlecchino's motley after all. If Pierpoint's speeches are the work of an absent authority and Zagreus's minor improvisations are the vain flutterings of democracy, neither ultimately carries the day. The revolution at the level of culture that Lewis believed to be a necessary catalyst for change was in the end nothing more than the stalking horse of a privileged but talentless elite, the gilded bolshevism of the wealthy aristocrat. The commedia metaphor and images combine to create a complex, layered aesthetic that brings together every aspect of the novel – it is the most developed and detailed aspect of his social satire and of the biographical elements that distracted early readers, it is central to the novel's strong visual bias and to Lewis's external method, and it informs his socio-political critique.

NOTES

1. Lewis, *The Apes of God*, p. 354.
2. Craig, 'Critics Criticised' in *The Mask*, 1912, 5, p. 183.
3. 'A Reader's Report for an American Publisher', in Lewis, *Satire and Fiction*, p. 130.
4. Swinerton, Aldington, in Lewis, *Satire and Fiction*, pp. 35, 23.
5. Mais, in Lewis, *Satire and Ficiton*, pp. 34, 16.
6. Munton, 'Wyndham Lewis: The Transformations of Carnival', in *Wyndham Lewis – Letteratura/Pittura*, p. 152.
7. Caracciolo, 'Mr Punch, Zoroastrianism and Relativity' in *Enemy News*, 18, pp. 28–31.
8. Lewis, *The Apes of God*, pp. 361, 410.
9. Ibid. p. 355.
10. Gordon, *Lazzi: The Comic Routines of the Commedia dell'Arte*, p. 9.
11. Lewis, *The Apes of God*, p. 244.
12. Ibid. p. 168.
13. Riccoboni, quoted in Sand, *A History of the Harlequinade*, p. 63.
14. Lewis, *The Apes of God*, p. 400.
15. Sand, *A History of the Harlequinade*, p. 65.
16. Smith, *The Commedia Dell'Arte – A Study in Popular Italian Comedy*, p. 36.
17. Lewis, *The Apes of God*, p. 329.
18. Ibid. pp. 335, 328.
19. Ibid. p. 422.
20. Lima, *Stages of Evil: Occultism in Western Theater and Drama*, p. 50.
21. Henke, *Performance and Literature in the Commedia Dell'Arte*, pp. 55–60.
22. Lewis, *The Apes of God*, p. 423.
23. Ibid. p. 203.
24. Storey, *Pierrot – A Critical History of a Mask*, pp. 9–19.
25. Gordon, *Lazzi: The Comic Routines of the Commedia dell'Arte*, p. 17.
26. Lewis, *The Apes of God*, p. 200.
27. Mic, *La Commedia Dell'Arte ou le Théatre des Comédiens Italiens des XVIe, XVIIe and XVIIIe Siècles*, p. 47.
28. Sand, *A History of the Harlequinade*, p. 22.
29. See for example Duchartre, *The Italian Comedy*, p. 251.
30. Scala, *Flavio The Fake Magician*, cited in Sand, *A History of the Harlequinade*, pp. 232–2.
31. Lewis, *The Apes of God*, pp. 251–2.
32. Baudelaire, *De l'Essence de Rire et Généralement du Comique dans les Arts Plastiques*, in *Oeuvres Complètes*, p. 380 (my own translation).
33. Rudlin, *The Commedia Dell'Arte: An Actor's Handbook*, p. 95.
34. Gordon, *Lazzi: The Comic Routines of the Commedia dell'Arte*, p. 29.
35. Lewis, *The Apes of God*, p. 386.
36. Rudlin, *The Commedia Dell'Arte: An Actor's Handbook*, p. 103.
37. Lewis, *The Apes of God*, p. 167.
38. Duchartre, *The Italian Comedy*, p. 162.
39. Oreglia, *The Commedia Dell'Arte*, p. 71.
40. Duchartre, *The Italian Comedy*, p. 161; Lewis, *The Apes of God*, p. 151, 400.
41. Lewis, *Satire and Fiction*, p. 46.
42. Ibid.
43. Lewis, *Men Without Art*, p. 288.
44. Lewis, *The Apes of God*, pp. 274, 593.

45. Lewis, *Men Without Art*, p. 123.
46. Kenner, *Wyndham Lewis*, pp. 103–4.
47. Lewis, *The Apes of God*, pp. 180, 187.
48. Ibid. p. 181.
49. Ibid. pp. 186, 187.
50. Ibid. pp. 190, 205.
51. Ibid. p. 68
52. Ibid. p. 280.
53. Lewis, *Tarr*, p. 6.
54. Ibid. p. 85.
55. Gordon, *Lazzi: The Comic Routines of the Commedia dell'Arte*, p. 15.
56. Ibid. p. 12.
57. Lewis, *The Apes of God*, p. 31.
58. Ibid. p. 231.
59. Lewis, *Men Without Art*, p. 288.
60. Ibid. p. 134.
61. Ibid. p. 135.
62. Bauer-Heinhold, *Baroque Theatre*, p. 34.
63. Smith, *The Commedia Dell'Arte*, p. 214.
64. 'Critics Criticised', *The Mask*, 5.2, July 1912, pp. 182–3.
65. 'An Improvisation by Count Carlo Gozzi', *The Mask*, 4.2, October 1911, p. 123.
66. Duchartre, *The Italian Comedy*, p. 91; 'Biographical Notes' in 'The Pre-Shakespearean Stage, Some Facts About It', *The Mask*, 6.2, October 1913, p. 155.
67. Lewis, *The Apes of God*, pp. 349, 350.
68. Ibid. pp. 352, 353, 352.
69. Ibid. p. 352.
70. Aercke, *Gods of Play: Baroque Festive Performance as Rhetorical Discourse*, p. 27.
71. Ibid. p. 39.
72. Lewis, *The Apes of God*, p. 484.
73. Ibid. p. 567.
74. Edwards, *Wyndham Lewis: Painter and Writer*, p. 344.
75. Ibid. p. 344.
76. Henke, 'Representations of Poverty in the Commedia dell'Arte', *Theatre Survey*, 48.2, pp. 234, 230.
77. Gordon, *Lazzi: The Comic Routines of the Commedia dell'Arte*, pp. 21, 22.
78. Sitwell, *Laughter in the Next Room*, p. 212.
79. Perkins, *A Very British Strike, 3 May–12 May 1926*, p. 219.
80. Henke, 'Representations of Poverty in the Commedia dell'Arte', pp. 236–7.
81. Lewis, *The Apes of God*, p. 483.
82. Sitwell, *Laughter in the Next Room*, p. 218.
83. Ibid. p. 221.
84. Lewis, *The Apes of God*, p. 267.
85. Ibid. p. 266.

CONCLUSION

To examine these particular writers and their work is to see baroque modernism as an aesthetic of human embodiment. That body may fracture, stand transfixed, move with exceptional grace and beauty, or spill over into other bodies, but it remains inextricably bound to the world of matter. In this bias, baroque modernism challenges the ability of the spoken and written word to capture and convey truth and sets itself apart from many examples of early and high modernist innovation. The manifestos of Vorticism, Futurism and Die Brücke had matched bold aims with bold print, as they privileged the printed word, making it a key part of experiment and expression. Marinetti's visual disruptions of typography and syntax led him to favour nouns at the expense of verbs and adjectives, and he believed that he could convey meaning simply through the scale of his typography and its position on the page. Along with other Futurists, such as Guillame Apollinaire, Marinetti worked with the conviction that the printed word presented in different proportions and designs could achieve a seamless blending of painting and poetry called 'parole in libertà'. Likewise, the Synthetic Cubism of Braque and Picasso had dispensed with Analytical Cubism's muted colours in favour of collage and the use of non-painterly effects and materials, vestiges of the printed word such as tickets and newspaper cuttings. For the baroque modernists, however, experience and knowledge of the world were neither captured nor sustained by language. In the silences of baroque, creaturely lament and the wordless cries of the night-world's protagonists, in the unscripted dance performances that follow the mute wave patterns of the natural world, in the commedia actor's intuitive responses to his colleague's actions and gestures, and in the wealth of emotion and tension captured by Schrei's sculptured bodies, modernism's baroque texts and performances undermined reason, intellect and the spoken and written word in favour of extemporisation, action, silence and sensual intuition. Where the subject tried to fix meaning with language, they could go no further than the relentless but futile rhythm of allegory. The modern baroque sensibility also shows an increased awareness of the susceptibility of the subject, and that subject's relationship to the object world is playfully renegotiated.

In the high modernist work of Craig and Duncan, the baroque is theorised as a force of creative renewal for their respective performance arts. For Craig, the cataloguing of sources went no further than collating, celebrating and sharing commedia's potential in *The Mask* and subsequent publications, although the archive of material recorded in that journal is an exceptional achievement in itself. The commedia talents and practices that he recorded and made available for readers before and after the First World War remained academic rather than applied visions, images of the masked, disciplined actor and techniques of stagecraft that fed into his ideal of the Ubermarionette. The baroque aesthetic set out with such attention to detail in *The Mask* between 1910 and 1924 centred on recognition and not assimilation. Both he and Duncan use a combination of physical discipline and rehearsed movement to inform the final improvisation and spontaneity of the actor or dancer's performance, and both theorise a baroque aesthetic that promotes an awareness of, and ability to respond to, the body as a privileged means of expression. Isadora Duncan was ultimately concerned with human nature and human behaviour, and as her work became increasingly politically and socially inflected, it is easy to see how monist convictions fostered her ambitious goals for dance and for her schools in Russia and Germany. The monist vocabulary of her theory was charged with a fashionable evolutionary significance, thanks to Haeckel's research and publications, and this allowed her to align the choreography of the modern female dancer with progress and a relentless adapting and perfecting of form. Rather than the stream of thought that characterised the internalised aesthetic of Joyce and Woolf, Duncan's stream of thought becomes an essential and intimate counterpart of the changes of *motion and rest* in the body, and her interpretation of mind is that it constitutes the expression of the successive states of that body. Humans become dependent beings and a prey to external, empirical forces, not only in their physical embodiment, but in their very thoughts and emotions. In all of the baroque modernisms discussed, we witness a narrative pull away from internalisation and psychological detail in favour of an externalised perspective.

Barnes follows the dramatists of the Expressionist period in looking to seventeenth-century allegory and the Trauerspiel for inspiration. The world of

Expressionist drama that she encountered in Provincetown and Berlin resurrected a period of history that had already inspired her writing through the baroque hagiography. Expressionism conferred new value and significance on baroque literature in general, and on the aesthetic and historical context of Trauerspiel in particular. By examining these original forms alongside interpretations of allegory by Benjamin, Baudelaire and Barnes, it becomes possible to translate this aesthetic from the seventeenth century to a modern context, where it proves peculiarly well suited to express the experience of commodified capitalist society. My analysis of Dr O'Connor as *Nightwood*'s court intriguer and Robin as the novel's despot challenges Emily Coleman's sense of discontinuity between the opening chapter and the rest of the novel. The novel's links with the characters and setting of the baroque Trauerspiel establish the court, the figure of the Jew, and Vienna's fall from an inclusive social and political programme, as a framework for the entire novel. Barnes's use of precise moments of contemporary history shot through with a post-lapsarian narrative of suffering provides the novel's final pages with a bleak interpretation in which *Nightwood*'s characters are cut off from all hope of redemption. She makes use of distinctive Schrei vocal and gestural techniques that evolve from her diverse experience of Expressionist drama and production styles, but, however strong the similarities between her writing and theatrical Expressionism, she was ultimately making use of an aesthetic that brought together and formalised images and ideas that had been present in her own writing for many years. While Schrei and the commedia dell'arte both made use of graphic, heavily stylised forms, and showed a determination to transcend the actor's personality, Barnes borrows from one aesthetic in order to shape the human body into hollow, allegorical emblems, while Craig borrows from the latter genre in order to redeem the art of theatre in its entirety.

Barnes's use of allegory in every aspect of *Nightwood*'s composition from imagery to the physicality of her characters places her outside the symbolic unity of modernism promoted by Eliot. To see just how far beyond this modern literary tradition the novel had taken her, it is helpful to turn to Leo Bersani's *The Culture of Redemption* (1990). Bersani writes against the idea 'that the work of art has the authority to master the presumed raw material of experience in a manner that uniquely gives value to, perhaps even redeems, that material', arguing that such a view of 'art's beneficently reconstructive function in culture depends on a devaluation of historical experience and of art'.[1] Bersani's text is directed against works that seek not only to save us from the catastrophes of history, but the catastrophes of sexuality as well. He discusses the work of Baudelaire and Nietzsche as examples of literature without redemptive authority, and I would suggest *Nightwood* as an additional text for this list. By superimposing the story of Robin and Nora's love affair onto the details of the Trauerspiel, Barnes has combined a sexual catastrophe with a catastrophe of history. The history of the Fall, the aftermath of the baroque Thirty Years War, and its modern counterpart, the First World War, are a critical part of the novel's significance and structure. Some fifty years before Bersani delivered his critique of the modern imperative to redeem, Barnes had created a novel in which she not only rejects the redemptive aesthetic in favour of unmitigated historical ruin and catastrophe, but her use of allegory pre-empts Bersani's conclusion that art 'cannot have the unity, the identity, the stability of truth; it does not belong to the world of perfectly intelligible ideas'.[2]

In his 1918 pamphlet, *The Caliph's Design*, Wyndham Lewis had responded to the chaos of the post-war period with tropes of totality that he believed would allow art to offer redemptive possibilities.[3] He urged the artist and the engineer to join forces in theorising and designing a new role for architecture as a way of transcending the inert, docile qualities of aestheticism, while maintaining its aristocratic organisation. He claimed that avant-garde architecture should be experimental and accomplished, but also prophetic, ushering in an aspirational new mode of living. His proposals for architectural reform use utopia as an epistemological tool to present and consolidate certain types of instruction, thought, feeling and interaction within society, while privileging the will of the artist. The plan for a radical, monumental restructuring of communal spaces was a means to social integration and harmony, but nevertheless sought to promote a sense of awe among the general public, representing ideological manipulation on a vast but peaceably executed scale. *The Caliph's Design* situated itself at the tense boundary between art and politics that so often troubled Lewis, while showing an awareness of the need to extend the public significance and impact of art and a commitment to a particular scale of artistic involvement.

As Lewis wrote *The Apes of God* in the late 1920s, it seems that all hope of redeeming modernist society and culture through artistic innovation had faded. He clearly felt that liberalism and democracy offered only trifling freedoms and sham privileges, while the Apes were capable of producing nothing that Lewis would dignify as art and they showed no interest in enlightening the wider public. Art's potential to influence had been reduced to the promotion of personal celebrity. The hypersubjectivity of allegory set out through the voice of Dr O'Connor and *Nightwood*'s narrator finds its parallel in Lewis's novel in the constantly displaced subjectivity of the Apes, as we are asked first to see through the eyes of Dan Boleyn, then to engage with the rather captivating but unpredictable Zagreus, and finally with Pierpoint, the absent authority to whom most threads of discourse and opinion lead. High modernist novels such as Virginia Woolf's *To The Lighthouse* had endeavoured to create unity by allowing multiple subjectivities to play against one another within the same instant of time. The thoughts of Mrs Ramsay jostle and overlap with those of her family and house-guests as Woolf creates an aesthetic of simultaneity.

Lewis's satire has taken this idea of synchronicity to its destructive extreme; rather than the thoughts of several subjectivities converging to offer a detailed perspective, we are given several converging perspectives and opinions, each one a bland but exact imitation of another mind. The Apes are like the beautiful wooden matryoshka dolls from Russia that nest one inside another. As the reader discovers one subjectivity to be hollow, flawed and lacking in originality, they open another and so on, until upon dismantling Pierpoint, in the space where we would expect to find the tiniest doll and an authorial voice offering hope and values of affirmation, we find nothing at all. Just as in his final scene, Matthew O'Connor realises that his anecdotes and allegories are in vain, so, at the end of the novel, Dan Boleyn shreds his painstakingly compiled catalogue of the Apes. Both have failed to assign meaning to their world. Barnes withholds the final apotheosis of allegory and the presence of God in her reworking of the Trauerspiel and Lewis offers the reader a similar twist in the original form by failing to offer the resolutions and reconciliations of the commedia genre.[4]

So how do these two late-modernist texts relate to Lukács's critique of modernist art-forms? Lukács structures capitalist society with its economic and social relations as a closed, integrated whole, an objective world that exists quite independently of the subject's consciousness. The hypersubjectivity of allegory within the baroque and Expressionist traditions, and its re-emergence in *Nightwood*, does nothing to attest to this underlying capitalist totality. While Lukács alleges that the good realist writes to distinguish between the 'appearance' and the 'essence', that is to say, between the consciousness of his characters, and the independent objective world, the ultimate reality or 'essence' pursued by the allegorist is entirely dependent upon their individual subjectivity. Bloch's sense that there may be real fissures in the inter-surface relationships captured by modernist literature proves to be a fitting verdict on Barnes's novel. The stabilising distinction between a subjective immediacy and an authentic social reality is overthrown because our sense of the night-world owes so much to Dr O'Connor and the narrator, both of whom favour allegorical techniques. Jenny Petherbridge and her emotional and material alliances, and the Finnian Shaw habit of exchanging hospitality and patronage for flattering newspaper coverage, notoriety and publications containing their own work, all represent striking embodiments of Lukács's sense of the fetishised commodity as a blueprint for all social relationships within capitalist society. Fragmented patterns and alienated experiences predominate because this is the reality of both form and content within modernity; there is no secretly apprehended unity accessible only to the realist writer and the disciple of Lukács's theories. More significantly still, Lukács emphasises the dichotomy of life under capitalism – irrational human suffering and melancholy instigated by the rationalisation of all aspects of existence, and he identifies the working class as the force that will finally overwhelm reification. In *The Apes of God*, the working class and their revolutionary potential have the rather sly, lethargic and disreputable Archie Margolin as their representative, and a less subversive figure would be hard to find. As to the miners of the General Strike, from the vantage point of the novel's publication, we know they are soon to be betrayed and forgotten. Barnes, meanwhile, locates the night-world firmly within Lukács's context of irrational suffering and lament, and her focus is the dispossessed and alienated class towards whom Lukács directs his hopes. As Robin and Dr O'Connor make their final descent into the depths of allegorical form at the novel's conclusion, and as Lady Fredigonde and her Victorian culture of decay vanish in the arms of Zagreus, it becomes clear that, for Barnes and Lewis, the reified world of capitalism is the only world attainable for their characters; modernism holds nothing of promise with which to replace it.

The baroque of late modernism was a vision that was both poignant and full of misgiving. As late-modernist writers and artists faced the difficulties of a fickle capitalist marketplace, the baroque summoned up the spectre of extravagant artistic patronage; as they looked on with either hope or suspicion at Europe's strengthening dictatorships, the baroque showed them its own blueprints for absolute rule and the politics of spectacle; and as they faced a profane world cut off from God's grace, the baroque reminded them that this had always been the case. When the Nazis began their attack on existing art-forms with the Bauhaus as a school of architecture, before going on to make Socialist architecture the cornerstone of their own cultural programme, modernism looked back at the baroque's own determination to consolidate absolute rule through architectural icons. Rather than explore symbols and narratives that might contain and order modernity within a single aesthetic, late modernism allows the unexpected, the incoherent, the fractured and the imperfect into its own aesthetic without flinching, but also without sacrificing high modernism's pride in a formal aesthetic after all. The formal mastery of high modernism, in particular, its recourse to the symbols and patterns of myth, represented an antidote or corrective for the sense of alienation and the loss of religious and secular values that defined modernity. *The Apes of God* and *Nightwood* offer their own developed formal aesthetic, one that unifies every aspect of the novel from character to language, but that late-modernist aesthetic underlines rather than offsets a loss of hope, values and spiritual consolation. Set in the context of modernism the baroque is contained neither historically nor conceptually by the long seventeenth century, but represents a way of mediating between past and present, bringing to light the rather bleak, obscure counterpart of high modernism, an aesthetic that is in many ways a contradiction, or anti-modernism.

Notes

1. Bersani, *The Culture of Redemption* (Cambridge, MA: Harvard University Press, 1990), p. 1.
2. Ibid. p. 2.
3. For a discussion of this text and utopian modernist architecture, see Armond, 'Wyndham Lewis and the Parables of Expressionist Architecture', *Modernist Cultures*, 9.2, Autumn 2014, pp. 282–303.
4. Gąsiorek, *Wyndham Lewis and Modernism*, p. 75, sets out *The Apes of God*'s own narrative of the Fall, interpreting Lewis's Apes according to the patristic tradition, whereby Satan was the first simian dei: 'envy of God's primacy and an abject desire to rival his creative power figure prominently in this account of the fall' .

BIBLIOGRAPHY

ARCHIVAL MATERIAL

Djuna Barnes Papers, Special Collections and University Archives, University of Maryland Libraries, Maryland, USA.

Emily Holmes Coleman Papers, University of Delaware, Newark, Delaware, USA.

PUBLISHED MATERIAL

Note: I have only included books in the bibliography that are significant for my own analysis of modernism and the baroque.

Aercke, Kristiaan P. (1994) *Gods of Play: Baroque Festive Performance as Rhetorical Discourse* (New York: State of the University of New York Press).

Adorno, Theodor, Walter Benjamin, Ernst Bloch, Bertolt Brecht and Georg Lukács (1977) *Aesthetics and Politics*, with an afterword by Frederic Jameson (New York: Verso).

Armond, Kate (2012) 'Allegory and Dismemberment: Reading Djuna Barnes's *Nightwoood* through the forms of the Baroque Trauerspiel', *Textual Practice*, 26.5, October.

Armond, Kate (2013) 'Cosmic Men – Wyndham Lewis, Ernst Haeckel and Paul Scheerbart', *Journal of Wyndham Lewis Studies*, 4, pp. 41–62.

Armond, Kate (2014) 'Wyndham Lewis and the Parables of Expressionist Architecture', *Modernist Cultures*, 9.2, pp. 283–303.

Armond, Kate (2015) 'A Paper Paradise – Ernst Bloch and the Crystal Chain', in David Ayers, Benedikt Hjartarson, Tomi Huttunen and Harri Veivo (eds) *Utopia – The Avant-Garde, Modernism and (Im)possible Life* (Walter de Gruyter: Berlin), pp. 259–74.

Bal, Mieke (1999) *Quoting Caravaggio: Contemporary Art, Preposterous History* (Chicago: University of Chicago Press).

Barnes, Djuna (1925) 'The Earth' in *Smoke and Other Early Stories* (London: Virago).

Barnes, Djuna (1942) 'The Perfect Murder' in *The Harvard Advocate*, 75 *Anniversary Edition*.

Barnes, Djuna (1949) *Nightwood*, with an introduction by T. S. Eliot (London: Faber and Faber Publishing). Originally published 1936.

Barnes, Djuna (1955) *Nightwood – The Original Version and Related Drafts*, ed. Cheryl Plumb (Normal: Dalkey Archive Press). Originally published 1936.

Barnes, Djuna (1962) 'Cassation' in *Spillway and Other Stories* (London: Faber and Faber).

Barnes, Djuna (1979) *Ryder* (Normal: Dalkey Archive Press). Originally published 1928.

Barnes, Djuna (1985) *Interviews*, ed. Alyce Barry (Washington, DC: Sun and Moon Press).

Barnes, Djuna (1994) *The Book of Repulsive Women: 8 Rhythms and 5 Drawings* (Los Angeles: Sun and Moon Press).

Barnes, Djuna (1999) *Ladies Almanack* (Normal: Dalkey Archive Press). Originally published 1928.

Barnes, Djuna (2000) *The Antiphon* (Los Angeles: Green Integer Publishing). Originally published 1958.

Baudelaire, Charles (1972) *Les Fleurs du Mal* (Paris: Gallimard). Originally published 1861.

Baudelaire, Charles (1975) *Oeuvres Complètes*, ed. C. Pichois (Paris: Gallimard).

Bauer-Heinhold, Margarete (1967) *Baroque Theatre* (London: Thames and Hudson).

Beaumont, Cyril W. (1926) *The History of the Harlequin*, with a preface by Sacheverell Sitwell (New York: Benjamin Blom).

Benjamin, Walter (2006) *Central Park*, in Michael W. Jennings (ed.) *The Writer of Modern Life – Essays on Charles Baudelaire*, trans. Harvard Eiland, Edmund Jephcott, Rodney Livingston and Harm Zohn (Cambridge, MA: Belknap Press).

Benjamin, Walter (1999) *The Arcades Project*, trans. Howard Eiland and Kevin McLaughlin (Cambridge, MA: Belknap Press).

Benjamin, Walter (2003) *The Origin of German Tragic Drama*, intro. George Steiner, trans. John Osbourne (London and New York: Verso). Originally published 1928.

Benjamin, Walter (2004) 'On Language as Such and on the Language of Man', in Marcus Bullock and Michael W. Jennings (eds) *Selected Works, Volume I, 1913–1926* (Cambridge, MA: Belknap Press).

Benson, Renate (1984) *German Expressionist Drama: Ernst Toller and Georg Kaiser* (London: Macmillan).

Bergman, Gösta M. (1977) *Lighting in the Theatre* (Stockholm: Almquist and Wiksell International).

Bersani, Leo (1990) *The Culture of Redemption* (Cambridge, MA: Harvard University Press).

Blau, Herbert (2009) 'From the Dreamwork of Secession to Orgies Mysteries Theatre', *Modern Drama*, 52.3, pp. 263–80.

Bloch, Ernst (2007) 'Discussing Expressionism', *Aesthetics and Politics*, with an afterword by Frederic Jameson (New York: Verso). Originally published 1935.

Bölsche, Wilhelm (1931) *Love-Life in Nature* (London: J. Cape).

Bronnen, Arnolt (1922) *Vatermord: Schauspiel in der Fassurgen von 1915 und 1922* (Munich: Edition und Kritik).

Brust, Alfred (1921) *Die Wölfe. Ein Winterstück* (Munich: Kurt Wolff).

Brust, Alfred (1968) *The Wolves: A Winter Play*, trans. J. M. Ritchie, in Ritchie, *Seven Expressionist Plays: Kokoschka to Barlach* (London: Alder and Boyars).

Buci-Glucksmnan, Christine (1994) *Baroque Reason: The Aesthetics of Modernity*, trans. Patrick Camiller, intro. Brian S. Turner (London: Sage Publications).

Buck-Morss, Susan (1989) *The Dialectics of Seeing – Walter Benjamin and the Arcades Project* (Cambridge, MA and London: MIT Press).

Calabrese, Omar (1992) *Neo-Baroque: A Sign of the Times*, trans. Charles Lambert (Princeton: Princeton University Press).

Caracciolo, Peter (1983) 'Mr Punch, Zoroastrianism and Relativity', *Enemy News*, 18, pp. 28–31.

Caselli, Daniela (2009) *Improper Modernism: Djuna Barnes's Bewildering Corpus* (Burlington, VT: Ashgate).

Conti, Count (1928) *The Reign of the House of Rothschild*, trans. Brian and Beatrice Lunn (London: Victor Gollancz).

Craig, Edward Gordon (1923) *Scene*, foreword and intro. John Masefield (London: H. Milford, Oxford University Press).

Cysarz, Herbert (1924) *Deutsche Barockdichtung: Renaissance, Barock, Rokoko* (Leipzig: Haessel).

Deleuze, Giles (1993) *The Fold: Leibniz and the Baroque* (Minneapolis: University of Minnesota Press).

d'Ors, Eugenio (1945) *Del Barocco* (Milan: Rosa e Ballo). Originally published 1935.

Dubois, Claude-Gilbert (1995) *Le Baroque en Europe et en France* (Paris: Presses Universitaires de France).

Duchartre, Pierre Louis (1966) *The Italian Comedy: The Improvisations, Scenarios, Lives, Attributes, Portraits and Masks of the Illustrious Characters of the Commedia dell'Arte*, trans. Randolph T. Weaver (New York: Dover Publications). Originally published 927.

Duncan, Irma (1959) *Isadora Duncan: Pioneer in the Art of Dance* (New York: New York Public Library).

Duncan, Isadora (1928) *The Art of Dance*, ed. and intro. Sheldon Cheney (New York: J. J. Little and Ives).

Duncan, Isadora (1968) *My Life* (London: Victor Gollancz). Originally published 1928.

Duncan, Isadora (1976) *Your Isadora: The Love Story of Isadora Duncan and Gordon Craig Told Through Letters and Diaries*, ed. Francis Steegmuller (New York: Random House). Originally published 1974.

Duncan, Isadora (1994) *Isadora Speaks: Writings and Speeches of Isadora Duncan*, ed. and intro. Franklin Rosemont, preface Ann Barzel (Chicago: Charles H. Kerr). Originally published 1917.

Edschmid, Kasimir (1920) *Tribune der Kunst und Zeit Eine Schriftensammung – Uber den Expressionismus in der Literatur und die Neue Dichtung* (Berlin: Erich Reib Verlag).

Edwards, Paul (2000) *Wyndham Lewis: Painter and Writer* (New Haven, CT: Yale University Press).

Eliot, T. S. (1921) 'The Metaphysical Poets', in Vincent B. Leitch, William E. Cain, Laurie Finke and Barbara Johnson (eds) *The Norton Anthology of Theory and Criticism* (New York: W. W. Norton and Co.).

Ferris, David S. (ed.) (1996) *Walter Benjamin: Theoretical Questions* (Stanford: Stanford University Press).

Frese Witt, Mary Ann (2014) *Metatheater and Modernity: Baroque and Neobaroque* (Madison, WI: Fairleigh Dickinson University Press). Originally published 2013.

Fuerst, Walter R., and Samuel Hume (1967) *Twentieth Century Stage Lighting* (New York: Dover Publications). Originally published 1929.

Gąsiorek, Andrzej (2004) *Wyndham Lewis and Modernism* (Tavistock, Devon: Northcote House Publishers Ltd).

Gerstenberger, Donna (1993) 'Modern (Post) Modern: Djuna Barnes among the Others', *Review of Contemporary Fiction*, 13.3, pp. 33–40.

Gillespie, Gerald Ernest Paul (1965) *Daniel Casper von Lohenstein's Historical Tragedies* (Columbus: Ohio State University Press).

Goering, Reinhard (1977) *Seeschlatt (Seabattle) – The German Text with an English Translation*, trans. Ingebor H. Solbrig (Stuttgart: Akademischer Verlag Hans-Dieter Heinz). Originally published 1916.

Gordon, Donald E. (1987) *Expressionism – Art and Idea* (New Haven, CT and London: Yale University Press).

Gordon, Mel (1975) 'German Expressionist Acting', *The Drama Review*, 19.3, pp. 34–50.

Gordon, Mel (1983) *Lazzi: The Comic Routines of the Commedia dell'Arte* (New York: Performing Arts Journal Publications).

Grace, Sherill E. (1989) *Grace, Regression and Apocalypse: Studies in North American Literary Expressionism* (Toronto: University of Toronto Press)

Green, Martin, and John Swan (1986) *The Triumph of Pierrot – The Commedia Dell'Arte and the Modern Imagination* (New York: Macmillan).

Green, V. H. H. (1952) *Renaissance and Reformation – A Survey of European History between 1450 and 1660* (London: Edward Arnold Publishers Ltd).

Greene, Graham (1936) 'Fiction Chronicle', *The Catholic Tablet*, November, pp. 678–9.

Gilbert-Dubois, Claude (1995) *Le Baroque en Europe et en France* (Paris: Presses universitaires de France).

Haeckel, Ernst (1904) *Die Lebenswunder* (Stuttgart: Alfred Kröner)

Haeckel, Ernst (1913) *The Riddle of the Universe at the Close of the Nineteenth Century*, trans. Joseph McCabe (London: Watts and Co.).

Hagen, Joshua (2008) 'Parades, Public Space and Propaganda: The Nazi Culture Parades in Munich', in *Geografiska Annaler: Series B, Human Geography*, 90.4, pp. 349–67.

Hamman, Brigitte (1999) *Hitler's Vienna – A Dictator's Apprenticeship* (Oxford: Oxford University Press).

Hampshire, Stuart (1987) *Spinoza: An Introduction to his Philosophical Thought* (Harmondsworth: Penguin Books). Originally published 1952.

Hanfstaengl, Ernst (1957) *Hitler: The Missing Years* (London: Eyre and Spottiswoode).

Harrison, Jane Ellen (1948) *Ancient Art and Ritual* (London: Oxford University Press). Originally published 1913.

Hasenclever, Walter (1984) *Humanity*, trans. Walter H. Sokel and Jacqueline Sokel, in Walter H. Sokel (ed.) *Anthology of German Expressionist Drama: A Prelude to the Absurd* (London: Cornell University Press).

Hawkins, Desmond (1937) 'Views and Reviews', *The New English Weekly*, 29 April, p. 51.

Henke, Robert (2002) *Performance and Literature in the Commedia Dell'Arte* (Cambridge: Cambridge University Press).

Henke, Robert (2007) 'Representations of Poverty in the Commedia Dell'Arte', *Theatre Survey*, 48.2, pp. 229–46.

Hoover, Calvin B. (1993) *Germany Enters the Third Reich* (London: Macmillan and Co. Ltd).

Idol, John L. (1979) 'Burton's Use of Illustrative Emblems', *Renaissance Papers*, pp. 19–28.

Innes, Christopher (1993) *Avant-Garde Theatre 1892–1992* (London: Routledge).

Jahn, Hanns Henny (1919) *Pastor Ephraim Magnus* (Berlin: S. Fischer Verlag).

Jaynes, Jeffrey (1996) 'Review of *The Fabricated Luther: The Rise and Fall of the Shirer Myth*', *The Sixteenth Century Journal*, 27.2, pp. 515–17.

John, Augustus (1964) *Finishing Touches*, ed. and intro. Daniel George (London: Jonathan Cape).

Judson, Pieter M. (1996) *Exclusive Revolutionaries: Liberal Politics, Social Experience and National Identity in the Austrian Empire* (Ann Arbor: University of Michigan Press).

Kaiser, Georg (1920) *From Morn to Midnight: A Play in Seven Scenes*, trans. Ashley Dukes (London: Hendersons Publishing).

Kaivola, Karen (1993) 'The Beast Turning Human: Constructions of the Primitive in "Nightwood"', *The Review of Contemporary Fiction*, 13.3, p. 172.

Kannestine, Louis (1977) *The Art of Djuna Barnes: Duality and Damnation* (New York: New York University Press).

Kaup, Monika (2005) 'The Neobaroque in Djuna Barnes', *Modernism/ Modernity*, 12.1, January, pp. 85–110.

Kenner, Hugh (1954) *Wyndham Lewis* (London: Methuen and Co. Ltd).

Klibansky, Raymond, Erwin Panofsky and Fritz Saxl (1964) *Saturn and Melancholy: Studies in the History of Natural Philosophy, Religion and Art* (London: Thomas Nelson and Sons Ltd); first published as Erwin Panofsky and Fritz Saxl (1923) *Durer's Melencolia 1: eine quellen- und typengeschichteliche Untersuchung* (Leipzig: Teubner).

Klossowski de Rola, Stanislas (1973) *Alchemy – The Secret Art* (London: Thames and Hudson).

Kreymborg, Alfred (1918) *Lima Beans; Manikin and Minikin*, in *Plays for Poem-Mimes* (New York: The Other Press).

Kreymborg, Alfred (1920) *Vote the New Moon*, in *Plays for Merry Andrews* (New York: The Sunrise Turn).

Kuhns, David F. (1997) *German Expressionist Theatre – The Actor and the Stage* (Cambridge: Cambridge University Press).

Kuna, F. (1963) 'T. S. Eliot's Dissociation of Sensibility and the Critics of Metaphysical Poetry', *Essays in Criticism*, July, 13.3, p. 241.

LaMothe, K. (2006) *Nietzsche's Dancers – Isadora Duncan, Martha Graham, and the Revaluation of Christian Values* (London: Palgrave Macmillan).

Lasko, Peter (2003) *The Expressionist Roots of Modernism* (Manchester: Manchester University Press).

LeBoeuf, Patrick (2010) 'On the Nature of Edward Gordon Craig's Ubermarionette', *Theatre Quarterly*, 26.2, pp. 102–14.

Lee, Judith (1991) 'Nightwood – The Sweetest Lie', in Mary Ann Broe (ed.) *Silence and Power – A Reevaluation of Djuna Barnes* (Carbondale: Southern Illinois Press).

Lewis, Wyndham (1926) *The Art of Being Ruled* (London: Chatto and Windus).

Lewis, Wyndham (1927) *The Wild Body* (London: Chatto and Windus).

Lewis, Wyndham (1928) *Tarr* (London: Chatto and Windus). Originally published 1918.

Lewis, Wyndham (1930) *Satire and Fiction, Enemy Pamphlet No. 1* (London: The Arthur Press).

Lewis, Wyndham (1931) *The Apes of God* (London: Nash and Grayson).

Lewis, Wyndham (1931) *The Diabolical Principle and the Dithyrambic Spectator* (London: Chatto and Windus).

Lewis, Wyndham (1964) *Men Without Art* (New York: Russell & Russell). Originally published 1934.

Lewis, Wyndham (1965) *The Childermass* (London: Calder Publications Ltd).

Lewis, Wyndham (1969) *The Caliph's Design*, in Walter Michel and C. J. Fox (eds) *Wyndham Lewis on Art: Collected Writings 1913–1956* (New York: Funk and Wagnalls). Originally published 1918.

Lewis, Wyndham (1977) *Mrs Dukes' Million* (Toronto: Coach House Press).

Lewis, Wyndham (1989) *Creatures of Habit and Creatures of Change: Essays on Art, Literature and Society 1914–56* (Santa Rosa, CA: Black Sparrow Press).

Lima, Robert (2005) *Stages of Evil: Occultism in Western Theater and Drama* (Lexington: University Press of Kentucky).

Loewenthal, Lillian (1993) *The Search for Isadora: The Legend and Legacy of Isadora Duncan* (Princeton: Princeton University Press).

Longworth, Deborah (forthcoming) *The Sitwells: Ornamental Modernism* (Oxford: Oxford University Press).

Lukács, Georg (1980) *Georg Lukács: Essays on Realism*, ed. and intro. Rodney Livingstone, trans. David Fernbach (London: Lawrence and Wishart).

Lukács, Georg (1980) 'Expressionism: Its Significance and Decline', in Rodney

Livingstone (ed.) *Georg Lukács: Essays on Realism* (London: Lawrence and Wishart). Originally published 1934.

Lukács, Georg (1983) *The Destruction of Reason* (London: Merlin Press).

Lukács, Georg (2007) 'Realism in the Balance', in Theodor Adorno, Walter Benjamin, Ernst Bloch, Bertolt Brecht and Georg Lukacs, afterword Frederic Jameson, *Aesthetics and Politics* (New York: Verso).

McAlmon, Robert (1938) *Being Geniuses Together 1920–1930*, rev. Kay Boyle (London: Michael Joseph).

McGovern, Montgomery (1941) *From Luther to Hitler: the History of Fascist-Nazi Political Philosophy* (New York: Houghton Mifflin Company).

MacGowan, Kenneth, and Robert Edmond Jones (1923) *Continental Stagecraft* (London: Benn Brothers Ltd).

Maravall, José Antonio (1983) *Culture of the Baroque: Analysis of a Historical Structure*, Theory of History and Literature Volume 25, trans. Terry Cochran (Minneapolis: University of Minnesota Press). Originally published 1975.

Marcus, Jane (1991a) 'Laughing at Leviticus: *Nightwood* as Circus Epic', in Mary Ann Broe (ed.) *Silence and Power* (Carbondale: Southern Illinois Press).

Marcus, Jane (1991b) 'Mousemeat: Contemporary Reviews of *Nightwood*' in Mary Ann Broe (ed.) *Silence and Power* (Carbondale: Southern Illinois Press).

Marx, Karl (2009) *Das Kapital*, intro. Serge L. Levitsky (Washington, DC: Regnery Publishing Ltd). Originally published 1867.

The Mask: A Quarterly Journal of the Art of Theatre (1909–1929), ed. Edward Gordon Craig (Florence: The Arena Goldoni), reissued 1967 with index by Loreli Guidry (New York: Benjamin Blom).

Matthews, Stephen (2006) 'T. S. Eliot's Chapman: "Metaphysical" Poetry and Beyond', *Journal of Modern Literature*, 9.4, pp. 22–43.

Matthews, Stephen (2013) *T. S. Eliot and Early Modern Literature* (Oxford: Oxford University Press).

May, Arthur J. (1960) *The Hapsburg Monarchy 1867–1914* (Cambridge, MA: Harvard University Press).

May, Arthur J. (1966) *Vienna in the Age of Franz Joseph* (Norman: University of Oklahoma Press).

Menninghaus, Winifred (1988) 'Walter Benjamin's Theory of Myth', in Gary Smith (ed.) *On Walter Benjamin: Critical Essays and Recollections* (Cambridge, MA: MIT Press).

Mic, Constant (1913) *La Commedia dell'Arte ou le Théâtre des Comédiens Italiens des XVIe, XVIIe and XVIIIe Siécles* (Paris: Schiffrin).

Miller, Tyrus (1999) *Late Modernism: Politics, Fiction and the Arts between the World Wars* (Berkeley and London: University of California Press).

Miller Lane, Barbara (1968) *Architecture and Politics in Germany – 1918–1945* (Cambridge, MA: Harvard University Press).

Mitchell, Breon (1973) 'Expressionism in English Drama and Prose', in Ulrich Weisstein (ed.) *Expressionism as an International Literary Phenomenon* (Paris: Didier Press).

Munton, Alan (1982) 'Wyndham Lewis and the Transformations of Carnival', in Giovanni Cianci (ed.) *Wyndham Lewis – Letteratura/Pittura* (Palermo: Sellerio Editori).

Ndalianis, Angela (2004) *Neo-Baroque Aesthetics and Contemporary Entertainment* (Cambridge, MA: MIT Press).

Nelson, I. (1993) 'Baroque', in Alex Preminger and T. V. F. Brogan (eds) *The New Princetown Encyclopaedia of Poetry and Poetics* (Princeton: Princeton University Press). Originally published 1965.

Nicholls, Peter (1995) *Modernisms: A Literary Guide* (London: Macmillan).

Oreglia, Giacomo (1968) *The Commedia Dell'Arte*, trans. Lovett F. Edwards (London: Methuen & Co.).

O'Shanahan, William (1962) 'The Rise and Fall of the Third Reich: A History of Nazi Germany', *The American Historical Review*, 68.1, October, pp. 126–7.

Ovid (1986) *Metamorphoses*, trans. and intro. Mary Innes (Harmondsworth: Penguin Books).

Panofsky, Erwin, and Fritz Saxl (1923) *Durer's Melencolia 1: eine quellen- und typengeschichteliche Untersuchung* (Leipzig: Teubner), later extended with Raymond Klibansky to become *Saturn and Melancholy: Studies in the History of Natural Philosophy, Religion and Art* (1964).

Parsons, Deborah (2003) *Djuna Barnes* (Tavistock, Devon: Northcote House Publishers).

Parsons, Deborah (2007) 'Djuna Barnes: Melancholic Modernism', in Morag Shiach (ed.) *The Cambridge Companion to the Modernist Novel* (Cambridge: Cambridge University Press).

Patterson, Michael (1981) *The Revolution in the German Theatre, 1900–1933* (Boston, MA and London: Routledge and Kegan Paul).

Perkins, Ann (2007) *A Very British Strike, 3 May–12 May 1926* (London: Pan Books).

Peucker, Brigitte (2004) 'Fascist Choreography: Riefenstahl's Tableaux', *Modernism/Modernity*, 11.2, pp. 279–97.

Pinnow, Hermann (1996) *History of the Germany: People and State through a Thousand Years*, trans. Mabel Richmond Brailsford (London: George and Unwin Limited). Originally published 1933.

Plumb, Cheryl (1993) 'Revising Nightwood: A Kind of Glee of Despair', *The Review of Contemporary Fiction*, 13.3. pp. 149–59.

Preston, Carrie J. (2005) 'The Motor in the Soul: Isadora Duncan and Modernist Performance', *Modernism/Modernity*, 12.2, pp. 273–89.

Ritchie, J. M. (1976) *German Expressionist Drama* (Boston: Twayne Publishers).

Roberts, Gareth (1994) *The Mirror of Alchemy: Alchemical Ideas and Images in Manuscripts and Books From Antiquity to the Seventeenth Century* (London: The British Library Press).

Rosenfeld, Gavriel D. (1994) 'The Reception of William L. Shirer's *The Rise and Fall of the Third Reich* in the United States and West Germany, 1960–62', *Journal of Contemporary History*, 29.1, pp. 95–128.

Rudlin, John (1994) *The Commedia Dell'Arte: An Actor's Handbook* (London and New York: Routledge).

Rühle, Günther (1967) *Theater für die Republik, 1917–1933* (Frankfurt am Main: S. Fischer Verlag).

Sachar, Abram Leon (1930) *A History of the Jew* (New York: A. A. Knopf).

Samuel, Richard H., and R. Hinton Thomas (1939) *Expressionism in German Life, Literature and the Theatre (1910–1924)* (Cambridge: W. Heffer and Sons Ltd).

Sand, Maurice (1915) *A History of the Harlequinade*, Vol. 1 (London: Martin Secker).

Scheffauer, Herman George (1924) *The New Vision in the German Arts* (London: Ernest Benn Ltd).

Schürer, Ernst (2005) 'Provocation and Proclamation, Vision and Imagery: Expressionist Drama between German Idealism and Modernity', in Neil H. Donahue (ed.) *A Companion to the Literature of German Expressionism* (New York: Camden House Press).

Shirer, William (1960) *The Rise and Fall of The Third Reich* (London: Pan Books). Originally published 1959.

Siemon-Netto, Uwe (1995) *The Fabricated Luther: The Rise and Fall of the Shirer Myth* (St Louis: Concordia Publishing House).

Simonson, Mary (2013) *Body Knowledge: Performance, Intermediality, and American Entertainment at the Turn of the Twentieth Century* (Oxford: Oxford University Press).

Singer, Alan (1984) 'The Horse Who Knew Too Much: Metaphor and the Narrative of Discontinuity in *Nightwood*', *Contemporary Literature*, 25.1, pp. 66–87.

Sitwell, Osbert (1949) *Laughter in the Next Room* (London: Macmillan).

Sitwell, Sacheverell (1928) *German Baroque Art* (New York: George H. Doran Company). Originally published 1927.

Sitwell, Sacheverell (1951) *Southern Baroque Art* (London: Camelot Press). Originally published 1924.

Sitwell, Sacheverell (1952) *Cupid and the Jacaranda* (London: Macmillan).

Smith, Winifred (1912) *The Commedia Dell'Arte – A Study in Italian Popular Comedy* (New York: Columbia University Press).

Sokel, Walter H. (1959) *The Writer in Extremis – Expressionism in Twentieth-Century Literature* (Stanford: Stanford University Press).

Spinoza, Benedict de [Baruch] (1996) *Ethics* (London: Penguin Classics). Originally published 1677.

Stange, Martina (2005) 'Melancholia, Melancholia: Changing Black Bile into Black Ink in Djuna Barnes's *Nightwood*', in in Elizabeth Podnieks and Sandra Chait (eds) *Hayford Hall: Hangovers, Erotics and Modernist Aesthetics* (Carbondale: Southern Illinois University Press).

Storey, Robert (1978) *Pierrot – A Critical History of a Mask* (Princeton: Princeton University Press).

Strich, Fritz (1916) *Der lyrische stil des 17. Jahrhunderts*, in Franz Muncker, *Abhandlungen zur deutschen Literaturgeschichte, Festschrifte Franz Muncker zum 60. Geburtstage dargebracht* (Munich: C. H. Beck'sche Verlagsbuchhandlung).

Styan, J. L. (1982) *Max Reinhardt* (Cambridge and New York: Cambridge University Press).

Taggard, Genevieve (ed.) (1929) *Circumference: Varieties of Metaphysical Verse, 1456–1928* (New York: Covici Friede).

Taxidou, Olga (1998) *The Mask: A Periodical Performance by Edward Gordon Craig* (Singapore: Harwood Academic Publishers)

Tomlin, E. W. F. (1955) *Wyndham Lewis* (London, New York and Toronto: Longman's, Green and Co.).

Valgamae, Mardi (1972) *Accelerated Grimace: Expressionism in the American Drama of the 1920s* (Carbondale: Southern Illinois Press).

Walkowitz, Abraham (2000) *Line Dance: Abraham Walkowitz's Drawings of Isadora Duncan* (Newark, DE: University Gallery, University of Delaware).

Warnke, Frank J. (1972) *Versions of the Baroque* (New Haven, CT and London: Yale University Press).

Watanabe-O'Kelly, Helen (2002) *Court Culture in Dresden from Renaissance to Baroque* (New York: Palgrave Publishers Ltd).

Wedekind, Frank ([1910] 2007) *Spring Awakening*, trans. and intro. Jonathan Franzen (New York: Faber and Faber).

Weisbach, Werner (1921) *Der Barock als Kunst der Gegenreformation* (Berlin: P. Cassirer).

Weisbach, Werner (1925) *Die Kunst des Barock in Italien, Frankreich, Deutschsland und Spanien* (Berlin: Propyl Aen-Verlag).

Weisstein, Ulrich (1973) 'Expressionism as an International Literary Phenomenon', and 'Vorticism: Expressionism English Style', in Weisstein (ed.) *Expressionism as an International Literary Phenomenon* (Paris: Didier Press).

Wellek, René (1963) 'The Baroque', in Stephen Nichols (ed.) *Concepts of Criticism* (New Haven, CT and London: Yale University Press).

Wiener, Peter F. (1945) *Martin Luther – Hitler's Spiritual Ancestor* (London: Hutchinson and Co. Ltd).

Whitman, Sidney (1898) *Austria* (London: Fisher Unwin).

William, Crown Prince of Germany (1922) *Memoirs of the Crown Prince of Germany* (New York: Scribners).

Williamson, Alan (1964) 'The Divided Image: The Quest for Identity in the Works of Djuna Barnes's, *Critique*, 7, pp. 58–74.

Wölfflin, Heinrich (1950) *Principles of Art History – The Problem of the Development of Style in Later Art*, trans. M. D. Hottinger (New York: Dover Publications). Originally published 1932.

Wölfflin, Heinrich (1971) *Renaissance and Baroque* (London: Fontana-Collins). Originally published 1964.

Worringer, Wilhelm (1927) *Form in Gothic*, ed. and intro. Herbert Read (London: Putnam).

Worringer, Wilhelm (1997) *Abstraction and Empathy: A Contribution to the Psychology of Style*, trans. Michael Bullock, intro. Hilton Kramer (Chicago: Ivan R. Dee Publishers).

Zedlitz-Trützschler, Robert von (1924) *Twelve Years at the Imperial German Court* (London: Nisbet and Co.).

INDEX